SOCIAL MOVEMENTS
PAST AND PRESENT

Irwin Sanders, Editor

THE ANTINUCLEAR MOVEMENT

THE ANTINUCLEAR MOVEMENT

JEROME PRICE

TWAYNE PUBLISHERS

THE ANTINUCLEAR MOVEMENT
SOCIAL MOVEMENTS PAST AND PRESENT

Copyright © 1982 by G. K. Hall & Company
All Rights Reserved
Published by Twayne Publishers
A Division of G. K. Hall & Company
70 Lincoln Street
Boston, Massachusetts 02111

Book production and design
by Barbara Anderson

This book was typeset in
10 point Times Roman with Univers display type
by Compset, Inc. of Beverly, Massachusetts.

Printed on permanent/durable acid-free paper
and bound in the United States of America

Library of Congress Cataloging in Publication Data

Price, Jerome
    The antinuclear movement.

(Social movements past and present)
Originally presented as the author's thesis (Ph.D.—Rutgers University)
Bibliography: p. 192
Includes index.
1. Antinuclear movement—United States
I. Title. II. Series.
HD9698.U52P74   1982   322.4'4   82-11842
ISBN 0-8057-9705-X

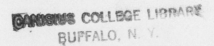

CONTENTS

ABOUT THE AUTHOR

Jerome B. Price was born in Tampa, Florida. After living near London, England, his family moved to Mississippi, where he graduated from Millsaps College. He completed the M.A. degree at Western Kentucky University and then worked in Germany before attending Rutgers University. Since receiving his Ph.D. in sociology at Rutgers in 1979, he has taught at Virginia Polytechnic Institute and State University and the University of Maine at Presque Isle.

PREFACE

When the search began for alternative sources of energy to replace fossil fuels, nuclear power seemed to be the solution to our energy problems. Proponents claimed that it was a clean and safe source of energy with a "flawless record" and was one of the twentieth century's greatest scientific and technological achievements. By controlling the process of the fission of atoms enormous quantities of energy could be released to provide heat that would run electric turbines indefinitely.

This new confidence that we had a source of energy that would free us from dependence on imported oil and provide nations with a plentiful supply of energy for eons without any threat to human life has been seriously eroded. Opponents of nuclear power assert that it is already a "failed technology" that has existed only because of massive government subsidies. The possibility of nuclear accidents, such as the one at Three Mile Island, and uncertainty over what can be done with radioactive wastes continue to be a major source of contention between antinuclear activists and the nuclear establishment.

When I first became interested in the antinuclear movement, it was in the context of a dissertation proposal to analyze the role of scientists in the process of policy formation in Project Independence. It was soon apparent to me that the focus of government energy policy was nuclear power, and I decided to narrow my study to see why nuclear energy was thought to be preferable to other alternatives such as solar and hydroelectric power. It was disconcerting to discover that nuclear technology was not as safe as people generally assumed, and was moreover clearly linked to the problem of nuclear weapons proliferation.

As I became more deeply immersed in studying nuclear power and the controversy it was generating, I realized that a social movement was in the making. I initially followed the development of the movement as an interested observer, but soon this interest developed into active participation. Most participants do not realize they are involved in a social movement, believing that involvement in a movement is defined solely by attendance at rallys and demonstrations. But membership in social movements also involves the activity of less tangible attributes such as one's political and social conscience. During the 1960s the larger "Movement" included civil rights activism, revolutionism, anti-Vietnam War activities, and at least sympathetic support for a myriad of groups articulating a new political consciousness. What puts the antinuclear movement in this same stream is the common spirit of social change.

The antinuclear movement has provided a view of the world and of political activity for a new generation that keeps the liberal tradition alive in an era in which religious fundamentalism and the New Right philosophy appear to be in ascendance. The 1960s generation was bequeathed the vestiges of a plantation society, militarism in Southeast Asia, and oppressive cultural traditionalism. The generation of the 1970s and 1980s are the heirs to radioactive wastes, potential "core meltdowns," and a world of two nuclear superpowers and innumerable smaller nuclear-armed nations. The catalysts that press people into social action may change from generation to generation, but the fight for liberalism continues to enjoy a steady infusion of energy.

While Seabrook and Diablo Canyon are media events that garner much attention, the locus of the antinuclear movement is in a plethora of environmentalist, labor, church, women's, and local citizens' activist groups. While younger participants in the movement have the freedom to demonstrate outside nuclear power plants, others choose to be more restrained and devote themselves to petitioning and other less visible movement activities. Organized groups such as the Union of Concerned Scientists or the Natural Resources Defense Council rely on professionals—scientists, lawyers, and others—who are able to sustain themselves while fighting powerful interests. This is a tribute to the viability of the democratic process in the United States during a period that is seemingly dominated by archconservatives.

Some observers believe that the antinuclear movement is now defunct, or irrelevant, because few nuclear power stations are being ordered despite the renewed commitment of the federal government to expansion of nuclear power plant construction. Nothing could be further from the truth. By the end of this decade the number of nuclear power plants in operation will almost double, while aging plants increase the risk of accidents, and radioactive wastes continue to accumulate. A moratorium on the development of nuclear power has not been achieved.

The plan of the book is first to give an overview of the history and origins of the antinuclear campaign and to show how it grew into a movement of great significance. I have explored the values of diverse antinuclear groups, their organizational history, and their ideology. The historical precursors of the antinuclear movement in the 1950s and the episodic antinuclear protests of the 1960s are the backdrop to its environmentalist phase and its eventual emergence as a distinctive movement. The nuclear issue has now spanned three decades and has spawned a movement that is as strong in Western Europe as in the United States.

Subsequent chapters are concerned with main subgroups within the movement: environmentalists, scientists, and direct action groups. Each group has contributed in unique ways to the antinuclear movement. These chapters describe these people and the organizations they created to bring about social change. After reading the overview of the movement, the reader may want to turn to the first appendix, which is an excursion into the general social science theory of social movements, specifically resource mobilization and social action theory. A second appendix is included to give some knowledge of the nuclear fuel cycle and the structure of the nuclear industry to those who are not certain how nuclear energy is used to produce electricity.

After analyzing and describing environmentalists, scientists, and direct action groups, I have looked at the consequences of the antinuclear movement, concentrating on the energy policy of the Carter administration, on public opinion, and on international nuclear policy. The greatest impact of the movement was on the Democratic Party in the late 1970s. We have yet to see if reversal of priorities in the Reagan Administration will succeed in turning around those gains of the antinuclear movement.

The final chapter attempts to place the movement in the context of more general problems facing modern societies.

Social movements are constantly undergoing change, and the antinuclear movement is no exception. Many new groups and coalitions have come into existence, and tactics are changed when efforts meet with failure. The challenge of studying social movements exists in the fact that they are not phenomena frozen in time but rather are made up of living, acting people who are always redefining the meaning of their role in the movement and creating innovative strategies for change.

Jerome Price

ACKNOWLEDGMENTS

I am especially indebted to Bernard Goldstein, director of my dissertation at Rutgers University, and to the other members of my thesis committee, Jackson Toby, Harry Bredemeir, and William McLean. John Leggett and Irving Louis Horowitz were also helpful in the initial organization of my research ideas. I began to revise the manuscript when I was a Visiting Assistant Professor of Sociology at Virginia Polytechnic Institute and State University, and completed it at the University of Maine at Presque Isle. I am grateful to my colleagues, friends, and students at these institutions for their support.

In particular I wish to acknowledge the encouragement and advice given to me by Irwin Sanders of Boston University, who is editor of the Social Movement Series of which this volume is a part. I also appreciate the help of Caroline Birdsall, senior editor; John LaBine, associate editor; and Janet Quimby, manuscript editor, at Twayne Publishers. Although I take all responsibility for the content of the book, I would like to thank the following people for their support or their review of my work: Clifton Bryant, Virginia Polytechnic Institute and State University; Michael Hughes and Michael Wood, also at Virginia Tech; Irene Dabrowski, St. John's University in Staten Island; Ward Gerow, William Davidshofer, George Hall, and Ken Taylor, University of Maine at Presque Isle; Kathleen McPherson, University of Southern Maine; Alan Schnaiberg, Northwestern University, and James Dunleavy, judge of probate in Aroostook County, Maine.

My deepest gratitude is to Claudia Pott, my parents, and my brothers and sisters. They all helped in their own way.

CHAPTER 1
The Emergence of the Movement

Along the beautiful coastal area near Wiscasset, not far from Bar Harbor and Acadia National Park, the large dome of Maine Yankee, a nuclear power plant, rises above the surrounding forest. Although this seemingly innocuous power station produces one third of Maine's electricity, the people of that state were given the choice of shutting down the plant in order to force the utilities to actively pursue alternative sources of energy. If the Maine Nuclear Referendum had succeeded, it would have set a national precedent by closing down an existing nuclear power plant and would have represented a substantial victory for the antinuclear movement.[1] Even though the referendum failed, over forty percent of the voters did express their opposition to nuclear energy.

In a small state with barely over one million inhabitants, many of whom struggle as potato farmers in northern Aroostook County or depend on the seasonal tourist trade or public relief, why would such a large proportion of voters be willing to risk the severe economic effects of having to import more foreign oil should Maine Yankee close? Although nearly sixty percent voted against the shutdown primarily because of an unwillingness to pay higher electricity bills, the results of the referendum were widely perceived as a vote of no confidence in nuclear power but in support of energy alternatives such as solar, wind, and hydroelectric power.

The act of voting is simple, but understanding the complex issues involved in the controversy and the conflicting interests of competing groups is much more complicated. The groups and organizations that

1

formed the opposition to Maine Yankee under the banner of the Maine Nuclear Referendum Committee are similar to hundreds of antinuclear groups which have emerged in every state and in many Western European nations. The Maine Nuclear Referendum also produced an adversary situation in which pronuclear groups formed a countermovement under the auspices of Save Maine Yankee. Hundreds of thousands of dollars were spent to woo the electorate to one position or another. The nuclear issue is, therefore, no longer the special province of governments and industry; it is a public issue in which citizens are now playing a decisive role.

How did the antinuclear movement emerge, and what are the goals and ideology of groups active in the movement? What is the history of the controversy over nuclear power? How did the movement grow and then through a process of diffusion become a force in the politics of nuclear energy in Western Europe? Has the movement been successful? These questions do not lend themselves to easy answers, but we must have some understanding of them if we are to comprehend fully the implications of the movement against nuclear power.

Historical Precursors of the Antinuclear Movement

In August 1939, Eugene Wigner, Leo Szilard, and Albert Einstein wrote to President Franklin Roosevelt warning that Nazi scientists were investigating the feasibility of an atomic weapon based on the scientific possibility of a nuclear chain reaction. By 1942, the Manhattan Project, headed by General Groves, had been formed and eventually culminated in the explosions of atomic bombs over Hiroshima and Nagasaki, killing over 100,000 people. The age of atomic energy had begun.[2] With the conclusion of World War II, the administration of President Truman was committed to international control of the atom, although the Baruch Plan to establish an international corporation chartered by the United Nations for peaceful applications of nuclear energy got nowhere. A movement developed among scientists to prevent the control of nuclear energy by the military. These scientists had worked in the Manhattan Project, and their leader was J. Robert Oppenheimer. Their efforts helped to bring *civilian control of the atom* as mandated by the McMahon Act, which subordinated the military role to an operating or technical level.[3] But the scientists themselves were frequently maligned personally or denied security clearances in a military campaign to suppress their dissent.

Since the atom bomb became the symbol of nationalist obsession with military power, virulent anticommunism in what is known as the "McCarthy era" created an atmosphere in which dissent over nuclear policy was tantamount to treason. The aura of government secrecy in matters of nuclear energy was firmly established when Julius and Ethel Rosenberg were executed for allegedly giving vital atomic energy information to the Soviet Union.[4] On the other hand, many scientists were liberal and internationalist. Franz Schurmann has argued that this conflict between nationalists and internationalists was only resolved on the basis of a bipartisan ideology of national security.[5] Liberals looked toward the United Nations as the solution to the problems of war and revolution that were symbolized by Germany and Russia: the United Nations would facilitate demilitarization and the transfer of surplus wealth to the poor. On the other hand, nationalists viewed Britain as a symbol of international capitalism and Russia as the symbol of the revolutionary poor, and instead rallied to the cause of General MacArthur and Chiang Kai-shek to prevent the spread of communism. The compromise doctrine of national security established that any policy decisions regarding nuclear energy would be made by the federal government and the military.

The successful efforts of J. Robert Oppenheimer and the Federation of American Scientists to prevent full military control of the atom backfired on them, as the cold war erupted domestically in the McCarthy movement. National security issues brought before the public had the effect of placing the suspicion of communism on those who would be critical of such a sensitive area as nuclear policy. The military had opposed sharing atomic secrets with the Soviet Union as provided for in the Baruch Plan and proposals of Henry Stimson, the Secretary of War. After the Soviet Union detonated their atomic bomb in 1949, President Truman decided to commit the nation toward developing a fusion weapon on the advice of scientist Edward Teller. Yet, the Soviet Union exploded a fusion device only ten months after the Americans.[6] In what many today believe was an extreme act of scapegoating, the Rosenbergs were tried for espionage in passing nuclear secrets to the Russians and were executed for their treason. Scientists lost their administrative power over nuclear energy to other government appointees. The scientists were then discredited by an investigation into national security by a congressional committee under Senator Hickenlooper, with the dramatic subsequent loss of security clearance for J. Robert Oppenheimer.

The next major development was the Atoms-for-Peace proposal, made by President Eisenhower before the United Nations, calling for international cooperation and the sharing of nuclear materials. This proposal proved to be infamous, for twenty years later, India detonated an atomic bomb with materials supplied by Canada under the Atoms-for-Peace program. While the slogan "atoms for peace" could be used for propaganda advantages in American relations with nonnuclear nations, the program would also allow limited control over nuclear research that might lead to nuclear weapons development in other parts of the world. This has been a feature of our government policy to the present day and is the basis for our stated refusal to export nuclear technology to nations that we believe will divert nuclear materials to nuclear weaponry.

Government control of commercial public power was at stake in the conflict between private utilities and public corporations in the Dixon-Yates controversy in the mid-1950s.[7] Legislation to establish the Tennessee Valley Authority was viewed by Republicans as "creeping socialism." However, the private enterprise advocates of commercial nuclear power were given support when President Eisenhower appointed Lewis Strauss, a New York financier, to head the Atomic Energy Commission. Later, the first civilian nuclear power plant was built under *private* control in Shippingport, Pennsylvania, utilizing a design taken directly from the early submarine reactors developed by the Navy. Government subsidies of nuclear research centers aided this development. Between 1939 and 1971, it is estimated that the government invested over $52 billion into atomic energy, with over half that amount spent for military programs.[8] Antinuclear critics argue that without the government subsidy of nuclear research and facilities, in particular the enrichment of uranium at plants in Tennessee, nuclear energy would be prohibitively expensive as a source of commercial power.

Radioactive fallout from nuclear weapons testing contributed to a new direction in the activities of scientists opposing government policies. The Nobel Peace Prize was awarded to Linus Pauling for his efforts to ban the testing of nuclear weapons in the atmosphere. Herman Müller, who was awarded a Nobel prize for his work with fruit flies, publicly warned that radiation could cause genetic mutations. A paper written by Müller was then suppressed by the Atomic Energy Commission.[9] During the late 1950s, the public began to express opposition to government military nuclear policy. Initially, this was indirectly expressed in an alienated youth movement, the beatniks, in the United States and Britain. The beatniks were the predecessors of hippies; their social accoutrements included sandals, jazz, bongo drums, and beards, and their "let's live for today" philosophy stemmed from a belief that we would die soon in a nuclear war. The cold war era was breaking apart, and when a young, liberal president was elected dramatic changes were set into motion. The culmination of these new trends was the Test-Ban Treaty, signed in 1962 by President John Kennedy, barring the detonation of nuclear weapons in the atmosphere.

Antinuclear Episodes

Several episodes occurred during the 1960s which indicated resistance to commercial as well as military uses of nuclear power. There was substantial resistance to atomic weapons, particularly in the Ban-the-Bomb movement in Britain. Under the spiritual leadership of Bertrand Russell, large marches from Aldermaston to London took place to protest the American Polaris missile base in Scotland and the use of Britain as an American military arsenal.[10] But it was in Wyoming County, Pennsylvania, that citizens became embroiled in a controversy over the proposed Meshoppen nuclear power plant.

The Meshoppen nuclear power plant was supported both by President Kennedy and Glenn Seaborg, then chairman of the Atomic Energy Commission. But a group of Quakers and a citizens committee comprised of dentists, county officials, businessmen, and housewives appeared before a Senate Select Committee to try to block the proposed reactor for fear of radiation danger.[11]

A scientist at the University of Pittsburg, Ernest Sternglass, began the controversy by warning of an increase in cancer deaths due to radiation from nuclear power plants. The issue was linked in the minds of local residents to the contamination of milk with strontium-90 from radioactive fallout. By associating nuclear reactors with infant deaths, Sternglass quickly gained a reputation as a prophet of doom. But he was joined in his scientific views by John Gofman, then a nuclear chemist and a physician at Livermore National Laboratory in California. An Atomic Energy Commission scientist assigned the task of refuting Sternglass initially concluded that Sternglass had underestimated the socioeconomic reasons for infant deaths in Wyoming County, *but* that there was a significant relationship between radioactivity and infant mortality. The Atomic

Energy Commission responded by having the scientist, Dr. Arthur Tampblin, submit all of his speeches to the commission for prior approval. A paper Tampblin was to have presented before the American Association for the Advancement of Science was censored, and his staff transferred to other departments.[12]

Sternglass, Gofman, and Tampblin became important leaders of the antinuclear movement in the early 1970s. Gofman is a member of the Committee on Nuclear Responsibility, while Tampblin became a professional staff member of the Natural Resources Defense Council. The elder critic of the 1950s, Linus Pauling, has also been active in the movement, two decades since his initial warnings of the dangers of radiation. The government policies of repression only resulted in more public and active dissent by scientists.

These earlier episodes of antinuclear activity in the 1960s dissipated somewhat with the signing of the Treaty of Nonproliferation of Nuclear Weapons in 1968 by President Lyndon Johnson, which placed nuclear materials used in commercial power in the United States under the regulatory power of the International Atomic Energy Agency. Social activists were also much more involved in the antiwar movement that reached its peak in the late 1960s, as well as the other movements for change that included constituencies among youth, women, blacks, prisoners, and numerous other aggrieved groups in American society.

The Environmentalist Phase (1968 to 1972)

The direction a social movement takes is very much influenced by the dominant events in the society as a whole. Although the earlier antinuclear episodes did not amount to a social movement, their concern was with the possible effects of low–level radiation from nuclear power plants on public health, including infant mortality and cancer. Scientific evidence has been produced to suggest that this fear is an exaggeration, but it arose because of the association of commercial nuclear power plants with nuclear weapons and radioactive fallout. However, the Kemeny Commission report on Three Mile Island concluded that one of the greatest inadequacies in knowledge is of the effect of low–level radioactive wastes on human organism.[13] The issue therefore has been revived.

Perhaps the most important effect of the early episodes was to lessen the power of the Atomic Energy Commission. Since its inception, the Atomic Energy Commission had been one of the most arrogantly directed agencies in the federal government. Atomic weapons had given America status as the international superpower, so it seemed almost natural for the onus of suspicion to fall on critics rather than on the guardians of nuclear secrets.

However, the real threshold for the emergence of a large-scale movement came along with the growth of the ecology or environmentalist movement. The attacks on a broad range of environmental problems such as air pollution, strip mining, water pollution, and the quality of life drew the attention of ecology groups to the issue of thermal pollution from nuclear power plants. The issue was not as emotion laden as radiation hazards and did not involve questions of national security. Since nuclear power plants discharge immense quantities of hot water from their cooling systems, ecology groups had legal ground for intervention. Several large fish kills occurred near a nuclear plant at Oyster Creek, New Jersey, and at a nuclear fuels reprocessing plant in West Valley, New York. The door was open to chip away at the authoritarian power of the Atomic Energy Commission. Environmentalist organizations discovered that they could use the National Environmental Policy Act to challenge the consequences of nuclear power on the ecology of local areas. In the landmark Calvert Cliffs federal court ruling, environmental impact statements became required before the Atomic Energy Commission could issue a construction permit for a nuclear power plant.

Thermal pollution was a short-lived issue, for the problem was not that severe and was one that could be corrected through the construction of cooling towers, although this added substantially to the cost of nuclear power plants. Some of the fish kills had been the result of accidental thermal discharges, and other evidence even indicated that the warmer waters around nuclear power plants were actually a breeding ground for several types of fish.

Some of the mystery of nuclear power was stripped away when citizen groups began to include the plants among their ecological concerns. But the most important result of the environmentalist phase was to pave the way for *legal intervention* in Atomic Energy Commission licensing hearings for new plants. The new confidence of citizen groups may have been reflected in the use of the term "nuclear energy" for commercial nuclear power, for the term "atomic energy" seems more associated with military power and unassailable government bodies such as the Atomic Energy Commission and the Joint Committee on Atomic Energy.

A typical conflict over nuclear power plants during the environmentalist phase was the controversy over Cayuga Lake, in upstate New York. Scientists and citizens feared ecological damage to the lake from a proposed nuclear power plant, although definitive scientific agreement on the possible extent of environmental damage was never firmly established. In her study of the Cayuga Lake controversy, Dorothy Nelkin found that scientists from nearby Cornell University were divided as to whether or not the credibility of science would be threatened by their taking a position on the issue with inconclusive evidence as to possible ecological damage.[14]

The university professors who opposed the Cayuga Lake nuclear power plant were joined by physicians, local politicians, the local Chamber of Commerce, the League of Women Voters, and the Sierra Club. Nelkin found that Republicans generally viewed the conflict from the perspective of the national interest in new energy supplies and the need for progress, while Democrats were more likely to be opposed to the plans for construction of a nuclear power plant. However, the subtle disagreement among scientists never became a rigid cleavage, although scientists who were involved in scientific research funded by the utility company were open to criticism from their peers in the scientific community. On the opposition side, policy analysis was more important to scientists who wrote public speeches, participated in citizen committees, and wrote position papers. Nelkin observed that the contribution of these scientists was diminished by both company management and critics in their eagerness to support their own point of view.[15]

The adversary process in legal hearings where citizen groups intervene evidently does not enhance the idea that scientists can provide the objective knowledge about nuclear power so that reasonable decisions can be made. When two political scientists observed licensing proceedings for proposed nuclear power plants in Midland, Michigan, and Vernon, Vermont (Vermont Yankee), they found it to be geared to the promotion of nuclear power and the confirmation of prior decisions to build the plants.[16] Intervenors in the hearings had limited financial resources, a lack of experts to provide technical criticisms, and frequently could not comprehend the testimony on complex technical questions given by the company scientists and engineers. Attorneys would seize upon the gaps in knowledge to portray them as a deliberate attempt to hide potentially damaging evidence, creating a situation whereby scientists avoided the hearings in order not to have their competency challenged by lawyers all too willing to embarrass them. The adversary process involving lawyers had little relation to normal scientific processes. Therefore, the small groups of citizens were consigned to helplessness before the "steamroller of agency arogancy, expert elitism, and stacked deck proceedings," leading the citizens to be prone to "know-nothingism, blind antitechnology and antigovernment sentiment, pessimism, and doom forecasting."[17]

Despite these problems, the tactic of citizen intervention quickly evolved as a major part of the strategy of the coalescing antinuclear movement. The right of intervention itself became a cause of liberal Democrats such as Senator Edward Kennedy of Massachusetts, who even tried to get federal funding for intervenor groups.

The Emergence of the Antinuclear Movement

Since nuclear energy was controversial from the very beginning, and a number of opposition movements existed, first among scientists, then among disenchanted beatniks, and finally among the professional upper middle class, the antinuclear movement that has garnered mass media publicity from the early 1970s to the present must be viewed as a continuation of earlier struggles. Nonetheless, it became a large-scale social movement with a distinct identity *only* after the devastating consequences of the 1973–1974 energy crisis. Certainly the Yom Kippur war between Egypt and Israel and the OPEC embargo on oil to supporters of Israel was a turning point in modern history. The ensuing energy crisis itself was the result of an accumulation of factors, but never before the early 1970s had energy shortages been so directly related to world political instability, mercantilist economic policies, and world recession. High inflation and unemployment turned the public away from the oil corporations that were thought to be culprits in the crisis, and a movement developed within the liberal wing of the Democratic party for divestiture of their holdings. Added to all of this was a profound loss of public confidence in political institutions after the forced resignation of President Nixon.

If the environmentalist phase of antinuclear activities had been modestly successful, it was because the government was favorably disposed to regulation of the environmental consequences of modern technology. After "brownouts" in the Northeast in 1970 due to electricity shortages, President Richard Nixon attempted to deal with the problem through the "Clean Energy" proposals. These were proposals for successful demonstration of the fast breeder reactor by 1980 and federal support for alternative energy resources. The fast breeder has the technological advantage of producing more fuel than it consumes, but it is nowhere near a successful demonstration, as funds were cut eight years later by President Carter. The other Clean Energy proposals were for increased federal monies for sulphur oxide control, conversion of coal into a gaseous fuel, underground transmission of electricity, offshore oil and gas leases, government reorganization of energy agencies, and assessment of solar energy by the National Aeronautics and Space Administration (NASA) and the National Science Foundation (NSF). Many of these proposals are still a major part of energy policy (solar energy, coal conversion), have already been accomplished (government reorganization of energy agencies), or are still embroiled in controversy (offshore oil and gas leases, the breeder reactor).

An awareness of an impending energy crisis already existed in the government with projections of an expansion in nuclear power plant capacity being the kingpin of energy policy. But the Arab oil embargo reversed priorities, for now the overwhelming aim of United States energy policy was to make the nation free from foreign disruption of energy supply. While the blueprint for energy security was being planned through Project Independence, government response to the immediate problem was to create an interim White House Federal Energy Office to deal with short-term problems of fuel allocation until strategic planning could become effective.

A struggle both within Congress and between Congress and the White House over government reorganization gave the antinuclear movement its first push into national significance.[18] President Nixon had asked Congress to create the Federal Energy Administration and the Energy Research and Development Administration, to be incorporated later into a large-scale Department of Energy. The interim plan was opposed by Senator Henry Jackson from the state of Washington, who wanted direct enactment of a Department of Energy. Dixie Lee Ray, chairman of the Atomic Energy Commission (and later governor of Washington State), supported the Nixon plan for a new agency to take over the research and management of nuclear installations and a second agency, the Nuclear Regulatory Commission, to be responsible for the licensing and regulation of nuclear power plants.

Conflict of interest between the promotion and regulatory functions of the Atomic Energy Commission was the first political issue of the coalescing antinuclear forces. They could not see how the Atomic Energy Commission could both promote and regulate nuclear power and believed this to be an obstacle toward directing a new energy agency to research alternative energy technologies as well as means of energy conservation. Congressional infighting among Senators Jackson, Ribicoff, and Kennedy and among Representatives Udall, Holifield, and McCormack made passage of a reorganization bill difficult. The real opening for antinuclear forces to become effectual came when Senator Ribicoff of Connecticut held hearings on amendments designed to strengthen safety requirements of nuclear power plants. Cooperating with Friends of the Earth and National Intervenors, Senator Edward Kennedy introduced an amendment requiring subsidization of antinuclear intervenors in regulatory and licensing hearings. In the House of Representatives, the amendments were vigorously opposed by the influential Representative Holifield of California. Senator Kennedy and Representative Udall of Arizona then pressed for assurances that the new energy agency would develop nonnuclear technologies as well as protect the environment.

Ralph Nader entered the battle by calling the commitment to nuclear power "technological suicide." When the Sierra Club and Friends of the Earth joined Nader and called for a moratorium on nuclear power development, the antinuclear movement was born. Senator Ribicoff held more hearings in March 1974 and began to warn of safety hazards from dependence on nuclear energy. Theodore B. Taylor, a nuclear physicist who designed many of the most advanced weapons for the Defense Department, appeared before the committee to warn of the dangers of nuclear theft and sabotage. His contentions were refuted by Dixie Lee Ray and Ralph Lapp, a nuclear consultant, and the interchange was broadcast on national television networks.

Representative Holifield was successful in blocking the Kennedy amendments to subsidize intervenors, and the way was cleared for the Energy Reorganization Act of 1974. The Atomic Energy Commission was abolished, and the Energy Research and Development Administration (ERDA) and an independent Nuclear Regulatory Commission (NRC) were established. President Gerald Ford appointed Robert Seamans, former Secretary of the Air Force, as director of ERDA, and William Anders, a former Atomic Energy Commission member, as chairman of the NRC. Despite new commitments and significant government reorganization, the ERDA budget did not reflect any departure from research expenditures for nuclear energy to conservation and alternative energy technologies. This would take the election of a Democratic candidate to the White House. When President Carter succeeded Ford, Congress went back to the original plan for a large energy superagency and created the Department of Energy (DOE) to replace ERDA, but the structure of the Nuclear Regulatory Commission was to remain secure until the accident at Three Mile Island.

A Synopsis of Significant Events in the Nuclear Controversy (1973 to 1980)

Almost as suddenly as the national political elite split in a divisive struggle over government reorganization to manage the energy crisis, resolution was swift and certain: the nuclear option was validated and commitment to it was strengthened. The antinuclear movement was born, and the momentum intensified from that point on.[19] The public had been awakened to the controversy through a CBS broadcast about dangers in the commercial nuclear power industry. Writing about Theodore Taylor, the physicist who had done nuclear weapons research, John McPhee sounded the alarm with the publication of *The Curve of Binding Energy* in 1974, a book that became essential reading for antinuclear groups forming throughout the nation.

Weakness had also been shown within the nuclear establishment. Shortly before its demise, the Atomic Energy Commission had released the Rosenbaum report regarding the inadequacy of nuclear safeguards and had dramatically overreacted to its own report by ordering armed guards around nuclear installations. Then Montsanto Mound Laboratory in Miamisburg, Ohio, discovered that plutonium was leaking into the Erie Canal. A flood of internal memoranda was covertly released from within the Atomic Energy Commission, confirming the suspicion that nuclear power was not as safe or clean as proponents believed.

The government countered by releasing a massive report on reactor safety completed by a research team under Norman Rasmussen at the Massachusetts Institute of Technology. Intended to be a definitive study showing the statistical improbability of a nuclear accident, the Rasmussen report was immediately challenged by both the Sierra Club and the Union of Concerned Scientists, groups that had been instrumental in preparing the ground for a movement with their criticisms of the safety of emergency core cooling systems in reactors.

When it was apparent that the battle on Capitol Hill had been lost, Ralph Nader organized the first antinuclear conference, Critical Mass '74, in Washington, D.C. Workshops were held and groups throughout the United States learned some of the basics for forming antinuclear organizations. At about the same time, Karen Silkwood, a worker at the Kerr-McGee plutonium reprocessing facility in Oklahoma, was killed in an automobile accident. Her death brought the National Organization of Women full-force into the antinuclear movement, and cast doubt on the safety of workers in nuclear facilities. The death also gave the movement a symbolic martyr, as well as bringing the women's and labor movements into the antinuclear controversy. With speculation that the accident may have been intended, the first activist to die as a result of participation in the movement may have occurred. This was analogous to the Kent State incident during the movement to end the war in Vietnam.

Natural events also brought the point home. A geologic fault that could result in an earthquake was discovered at Diablo Canyon in California, site of a nuclear power plant under construction. A few months later, a fire broke out at Brown's Ferry nuclear power plant in Alabama, burning through the cables controlling the emergency cooling system. If the reactor had not been shut down in time, a major nuclear accident could have occurred. Now the antinuclear movement gained more important publicity. In mid-1975, the American Physical Society released a study critical of reactor safety, while Representative Aspin requested the NRC to withdraw a license for the shipment of nuclear materials to South Korea, and Senator Henry Jackson publicly opposed nuclear exports to South Africa. Credibility was given to the antinuclear movement with this criticism of nuclear power from within the political and scientific establishment.

The Brown's Ferry incident prompted Governor Carey of New York to announce his support of a nuclear moratorium in that state, and a moratorium bill was introduced into the state legislature of Nebraska. Also in the Midwest, Businessmen and Professional People in the Public Interest of Chicago and the Izaak Walton League scored one of the first victories of the movement when they obtained a permanent stay against the Bailly nuclear power plant construction site because it was too near major population centers. However, the order was reversed by the U.S. Supreme Court four months later.

The need for international cooperation on the nuclear safeguards issue was demonstrated when West Germany announced the sale of a complete nuclear fuel cycle to Brazil, a nation that has not signed the Nuclear Nonproliferation Treaty. But President Ford responded only by asking Congress for private industry control of future uranium enrichment plants. Local groups, however, were becoming more active on issues related to the safety of plants in the United States. In Pennsylvania, LeHigh Common Cause voted to oppose nuclear power, while in Vermont the state legislature was persuaded by the Vermont Public Interest Research Group to pass a bill requiring legislative approval of new nuclear power plants. Colorado Public Interest Research Groups filed suit to force the Environmental Protection Agency to regulate radioactive water discharges from nuclear facilities (and later the U.S. Court of Appeals made the Environmental Protection Agency set water pollution standards for all nuclear facilities). In New York, the Safe Energy Coalition attempted to introduce a bill to prohibit the construction of any new nuclear power plants in the state but did not get legislative support, and in Iowa a citizens group blocked the licensing of a nuclear power plant until a commercial system could handle its wastes.

There was a lull in the movement during the summer of 1975 after this flurry of activity, but nuclear advocates were given a boost when Saudi Arabia announced a $15 billion electrification and desalinization plan that would include twenty-five agro-industrial complexes and a national power grid generated by nuclear power—despite the fact that uranium prices had now tripled, casting doubt on the future of nuclear fuel supply. Gulf Oil later pleaded nolo contendere to charges of price fixing in the uranium market with the Canadian government. In other areas of controversy, the NRC officially opposed the idea of a federal security force to protect nuclear materials, confronting the argument that nuclear power would require a national security state. In New York, the Council on Economic Priorities charged Con Edison with a misleading public relations campaign on savings claimed from operation of the Indian Point nuclear reactors, while Ralph Nader publicly requested the NRC and EPA to alert two hundred New Mexico uranium miners and their families that their drinking water contained high levels of radioactive substances. The awareness of the Karen Silkwood case prompted Billy Jack Productions to announce their intention to film a documentary on the strange circumstances surrounding her death.

Everywhere the nuclear establishment found itself on the defensive. A group called Citizen Alert opposed an ERDA decision choosing Nevada as the site for storage of high level radioactive wastes. Safe Power for Maine began a petition drive for a referendum calling for a seven–year moratorium on nuclear power, while Concerned Citizens of Tennessee opposed a proposed nuclear complex in Hartsville. National Public Radio Corporation filed a Freedom of Information suit against the Justice Department for access to the files of an investigation into the death of Karen Silkwood, and nuclear opponents scheduled an antinuclear rally in New York City to coincide with the one year anniversary of the death of Karen Silkwood. Ralph Nader groups requested that evacuation plans in the event of a nuclear accident be released, and coordinated efforts to block the automatic passing of uranium price increases to consumers. Two important suits were filed against the NRC with long range implications. The Natural Resources Defense Council, the Sierra Club, and Businessmen and Professional People in the Public Interest succeeded in getting the NRC to prepare an environmental impact statement on the handling of wastes from light water nuclear reactors, while the Sierra Club and the Natural Resources Defense Council filed a petition to intervene in hearings on the Clinch River Breeder Reactor project, along with the East Tennessee Energy Group. The movement seemed to be gathering more support and was becoming effective in the legal arena.

November 1975 brought the second Critical Mass antinuclear conference, with a candlelight vigil before the White House for Karen Silkwood. Ominous notes were sounded when South Africa announced their plans to construct a uranium enrichment facility using the West German Becker jet nozzle process and when the NRC decided to allow the limited recycling of plutonium. But the following month, the National Council of Churches released a statement condemning the "plutonium economy," while the Federation of American Scientists released a poll of 10 percent of its members showing that a majority were opposed to the rapid development of nuclear power. The base of support for the antinuclear movement was broadening and becoming more inclusive of diverse segments of society.

1976: The Nuclear Showdown

The antinuclear movement intensified and sharpened its struggle in 1976 by a frontal attack on the nuclear establishment. Since 1976 was both the year of the American Bicentennial and a presidential election, the movement's activities became even more significant.

The government seemed to be on the brink of finding some solutions to the nuclear safeguards problem. An international accord was reached on nuclear exports, but then details were not announced. Nationally, the Natural Resources Defense Council appealed the NRC decision to allow the interim recycling of plutonium as a violation of the National Environmental Policy Act *and,* in a new precedent, a violation of the Atomic Energy Act of 1954. After a meeting with representatives from the National Organization of Women, Senator Metcalf reopened the Karen Silkwood investigation. Across the nation, Stop Nuclear Power of Margate, New Jersey, intervened in hearings over proposed floating nuclear power plants off the Atlantic coast, an Iowa citizens group petitioned the NRC to revoke operating licenses for plants which repeatedly violate existing regulations, and Public Media Center of California filed a suit for fairness in radio time for antinuclear advertisements.

The first major political test for the movement was to be an initiative on nuclear safeguards on the California ballot, taking the issue directly to the people of a populous state. Early in the year, three engineers had resigned their positions in the nuclear industry to participate in the antinuclear movement in California, and a fourth engineer resigned his position in New York a few days later to work for the Union of Concerned Scientists. The resignations gave the movement a tremendous impetus, for they captured the attention of the mass media. While the media focus was on the initiative and the upcoming presidential election, antinuclear groups continued to hammer away at every level of government. The Union of Concerned Scientists, the Sierra Club, and the Natural Resources Defense Council filed a suit asking the NRC to withdraw a nuclear export license of Edlow International Company allowing them to ship nuclear materials to the Tarapur nuclear power plant in India. (This was eventually agreed to by President Carter, who in turn was overrruled by Congress in 1980, allowing shipment of nuclear fuel to India). This would be the first time international controls would be legally sanctioned by the NRC, rather than by international accord among governments. In Washington, D.C., the Silkwood case was summarily closed again, and the Supporters of Silkwood were organized to focus national attention on the case. Locally, legal petitions were directed to the problem of planning for a nuclear accident. Maine Public Interest Research Group filed a show cause order for evacuating plans in the event of an accident at Maine Yankee, and in Pennsylvania an antinuclear group demanded *immediate* emergency nuclear safeguards. Friends of the Earth attempted to have the Department of Transportation in New York City stop nuclear wastes from being transported through the city until an environmental impact statement was prepared.

The stage was being set for a confrontation in California. Meanwhile, the National Council of Churches voted in favor of a nuclear moratorium, and the NRC released a study of terrorist and sabotage threats against nuclear installation with the suggestion that an Army unit be trained to act against terrorist groups in the event an attack against a nuclear installation were to take place. At the site of the Indian Point reactors in New York, antinuclear activists were confronted by the plant workers, who felt their jobs were being threatened by the demonstrators, prompting the formation of a group called Environmentalists for Full Employment. In April, *Time* magazine made a startling revelation by reporting that Israel did have nuclear weapons at the secret Dimona installation in the Negev desert, and that the Israeli government had come to within thirty minutes of using the weapons in the 1973 Yom Kippur war. *Time* also reported that in 1972 an American commercial airliner with 108 passengers aboard had been shot down by Israeli jets after it strayed over the Dimona installation.

After an intensive campaign on both sides, including a massive infusion of funds by utility companies throughout the nation into the pronuclear Jobs & Energy organization and a "red alert" scare to nuclear power plants on the eve of balloting day, the California Nuclear Safeguards Initiative was defeated by a two-to-one margin. The movement was not stopped in California. In the same month, Jimmy Carter was nominated as the Democratic presidential candidate, with a party platform supporting the development of alternatives to nuclear power. Having been frustrated by the tactics of legal intervention and voter referenda, however, antinuclear groups turned to direct action. The Seabrook nuclear power plant construction site in New Hampshire was occupied by members of the Clamshell Alliance, followed by a second demonstration with two hundred arrests. Presidential candidate Carter announced his support of civil disobedience on the part of the Seabrook activists *if* they were willing to take the consequences of their actions. These demonstrations were immediately successful: a surprising victory for the movement came when the NRC issued a temporary moratorium on new licenses until a study could be completed of nuclear fuel reprocessing facilities and the handling of radioactive wastes. The suit had been filed by National Intervenors, the Natural Resources Defense Council, and the New England Coalition on Nuclear Pollution.

Direct action means confrontation with authorities. Charges were made by activists that the Federal Bureau of Investigation and the Central Intelligence Agency had monitored the activities of civilian antinuclear groups, and that the nuclear industry had funded background investigations into the Sierra Club, Friends of the Earth, Another Mother for Peace, the Union of Concerned Scientists, and Ralph Nader. Disclosures were made of FBI cooperation with an informer, Jacque Srouji, in preparing a book with derogatory information about the sex and drug life of Karen Silkwood by showing the informer 1,000 pages of files. A few months later, the informer disappeared.[20]

National attention then focused on the presidential election. Antinuclear groups prepared for referenda in six states that would be on the ballots. Internationally, Swedish Center party leader Falldin defeated the Social Democratic party in a struggle where his opposition to nuclear power was crucial to his victory. The parents of Karen Silkwood filed a suit against the Kerr-McGee Corporation charging responsibility in the death of their daughter. Shortly before the elections, the NRC dramatically issued shoot-to-kill orders in the event of any attempt to sabotage fourteen nuclear weapons facilities. The referendum results were less than dramatic; all the referenda were soundly defeated, and the antinuclear movement was at least temporarily routed.

During 1977 the antinuclear movement persisted by relying on the tactic of demonstrations.[21] These were localized conflicts involving the nuclear power plant under construction at Seabrook, New Hampshire, and the arrest of ninety protestors at Diablo Canyon in California. About a month after the Seabrook demonstrations, more than 3000 construction workers and company employees who called themselves the New Hampshire Voice of Energy staged a counterdemonstration in support of nuclear power outside of Seabrook, and in Charlestown, Rhode Island, pronuclear supporters disrupted a talk being given by Ralph Nader. These were the first inklings of a countermovement involving public participation. The greatest escalation of the movement occurred in Europe. Thousands of helmeted demonstrators carrying communist flags fought a three–hour battle with the police at the nuclear power plant site at Grohnde, West Germany, injuring fifty demonstrators and forty policemen. A protest of 30,000 people against the Super-Phenix breeder reactor at Creys-Malville in France left a person dead in a clash with the police, and in Italy 7,000 persons demonstrated against two nuclear power plants proposed in Monalto di Castro. The high point of the year, however, was in November, when President Carter vetoed the $80 million appropriation for the Clinch River breeder reactor in Tennessee. This and other government action was perhaps taking some of the steam out of the movement by incorporating its goals into public policy.

Demonstrations continued at Seabrook the following year, including one in which 20,000 people participated. Daniel Ellsberg, veteran of the antiwar movement of the 1960s and the Pentagon Papers controversy, was one of nineteen persons arrested during a demonstration outside the military nuclear wastes dump at Rocky Flats, Colorado. The Potomac Alliance demonstrated outside the White House over the Karen Silkwood case, arrests were made outside the Trojan nuclear power plant in Oregon, and 300 out of the 2,000 demonstrators of the Abalone Alliance were arrested at Diablo Canyon. The Ku Klux Klan entered the controversy by organizing a pronuclear demonstration outside Seabrook, while in the conservative South the first major demonstration took place outside the nuclear fuels reprocessing plant in Barnwell, South Carolina, with over 1,000 participants who called themselves the Palmetto Alliance. But generally the movement was slowing down. The greatest successes were again in November: during the 1978 off-year elections, the voters of Hawaii and Montana passed limited antinuclear referenda.

On March 28, 1979, the world was abruptly awakened to the perils of nuclear power when a complex series of human and mechanical errors resulted in the release of radioactive gases into central Pennsylvania. When the cooling system of the nuclear reactor at Three Mile Island malfunctioned, the reactor core began to overheat, raising the specter of a nuclear "meltdown." Reverberations from this near disaster were immediate. Shouting "We all live in Pennsylvania," 35,000 people attended an antinuclear rally in Hanover, West Germany, to oppose plans for an underground dump for nuclear wastes. In San Francisco, demonstrators played "dead" outside a utility office, and a "die-in" was held outside the office of the Philadelphia Electric Company.[22] Proposed bans on new nuclear power plants were introduced into state legislatures, although in Austin, Texas, voters approved a bond issue allowing the city to continue participation in a nuclear project. The largest antinuclear rally ever took place in Washington, D.C., involving an estimated 65,000 people, following a demonstration of 20,000 people in San Francisco.

According to the *New York Times* (May 7, 1979) the demonstrators in Washington, D.C., included representatives of the Communist party, the Socialist Worker's party, the Women's International League for Peace and Freedom, the Union of Concerned Scientists, the Grey Panthers, and the Gay Liberation Movement, among others. One month later there were more mass demonstrations throughout the world as June 5, 1979, became designated as International Anti-Nuclear Day by movement groups. Demonstrators were arrested in Oklahoma, Arkansas, and Massachusetts. Twenty thousand Dutch citizens turned out for a rally. Six hundred protestors out of an estimated 15,000 were arrested outside of the Shoreham, Long Island, nuclear power plant, and in Spain, one demonstrator was killed.[23]

The size of the demonstrations and the number of persons arrested grew larger and larger. In October, at Battery Park, New York, over 300,000 people turned out for a demonstration in which many of the movement people of the 1960s such as Jane Fonda reappeared. A few weeks later, 1,045 persons were arrested at the New York Stock Exchange. But then a new crisis diverted attention away from the nuclear issue. The takeover of the American Embassy in Iran and the subsequent crisis over the hostage situation "preempted" the antinuclear movement from the national media, and demonstrations were small and sporadic all through the following year.

International Diffusion of the Antinuclear Movement

Harrisburg became symbolic to antinuclear forces throughout the world. Initially, the diffusion of the antinuclear movement to Western Europe was facilitated by (1) the activities of ecology organizations with international affiliates, particularly Friends of the Earth; (2) the availability of criticisms of nuclear power published by the Union of Concerned Scientists; (3) publicity given to controversial studies of the Atomic Energy Commission in the international media; and (4) the activities of indigeneous citizen groups in Europe that often looked to their American counterparts for strategic and tactical leadership.

The movement became strongest in West Germany, Sweden, France, Holland, and Britain. Legal interventions were also initiated in Denmark, Norway, Switzerland, and Austria. Italy and Spain joined the list of those countries with strong opposition to nuclear power, and the movement has even begun to diffuse to Eastern Europe through Yugoslavia. Violence and bombings erupted in the French movement, while in West Germany the tactical action quickly escalated to sit-ins and demonstrations prior to similar tactics in Seabrook, New Hampshire. Violent resistance also emerged in Spain.

The protest against nuclear power in West Germany centered around opposition to a plant under construction in Whyl, a small town of two thousand residents near the Rhine.[24] Farmers were among the staunchest opponents because they feared the nuclear power plant would damage their fruit, vegetables, and vineyard. A sit-in that was a virtual takeover of the plant site by the farmers and villagers attracted conservationist groups, middle–class university students, and other citizens. These groups defined their tactics as "burgher initiatives," a form of citizen action embracing a wide variety of community issues. Radicals and procommunist students are usually excluded from burgher iniatives, although government leaders in Stuttgart attempted to portray all the demonstrators as radicals.

In Germany and France, the antinuclear movement not only resulted in massive demonstrations, but provided electoral support for antinuclear candidates.[25] Violent demonstrations occurred in Grohnde and Brokdorf, West Germany, and at the site of the Super-Phenix reactor in Fessenheim and the site of the Plogoff reactor in Quimper, France. Ecology parties—the "green movement"—used the issue to gain small proportions of the vote in national and municipal elections. As Dorothy Nelkin and Michael Pollack indicate, nuclear power came to represent anxieties over advanced industrial society such as the "industrialization of rural areas, the concentration of economic activities, the centralization of decision-making, and the incremental tendencies towards a tightening of police control."[26]

Nuclear policy in France is decided by the Council of Ministers under a shroud of secrecy, inhibiting opposition. Etienne Bauer describes the French nuclear opposition as "weakly organized ecologists who have almost no political power, and who can mobilize fewer people in France than in Scandanavia. They speak a passionate language, mixing serious arguments and apocalyptic delirium. To them, nuclear power appears to be more a symbol of a hateful form of civilization than a well-defined eco-technical and social problem."[27] Despite general public apathy, however, the use of violence in the antinuclear movement first occured in France.

In both France and Germany, radical left political parties and groups (but not the Communists) have been actively opposed to nuclear power, while socialist parties have been more ambivalent, either supporting a moratorium or a slower level of development of nuclear energy. Centrist parties, such as the Gaullists in France and the Christian Democrats in West Germany, have been the strongest advocates of nuclear energy and also most responsive to the large companies, including the state–owned nuclear company in France, Framatome, and Kraftwerks-union in West Germany.

Despite the growing strength of the antinuclear movement, France and Germany remain committed to nuclear power programs that are intended to eventually provide over one-half of their electricity. This is particularly true of France, whose commitment to nuclear power was reaffirmed by President Giscard D'Estaing after Harrisburg, and made more palatable to the public by promising that people living near a nuclear power plant would get a 15 percent reduction in their electricity bills.[28] With the socialist victory of Francois Mitterand, however, rapid expansion of nuclear power beyond projected plans is unlikely.

Swedish nuclear opposition includes the *Miljocentrum* ("Environment center"), *Faltbiolergna* ("Field biologists"), *Alternativ Stad* ("Alternative earth"), and *Jordens Vanner* ("Friends of the Earth"). The Center party, along with the Communist party, introduced parliamentary opposition to nuclear power in 1974 in Sweden, after Arthur Tampblin and Dean Abrahammson (two American nuclear critics) and Amory Lovins, British representative of Friends of the Earth, gave speeches in the country. Pronuclear speeches were given in Sweden by Dixie Lee Ray and Edward Teller. The Conservative party, with support from the Social Democrats, was able to pass a bill through the Swedish Parliament expanding the nuclear power program, although a majority of the public supported the opposition.

Some of the major arguments against nuclear power are diminished in Sweden because nuclear wastes are sent to England, and Sweden is not interested in nuclear weapons development. Nevertheless, the controversy took a different turn when Thorbjorn Falldin, the Center party leader, credited Swedish physicist Hannes Alfven with having awakened him to the hazards of nuclear power.[29] The 1976 election became a virtual referendum on nuclear power that contributed to the defeat of the Social Democratic party for the first time in forty-four years.

However, the coalition that gave the Center party victory in 1976 collapsed two years later, again over the nuclear issue, and this time the Liberal party gained power under the leadership of Ola Ulsten. Sweden has a very developed environmental consciousness, but most of the feasible hydroelectric sites have already been utilized. This accounted for the original commitment to nuclear power. The Center party had formerly been the Agrarian party but had broadened its rural orientation to a concern with the environment and the adverse effects of modernization, including centralization of government.[30] This predisposed them to opposition to nuclear energy.

When the Swedish government adopted a report that called for neither a phasing out of nuclear power nor a binding commitment to this source of energy, the issue began to die down in Sweden. Falldin then compromised his position and infuriated his supporters in the Center party, leading to his resignation in 1978. However, after Harrisburg the leader of the Social Democratic party, Olaf Palme, announced his support for a referendum on nuclear power, and the Liberal Prime Minister Ola Ulsten refused permission for two reactors to charge until after the referendum.[31] This referendum took place in March 1980, and antinuclear proposals were defeated, although the Swedish referendum only allows *limited* expansion of nuclear power to continue as a matter of public policy.

Violent opposition to nuclear power has also emerged in Spain, which depends heavily on hydroelectric power for electricity. There are three nuclear reactors operating in Spain and seven under construction, but these have engendered opposition from local citizens as well as the Socialist and Communist parties.[32] Some of this difficulty occurred in the Basque region, where a demonstrator was killed in a clash with the police. But the new opposition has emerged in the rural western provinces of Badajoz and Cáceres, near Portugal. At one point, 30,000 people defied a ban to demonstrate in the town of Villaneuva de la Serena, and mayors of seventeen towns declared opposition to the starting up of the two new reactors at Almarez until safety guarantees were made.[33]

In other European nations, the antinuclear movement has been somewhat muted. In 1979 Austrian voters refused to allow a $550 million reactor at Zwentendorf to be activated, and the Swiss now require parliamentary approval for the building of nuclear power stations. Of all European nations, only Denmark, with tremendous natural gas reserves, and Norway, an oil–rich nation, have no nuclear power programs. In Finland there has been little resistance to the construction of four nuclear power stations because they mean independence from Soviet oil.

The main reactor in Holland is at Borselles and is operated by a public corporation. A substantial minority of the Dutch public opposes nuclear power, including some scientists, doctors, and public action groups. While the largest labor unions favor the development of alternative energy sources, the Protestant labor unions support nuclear power. The Dutch government wants a nuclear program in order to conserve the depleting natural gas fields at Groningen, while opponents of nuclear power believe that the North Sea deposits of oil and gas are sufficient for Dutch needs. In a controversy in Rotterdam, the Labor party rejected plans to build a large nuclear reactor near the city. Holland also participates in a fast breeder reactor project called the SNR-300 that is being built at Kalkar in the southern part of West Germany. The project involves both countries as well as Belgium. The Dutch helped to pay for their part by levying a 3 percent tax on all electric bills. This "Kalkar tax" was strongly opposed, and seventy muncipalities refused to hand over revenues to be used for the SNR-300, forcing a compromise whereby the government allowed individuals to consign the three percent tax to alternative energy programs.[34]

In Belgium, the mayor of Huy ordered a local power station at Tihange to close down, although he was quickly overruled by the Belgian government. The same reactor was shut down in 1980 by striking workers, who occupied the control room and threatened to reduce its output.[35] Radicals in Italy are calling for a moratorium on nuclear power, while the socialists are preparing for a referendum on the issue. Britain has been moving ahead slowly with nuclear power, relying on a design for reactors that is British and has produced public concern for safety but not enough pressure for a moratorium.[36] The main problem now is concern for the design, since it is similar to the pressurized water reactor at Harrisburg.

Finally, there has been some diffusion of the antinuclear movement from Western to Eastern Europe. In Yugoslavia, a nation lacking in energy resources or a national power grid, the government planned to build the country's second nuclear reactor in the industrial region of the Dalmation coast, but local citizens were concerned about pollution and the tourist trade. Yugoslavs working in West Germany also returned with an idea of why antinuclear protest was gaining ground. Under public pressure, the government backed away from its plans to site a reactor near the beaches of Dalmatia.[37]

Outside of Europe significant antinuclear opposition has not yet developed in nations such as Japan or the various South American and Asian countries with existing or proposed nuclear reactors. Japan, however, has a substantial antinuclear movement that focuses on nuclear weapons. In Canada, opposition is growing but is not on the same level as in the United States. Twenty–two existing or planned reactors are in Ontario, three in Quebec, and one in New Brunswick. Canada also has significant uranium reserves in Ontario, and uses the unique CANDU reactor design that uses heavy water as a moderator and burns natural rather than enriched uranium. The Canadian government is particularly concerned with occupational health hazards to uranium miners, and several commissions and inquiries have been officially made into a wide range of problems. However, as Robert Paehlke observes, "the various environmental—particularly antinuclear—groups in Canada are not yet so firmly established as a respectable part of the decision-making process in Canada as in the United States."[38]

The Pronuclear Countermovement

A countermovement is a response to the social change advocated by the initial movement, usually being oriented to challenges from less powerful groups that are threatening a vested interest.[39] The nuclear industry is the main source of a pronuclear countermovement, for its interests are the most threatened by the antinuclear movement. There are two organizations that promote the general interests of the nuclear industry on political issues. These are the Atomic Industrial Forum and the American Nuclear Society.

The Atomic Industrial Forum is an international association of 625 organizations. As early as 1974, the Forum outlined its basic position that "sun worship" is not a solution to energy problems, and that as many as 40,000 workers had lost their jobs due to delays and cancellations in the construction of nuclear power plants as a result of "the backlash against authority and technology."[40] The American Nuclear Society is somewhat different, functioning as a professional, scientific, and educational organization. The Society also asserts that unemployment will result from conservation efforts, since industry and commerce are the major consumers of electrical energy.

These industry groups at first did not acknowledge the existence of a separate antinuclear movement, but adhered to the idea that they were being unduly attacked by an obstructionist environmentalist movement. The president of a third major pronuclear organization representing the utilities, the Edison Electric Institute, says for example that "the precipitous rush to solve environmental problems through legislation and the ensuing process of legislative interpretation undertaken by the courts has brought our nation to the edge of a real crisis in electrical energy supply."[41]

Nuclear proponents believe that nuclear energy is a clean and safe energy source that is vital to our national welfare and national security. They have a greater faith in technological progress than do their opponents. The litany of nuclear energy's merits might run as follows: nuclear power plants do not produce chemical air pollution, radioactivity is kept to minimal levels, uranium mining is safer than coal mining, no fatalities have occurred among the public as a result of the civilian nuclear power program, and nuclear accidents are improbable.

The pronuclear countermovement includes many groups other than those directly associated with the nuclear industry. Financial support comes from utilities and private corporations, as well as from construction workers, the Ku Klux Klan, and the John Birch Society. The role of the federal government is much more complex, for both proponents and opponents believe that the government is on the side of the opposite group.

Save Maine Yankee, the countermovement group mobilized to defeat the Maine Nuclear Referendum, is illustrative of how pronuclear groups operate. First, the organization raised over three quarters of a million dollars to fight the Maine Nuclear Referendum Committee, which only raised about $127,000 during the 1980 referendum battle. The donations to Save Maine Yankee came primarily from the pulp and paper industry in Maine, Stone and Webster (the Boston engineering firm that designed Maine Yankee), Procter and Gamble, Exxon Nuclear Corporation, General Electric, Maine Public Service, and Merrill, Lynch, Pierce, Fenner & Smith.[42] They also received a contribution from Winner/Wagner, the Los Angeles consultants who engineered the defeat of the 1976 Proposition 15 referendum in California.[43] The issues defined by Save Maine

Yankee were strictly economic: shutting down Maine Yankee would mean higher electricity costs and dependence costs and dependence on foreign oil.[44] With the money and the pocketbook arguments on their side, Save Maine Yankee achieved a modest victory in the Maine Nuclear Referendum.

Participating Groups

The antinuclear movement has existed in some form in the United States ever since the inception of atomic energy as a source of military weaponry in the Second World War, and the movement today is in many ways an outgrowth of early opposition to the military use of nuclear technology. In the last ten years, the movement peaked prior to the 1976 presidential elections, appeared to subside somewhat, and then intensified after the accident at the Three Mile Island nuclear power plant near Harrisburg, Pennsylvania. A movement against nuclear power did not suddenly emerge as a result of Three Mile Island, for there was cumulative disenchantment with nuclear energy that had begun long before the accident in Pennsylvania.

Prior to the accident at Harrisburg that came to symbolize all that is wrong with nuclear power, the antinuclear movement attracted perhaps no more than 1 percent of the American populace and a smaller number of adherents in Europe. Before the issue of nuclear energy was introduced into the 1976 presidential election campaigns, the most broad-based activity of the movement was the obtaining of four hundred thousand signatures on a Clean Energy petition. This petition was circulated by the Task Force Against Nuclear Pollution, which was based in Washington, D.C., using the good offices of Senator Mike Gravel of Alaska.[45] The Clean Energy petition simply called for a moratorium on nuclear power plants and the development of solar energy technology. Petitions were also circulated to have initiatives on nuclear energy put before the voters in state elections.

The individuals who sign a petition are not necessarily active participants in the movement; in any case, signing a petition is only a minimal form of political expression. Actual membership in an organization or group active in the antinuclear movement is a higher threshold of participation, but here again the number of active individuals rarely exceeds 10 percent of the total membership, and in most cases represents only a small nucleus of activists. Some organizations have a structure that enables members to vote on the objectives that are to be incorporated into the strategy of the group, such as Common Cause, while in other cases a local chapter of an organization may be intensively involved in a specific conflict over a nuclear power plant, as exemplified by the Sierra Club— although the Sierra Club is quite active at the national level. Many of the groups that have become enmeshed in the nuclear controversy are actually voluntary associations, often aligned with the environmentalist movement. Numerically, environmentalist and conservationist societies have the largest membership of these voluntary associations in the antinuclear movement, with the Sierra Club having the largest public following of all. Several large organizations, such as the National Wildlife Federation, have only been involved in the antinuclear movement through a public proclamation against nuclear power. But all of these voluntary associations have had some role in the antinuclear movement.

The mass base of the movement in the United States is not so much comprised of the vast membership of large organizations as it is of small groups scattered throughout small towns and metropolitan areas. The most active groups are to be found along the Eastern Seaboard and the West Coast, but groups can be found in every state. (The range of these groups is indicated in Appendix C with local groups being the most numerous but not the most influential.) After the accident at Three Mile Island, there was a proliferation of new groups in the movement, although organizations founded prior to Three Mile Island still formed the core of the movement. Ecology and environmentalist voluntary associations such as the Sierra Club, Friends of the Earth, and the Natural Resources Defense Council are the most likely to have a national or international membership. It was through these groups with international chapters that the movement diffused to European nations.

Social action theory is one of the main theoretical perspectives in sociology that I have used to analyze the antinuclear movement.[46] One of the axioms of this theory is that in order to understand social reality, we should look at the subjective orientations that individuals and groups have toward situations that are relevant to them.[47] What is their *frame of reference* when they react to events significant to the movement? When an antinuclear group responds to an event such as the nuclear accident at Three Mile Island, the social scientist must deal with the event as it appears from the point of view of the groups or individuals whose action is being analyzed. After the Three Mile Island accident, President Carter appointed a committee to study what happened. The report of the

Kemeny Commission might appear to be a more objective analysis than that given by antinuclear activists, but if a social scientist is studying antinuclear groups, their reaction and definition of the situation is what must be reported.

The political action taken by various antinuclear groups is guided by their own specific orientations, which include their beliefs about nuclear power, their own social values, and symbols that express their opposition. Groups members have ideas about what they consider a desirable state of affairs to be. They may, for example, want an energy technology that is compatible with their ideas about ecology and the environment. These dominant value orientations are intertwined with the motivation of individuals to act. Four main types of social action have been defined that represent the most important modes of activity given the existence of specific social values and motives. These are intellectual, expressive, moral, and instrumental types of social action.[48] For the hundreds of groups involved in the antinuclear movement, this typology is a useful way of indicating the differences in how groups perceive nuclear power.

Antinuclear groups with *intellectual* patterns of social activism, such as the Union of Concerned Scientists in Cambridge, Massachusetts, place an emphasis on their knowledge of nuclear technology. These scientist groups are the most influential antinuclear organizations, both within the movement and with the public, but are also the smallest. The opinions of scientists who support nuclear energy have become increasingly subjected to scrutiny by their peers for fear they are political opinions rather than scientific statements of facts. Some scientist organizations, such as the Federation of American Scientists, have maintained relative neutrality by only making carefully guarded statements on nuclear power, while others, such as the Committee on Nuclear Responsibility, appear to serve more as a propaganda forum for scientists predominantly from the biomedical fields. But the most influential group has been the Union of Concerned Scientists, which has provided much of the esoteric criticism of nuclear power. Its statements are utilized by movement groups throughout the world. The orientation of these scientists and their role in the movement is largely an intellectual one because they are the creators of knowledge and provide the rationale for the rejection of nuclear power plants on the basis of their technical inadequacies.

Some groups, exemplified by the National Council of Churches and the World Council of Churches, have a *moral* reaction to the social implications of nuclear technology. These organizations have defined and explored the ethical dilemmas of nuclear power for society. Should we accumulate large amounts of radioactive wastes that future generations must live with? Are we justified in selling nuclear technology to nations that might use it to develop nuclear weapons? While these questions represent central concerns of moralist groups, intellectual groups by comparison might be more concerned with the technological or economic merits of nuclear power relative to other sources of energy. In reality the types of social action overlap, but they do indicate something about the dominant orientations of groups.

The orientation of ecology and environmentalist organizations is generally that of *instrumental activism,* meaning that they wish to accomplish through their role in the movement the realization of the ideal values in our culture concerning self-reliance, appreciation of the natural environment, and efficient utilization of resources.[49] In the instrumental type of orientation, activists are motivated to attain desired states of affairs through rational means. Goals are specific but often related to a more general system of values. For example, the Black Lung Association developed in West Virginia to help coal miners afflicted with the black lung disease to receive benefits from the federal and state governments as well as other forms of compensation.[50] Many of the environmentalist groups in the antinuclear movement would fit this pattern of involvement. The Sierra Club, for example, values the preservation of the natural environment and therefore takes steps to block future nuclear power plants from being built.

The backbone of the antinuclear movement consists of organizations that have taken up the nuclear issue at their raison d'etre. They lead the action against the nuclear establishment, e.g., the federal government, the utility companies, oil corporations, and the manufacturers of nuclear technology. These organizations usually have strong regional support, as typified by the New England Coalition on Nuclear Pollution and the Clamshell Alliance in New England, and People for Proof, the Western Bloc, and the Abalone Alliance in the West. Two organizations, the Task Force Against Nuclear Pollution and the National Intervenors, did attempt during the earlier part of the movement to coordinate it on a national scale from their offices in the national capital. Their efforts, however, were overshadowed by the regional alliances of antinuclear groups.

The orientation of regional direct action groups is frequently *expressive* in nature; that is, their opposition to nuclear power is also a means of realizing more general political or social objectives. These groups would be opposed to nuclear power primarily because it represents an affront to larger social values that they hold. For example, in his study of the Campaign for Nuclear Disarmament (CND) in Great Britain. Francis Parkin found that the movement attracted individuals who were more opposed to broader features of British life than to nuclear weapons.[51] CND activists were likely to reject the monarchy in favor of republicanism, and were dissatisfied with many other aspects of British life. Another example of this type of group would be Supporters of Silkwood, a group that helped to create a kind of martyrdom for a woman who was a labor movement activist in a plutonium reprocessing plant in Oklahoma. Supporters of Silkwood was actually a spinoff group from the National Organization of Women, which had taken up the cause of Karen Silkwood after her mysterious death following her revelations of safety abuse at the plant where she worked.

Most of the regional groups reflect an antibusiness tenor and objectives that are congruent with the cultural countermovement, which has survived since its emergence in the late 1960s. Others, such as the Environmentalists for Full Employment, have attempted to forge an ideological linkage between the labor movement and the antinuclear movement. Direct action groups are the vanguard of the movement, a kind of movement elite whose status derives from direct confrontations that involve significant publicity by the mass media. They are not the theorists or intellectuals of the movement, but without them there would be no movement, only the ambitious efforts of interest groups.

Numerous other groups are only peripherally involved in the antinuclear movement. These include farmer organizations, the Piedmont Organic Movement, the Hudson River Sloop Restoration, the Women's Christian Temperance Union, and the 4-H Earthkeepers. Student organizations, labor union locals, and state political party organizations have also issued antinuclear proclamations to their constituencies.

The Goals and Ideology of the Antinuclear Movement

Because of the diversity and varying degree of involvement of groups active in the antinuclear movement, there is no consistency in the specific goals of these groups. However, for the movement as a whole an ideology exists that includes goals common to most groups. Movement goals will change or be redefined in the career of the social movement, and they may vary according to their generality or specificity. Thus, the goals may be to seek change in the core values of social institutions, or more peripheral values, but they always are criticisms of existing conditions. The ideology of a movement incorporates its goals and is a conception of alternative "utopian" ways of organizing the social order.

The goal of a moratorium on the further construction of nuclear power plants with alternative emphasis on solar energy development has been common to all organizations in the antinuclear movement, with variation in emphasis from group to group. One organization, the National Intervenors, experienced a succession or displacement of their antinuclear goals and became strictly an advocate of solar power. It now exists as a clearinghouse for information on solar energy. In fact, many groups have been more occupied with energy alternatives, such as solar power, than with the pitfalls of nuclear energy.

More commonly, the antinuclear goals of many organizations appear to be means of realization of a larger framework of organizational values not directly related to nuclear power. Voluntary associations such as the Wilderness Society are fundamentally more concerned with preservation of the natural environment than with the economic and social implications of nuclear technology. The technical characteristics of nuclear power plants become salient only insofar as they threaten the basic values of the Wilderness Society.

The ideology of the antinuclear movement reflects the heterogeneous doctrines of the peace, environmentalist, and labor movements. First, the ideology proclaims a danger of proliferation of nuclear weapons with the spread of nuclear power plants throughout the world. Scientists have been particularly vocal in arguing that arms control involving nations embroiled in conflict such as South Africa, Israel, Egypt, and South Korea must extend to control of exports of nuclear technology and fuels. Second, the ideology propounds a concern for the safety of nuclear power plants and the potential hazards to the natural and human environment. Environmentalist groups have been most activated by this dimension of antinuclear ideology. Third, the movement's ideology stresses doctrines of the labor movement by charging the nuclear industry and the federal government with a perceived failure to provide for the safety of workers in nuclear facilities or to invest in energy systems that are labor intensive, thereby creating more employment and business opportunity for those not affiliated with large corporations.

Some of the underlying assumptions of antinuclear ideology held by all groups are that (1) nations will acquire plutonium to produce nuclear weapons and will use those weapons; (2) that terrorists have the capability of diverting nuclear material for clandestine purposes; (3) that nuclear accidents are probable; (4) that radioactive wastes cannot be adequately disposed of; and (5) that alternative energy technologies can meet the nation's energy needs.

Temporal dimensions are a part of ideologies, and not just in the sense of the historical development of specific doctrines. Analytically, ideologies cover a complex time frame that is invested with social and political meaning. Nuclear power plants have only been in operation for two decades and were supposed to have been a peaceful application of an energy source that had brought unparalleled destruction to end the Second World War. The reinterpretation of this time frame by antinuclear activists is that nuclear technology is not inherently progressive, for its export to other countries for ostensibly peaceful purposes is the export of a potentially destructive technology.

There is also an awareness contained in this ideology that an imminent catastrophe involving a dangerous technology will be precipitated by the rush to meet world energy shortages with more nuclear power plants. The near future holds the likelihood of a nuclear accident bringing havoc to the affected area and the possibility of world disaster because of the accumulation of radioactive wastes. The ideology of the antinuclear movement depicts the present as a sequence of irreversible steps being taken by a monolithic nuclear industry in collusion with the government that may end up in tragedy.

Three generalized beliefs have diffused throughout the antinuclear movement. One is that nuclear technology is dangerous and cannot be entrusted to mankind for centuries to come. Another is the belief that solar energy and other energy alternatives are preferable to the ambiguity of nuclear power. Finally, activists believe that social institutions cannot cope with the consequences of a nuclear infrastructure or a "plutonium economy." A conservative skepticism of human nature is often an intrinsic part of these beliefs, and is accompanied by a faith that alternative energy technologies are perfectable or at least not life threatening. The ideology is against large-scale technological systems with concentrated control and advocates decentralized and less complex systems that are more "appropriate" to the needs of individuals.

The conservative or at least parochial nature of aspects of antinuclear ideology is implied in its sense of justice. Activists are the most critical when they state their arguments as a dilemma of whether the public interest will prevail over the private interests of the nuclear industry and the oil corporations. The enemies of the movement have been the nuclear industry, large oil corporations, elite academic scientists, federal bureaucrats, and to some extent, the Republican party. On the other hand, few groups have articulated any substantial concern for the economic impact of nuclear power in the Third World. The most disadvantaged minority groups or the masses of poor people in this nation or in other parts of the world have not been targeted as the groups which suffer the most as a consequence of energy shortages. Antinuclear ideology cuts across the lines of social class by depicting the conflict as one between an elitist nuclear establishment and consumers. It is middle–class activism, not explicitly on behalf of the lower class.

Conclusion

As the first major public referendum on the nuclear issue in the 1980s, the vote in Maine represents a more cautious approach to nuclear energy in the United States. This trend is also apparent in Western European nations such as Sweden and Austria. However, the controversy over nuclear power that began with Hiroshima and Nagasaki is far from over. The movement may be expected to take new directions, specifically over the issues of nuclear wastes reprocessing and the fast breeder reactor. As the issues become increasingly international, the antinuclear movement will also become more international and less dependent on events occurring within the United States.

The subsequent chapters of this book are concerned with the internal structure of the antinuclear movement, including the division of labor within the organizations, available resources, types of leadership, and coordination of activities. They also consider the social values of the main groups in the movement and how their activities relate to the significant events in the career of the antinuclear movement.

Notes and References

1. The referendum was on a proposed Nuclear Fission Control Act that would prohibit electric power generation from nuclear fission power plants in the State of Maine, including existing facilities. This would have resulted in shutting down Maine Yankee, the state's only nuclear power plant. The September 23 results were 59.1 percent "no" votes on the referendum, and 40.9 percent "yes" votes *(Maine Sunday Telegram,* 28 September 1980, p. 24A). One year later, a referendum to elect public utilities commissioners and to formally define state energy policy in terms of nonnuclear alternatives was also defeated. Not to be daunted, efforts by the Maine Nuclear Referendum Committee were underway to hold another referendum to close down Maine Yankee in five years by public mandate.

2. For a history of the Atomic Energy Commission between 1947 and 1952, see Richard G. Hewlett and Francis Duncan, *Atomic Shield* (University Park: Pennsylvania State University Press, 1974).

3. A good analysis of these early struggles against the military may be found in Stuart S. Blume, *Toward A Political Sociology of Science* (New York: Free Press, 1974).

4. See Walter and Miriam Schneir, *Invitation to an Inquiry: Reopening the "Atom Spy" Case* (Baltimore: Penquin Press, 1973).

5. Franz Schurmann, *The Logic of World Power* (New York: Pantheon Books, 1974).

6. For an insightful view of this decision see Barton J. Bernstein, "Roosevelt, Truman, and the Atomic Bomb, 1941–1945: A Reinterpretation," *Political Science Quarterly* 90 (Spring 1975): 23–69.

7. See Aaron Wildavsky, *Dixon-Yates: A Study in Power Politics* (New Haven: Yale University Press, 1962).

8. Corbin Allardice and Edward Trapnell, *The Atomic Energy Commission* (New York: Praeger, 1974).

9. Reported in Richard S. Lewis, *The Nuclear Power Rebellion* (New York: Viking, 1972).

10. See Francis Parkin, *Middle Class Radicalism: The British Campaign For Nuclear Disarmament* (Manchester, England: University of Manchester Press, 1968).

11. Richard S. Lewis, *The Nuclear Power Rebellion.*

12. Ibid.

13. *Report of the President's Commission on the Accident at Three Mile Island* (Washington, D.C.: Government Printing Office, 1979).

14. Dorothy Nelkin, *Nuclear Power and Its Critics: The Cayuga Lake Controversy* (Ithaca, N.Y.: Cornell University Press, 1971).

15. Ibid., pp. 70, 117–19.

16. Steven Ebbin and Raphael Kasper, *Citizen Groups and the Nuclear Power Controversy* (Cambridge: MIT Press, 1974).

17. Ibid., p. 4.

18. The struggle over government reorganization to meet the energy crisis is best documented in *National Journal Reports* during 1974 and 1975. For 1974, see January 12:59–61; February 16: 229–34; March 23: 439–41; April 20: 588–91; for 1975, see March 1:305–13; March 22:419–29; May 4: 647–58; June 29: 962–68; July 5: 983; November 2: 1635–44; December 14: 1868–70.

19. This synopsis of events was constructed from a variety of sources. The main sources were items from the *New York Times* and *People & Energy,* a newsletter published by the Center for Science in the Public Interest during 1975 and 1976 in Washington, D.C. The items were too numerous to warrant separate footnotes, and the events were carefully followed by the author during this time period.

20. Only to reappear with a published book, much of it focusing on Karen Silkwood. See Jacque Srouji, *Critical Mass* (Nashville, Tenn. Aurora Publishers, 1977).

21. These events during 1977 are summarized from items appearing in the *New York Times.*

22. See the *Philadelphia Inquirer,* April 1, 1979, for a detailed account of the Three Mile Island crisis.

23. This was the second death of an antinuclear demonstrator, the first having occurred during a demonstration in Fessenheim, France, in 1977.

24. A first report of the Whyl demonstrations appeared in the *New York Times* on August 28, 1975, in an article entitled "West German Farmer's Resistance Forces Review of Nuclear Power Plants." A follow-up analysis by William Sweet, "The Opposition to Nuclear Power in Europe" appeared in the *Bulletin of the Atomic Scientists* 33, no. 8 (1977): 40–47. See also John J. Berger, *Nuclear Power: The Unviable Option* (New York: Ramparts Press, 1977), p. 330–34. Whyl was the first demonstration of its kind in Western Europe.

25. Dorothy Nelkin and Michael Pollack, "Political Parties and the Nuclear Energy Debate in France and Germany," *Comparative Politics* (January 1980), pp. 127–41.

26. Ibid., p. 129.

27. Etienne Bauer et al., "Nuclear Energy—A Fateful Choice for France," *Bulletin of the Atomic Scientists* 32 (January 1976): 37–41.

28. "Giscard's Nuclear Salesmanship," *New Statesman* 99, no. 2549 (25 Jan 1980): 112.

29. Swedish nuclear opposition is documented in Lennard Daleus, "A Moratorium in Name Only," *Bulletin of the Atomic Scientists* 31, no. 8 (1975): 27–33.

30. Peter James, "The Nuclear Issue in Swedish Politics," *World Today* (December 1979), pp. 499–507.

31. Nancy E. Abrahams, "Nuclear Politics in Sweden," *Environment* 21, no. 714 (12 July 1980): 75.

32. Brian Trench, "Massive Protest May Stall Reactors," *New Statesman* 98 (9 November 1979): 716.

33. "Spain Sets Up Shop," *Economist* 273 (12 July 1979): 75.

34. Sweet, "The Opposition to Nuclear Power in Europe.": 40–47.

35. *New York Times,* (21 February 1980), p. 10.

36. "Going Nuclear, Slowly," *Economist* 273 (22 December 1979): 50–51.

37. Gabriel Tonay, "First Victory for East Europe's Anti-Nuclear Lobby," *New Statesman* 98 (9 November 1979). 716–17.

38. Robert C. Paehlke, "Canada—Three Nuclear Inquiries Conclude," *Environment* 21, no. 4, (May 1979): 41.

39. Tahi L. Mottl, "The Analysis of Countermovements," *Social Problems* 27, no. 5 (June 1980): 620–34. See also Stanley Albrecht, "Environmental Social Movements and Counter–Movements," in *Social Movements: A Reader and Source Book,* ed. Robert R. Evans (Chicago: Rand-McNally, 1973), pp. 244–62.

40. Atomic Industrial Forum, "The Nuclear Industry in 1974: The $80 Billion Giant as Underdog," news release, December 1974, New York.

41. W. Donham Crawford, "Energy Demand and the Electric Utility Industry," in *Energy and Public Policy* (New York: Conference Board, 1972), pp. 49–51.

42. *Bangor Daily News* (Bangor, Maine), 17 September 1980, pp. 1–2.

43. See chapter 4 for an analysis of the California referendum.

44. Save Maine Yankee, "Maine Yankee Shutdown Referendum Fact Sheet," Augusta, Maine, 1980.

45. Task Force Against Nuclear Pollution (TFNP), bimonthly "Progress Reports," from September 1974 to September 1975, Washington, D.C.

46. Social action theory has important roots in the work of Talcott Parsons, a social theorist affiliated with Harvard University until his death in 1979. Parsons contributed to sociological theory in two main areas. First, he developed the perspective known as structural functionalism that dominated American sociology for at least a quarter of a century. Basically, structural functionalism is a way of analyzing societies by looking at how institutions, cultural values, and social norms function to integrate people into a working society. Critics frequently argued that this focus on what makes society an integrated entity excludes

analysis of the conflicts that exist between social classes and other social group-
ings. This criticism has often obscured Parsons's contributions to the general
theory of social action. A good summary can be found in "An Outline of the
Social System," in *Theories of Society,* ed. Talcott Parsons et al. (New York: Free
Press, 1961), pp. 30–79.

47. Talcott Parsons, *The Structure of Social Action* (New York: Free Press,
1937).

48. This typology is developed by Talcott Parsons and Edward A. Shils in
Toward A General Theory of Action (Cambridge: Harvard University Press,
1951), part 2.

49. The concept of instrumental activism derives from the social theory of
Talcott Parsons and has been used in a variety of contexts. For example, see
Jackson Toby, "Inadequacy, Instrumental Activism, and Adolsescent Subcul-
ture," in *Explorations in General Theory in the Social Sciences,* ed. Jan Loubser
et al. (New York: Free Press, 1976), pp. 407–14.

50. Bennet M. Judkins, "The Black Lung Movement: Social Movements and
Social Structure," in *Research in Social Movements: Conflict and Change,* ed.
Louis Kriesberg (Greenwich, Conn.: Jai Press, 1979), pp. 105–29.

51. Francis Parkin, *Middle Class Radicalism.*

CHAPTER 2
Environmentalist Antinuclear Groups

Aldous Huxley defined ecology as the science of mutual relations of organisms with their environment and one another. Environmentalism suggests an ideology based on ecological values. The environmentalist movement mobilized a citizenry that in the 1960s became increasingly aware of environmental degradation of the natural resources on which they depend for their survival. The aesthetic unpleasantness of America was no less alienating than the real threats to public health. As Rice Odell, a conservationist, says:

People began to see for themselves what was happening to their environment—the hazes of pollution hovering in their cities, the filth in the streams, the maddening "No Swimming" signs on the beaches, the smelly and unsightly dumps, the urban sprawl, the interstate highways which punched through their neighborhoods, the shorelines and wetlands defiled by development, the flooded scenic rivers, the clear-cut and strip-mined lands, and the noise of airplanes.[1]

The 1960s saw catastrophic damage done to the environment, particularly in the Santa Barbara oil spill that spread crude oil over miles of coastal beaches in 1969. But success came to the movement during the same year, when Congress passed the National Environmental Policy Act (NEPA). A cabinet–level federal agency was created to control air and water pollution, pesticides, noise, safety conditions in coal mines, and development of coastal areas. The Environmental Protection Agency (EPA) had the power to enforce the new environmental regulations contained in a multitude of bills passed by Congress.

Many who were involved in the civil rights and antiwar movements viewed the environmentalist movement as a middle–class escape from the more pressing problems of social inequality and the war in Vietnam. With the passage of the National Environmental Policy Act, the movement appeared to be legitimized and not in direct confrontation with the political establishment. But environmentalists were not docile or politically inconsequential. During the early 1970s they confronted the oil companies over construction of the Alaska pipeline and offshore oil and gas drilling facilities. Utility companies could not meet legislated air and water pollution standards, particularly the sulfur oxide pollution from coal-burning electric generating plants, and initiated a major shift from coal to oil as a source of energy. One undesirable consequence was to put hundreds of coal miners out of work, but it can also be said that the lives of a number of coal miners were probably saved.[2] However, after the oil shocks given to the Western world by the Organization of Petroleum Exporting Countries (OPEC) in 1974 and 1978, the utilities began to convert back to coal again.

When the United Nations held an environmental conference in Sweden in 1972, establishing the United Nations Environmental Program as a permanent organization with headquarters in Nairobi, Kenya, the international diffusion of the movement gained impetus. Nonetheless, a major "brownout" in the Northeast the previous year, followed by the energy crisis of 1973–1974, brought a turning point to the movement. The federal government became more willing to trade off environmental quality for energy security. The environmentalist movement began to be viewed as an obstruction to urgent new national goals. Business had generally regarded environmentalism as obstructionist and accurately perceived the pendulum swinging back in their direction.

The movement was firmly established, however, and its success had been dramatically demonstrated by Earth Day in 1970. But activists began to shift from a participatory to a power strategy in environmentalist issues, and, as Allan Schnaiberg has also pointed out:

While public education campaigns have by no means disappeared in recent years, the core of the active environment movement today is focused on litigation, political lobbying, and technical evaluation rather than on mass mobilization for protest marches, petition-signing, and the like. Recent antinuclear coalitions like the Clamshell Alliance and its European counterparts have revived many of these earlier forms, though.[3]

The abundance of economic opportunities for ecologists and other professionals in the environmental field emerged with various court decisions and EPA requirements that environmental impact statements be completed before any construction of large-scale projects could occur. This made it appear that many of the participants in the environmentalist movement were actually technical specialists rather than movement activists. However, as Hans Kruse has argued:

If the main criterion of social movements is that they represent in a coherent and continuous way social aspirations which derive from a collective belief in the imminence of a dramatic occurrence, there is no doubt that environmentalism falls into this category.[4]

Several different subgroups may be identified within the environmentalist movement. For example, *eschatological* environmentalists call for zero population growth and an end to economic expansion as the only way to save the world from catastrophe. On the other hand, *chiliastic* environmentalists advocate accelerated economic growth and environmental management as the safest way to achieve a mass consumption society.[5]

In the earlier stages of the environmentalist movement, the ideology of groups was largely eschatological, viewing destruction of the environment from unparalled economic growth and development as almost inevitable unless radical steps were taken. The chiliastic orientation, however, slowly predominated as environmentalists realized that in many parts of the world the lack of economic development is an impediment to human survival. The Club of Rome, an influential environmental organization, once warned of onerous consequences that would affect populations experiencing rapid economic growth and depleting raw materials in their societies. Later, the Club of Rome officially reversed its position and advocated that expansion of economic capacity is crucial if the world is to provide for the basic needs of human populations.

All environmentalists hope to bring about changes in our cultural value systems in order that environmentalism become a part of our consciousness. Only in this way will the totality of decisions made regarding economic growth reflect cumulative reversal of the present environmentally destructive paths pursued by many societies. Environmentalists do not generally believe that technology can resolve the ecological crisis, for this is in great part created by an expanding population, the energy intensiveness of industrial societies, and a growth economy. We must, they argue, reduce our consumption of minerals and energy, control pollution from fossil fuels and other sources, have more efficient land use planning, and reduce population so that food supply is more balanced. These outcomes are more dependent on changes in the value systems of societies than the purely technological approaches to environmental management.[6]

There are four types of environmentalist groups that have been significant to the antinuclear movement.[7] First, there are groups that developed out of the conservationist and preservationist movements in the early twentieth century in the United States, such as the Sierra Club and the National Audubon Society. Because they are more traditional organizations that do not place social welfare or political reform high on their agenda for change, they are sometimes considered to be distinct from the contemporary environmentalist movement.[8] Nonetheless, both the Sierra Club and the National Audubon Society claim large memberships and have been substantially involved in controversies over nuclear power. Secondly, there is the eschatological type previously defined as environmentalists who call for zero population growth and an end to economic expansion. Friends of the Earth and the Environmental Alert Group are examples. Aside from their programs for change, eschatologists also envision total environmental catastrophe. There are subtle differences in these groups, much like the subtle difference between conservationists and preservationists. Some groups that view total disaster as imminent also foresee a utopian future that can emerge from eco-catastrophe, while others simply prophesy impending doom. Those groups with doomsday orientations are distinguished here as apocalyptic groups. Thus, the first two types are preservationist-conservationist groups and eschatological-apocalyptic groups.

The third group consists of the chiliastic environmentalists. These activists are liberal reformers who recognize the negative features of economic growth but are prepared to accept growth if steps are taken to provide for environmental protection and management of resources. Of particular importance here are the Ralph Nader consumer-environmentalist advocate organizations that have been deeply involved in the antinuclear movement, such as Congresswatch and the loose association of groups united under the slogan "Critical Mass" (The Citizens Movement to Stop Nuclear Power).

A fourth type includes environmentalist groups that are strictly utilitarian and purposive. These groups involve themselves in specific issues and use tactics that will bring about clearly defined changes. They do not have the same popular mass base as other groups, resembling elite foundations more than social movement organizations. They are, however, extremely effective when they bring litigation against their targets. Examples of this subtype of environmentalists are the Natural Resources Defense Council and Businessmen and Professional People in the Public Interest.

Perhaps these subtle ideological differences obscure the fact that all of these groups simply have varying ways of interpreting the ecology ideal and choose different tactical styles that symbolize their cause and the preferred means of bringing about change. All of the groups engage in a form of activity that I have defined as *instrumental activism.* When participating in the antinuclear movement, the involvement of environmentalist groups and organizations is usually a *means* to realize their interpretation of the ecology ideal. In the following pages, examples of how environmentalists have been involved in the antinuclear movement illustrate their unique role in the nuclear controversy.

Preservationist and Conservationist Groups: The Sierra Club and the Florida Audubon Society

When the board of directors of the Sierra Club voted in 1974 to oppose the construction of new nuclear power plants, the antinuclear movement gained an impressive endorsement, for the Sierra Club is one of the oldest and probably the most prestigious of all conservationist societies. The reasons initially given by the board of directors for opposing nuclear power were the potential threats to public health from radioactive wastes, as well as questions regarding the operating efficiency of nuclear power plants and the ability of the government to prevent the theft or diversion of nuclear materials.

The Sierra Club did not, however, issue a blanket approval of antinuclear goals. Nuclear power was only opposed in its present state of development. In other words, the Sierra Club feared an irreversible commitment to nuclear power before the solution of technological problems. Guarded in its judgement, the Sierra Club statement on nuclear power acknowledged that many environmentalists view nuclear power proponents as potential allies, for nuclear power reduces the air pollution caused by the burning of fossil fuels. Furthermore, nuclear energy avoids adverse consequences of strip mining for coal and marine drilling for oil and natural gas. Since the preservation of natural beauty is a core value of the Sierra Club, nuclear power plant construction could end plans to dam and flood scenic canyons for hydroelectric power.

Michael McCloskey, then executive director of the Sierra Club, wrote in the 1974 statement that

nuclear power is now undergoing severe questioning because it was a technology that was prematurely overstimulated and was managed by a less than competent bureaucracy. The premature expansion of the nuclear power industry resulted in poor government decisions which actually hurt the development of the technology.[9]

Local units of the Sierra Club have considerable autonomy and command of resources. In California, they have initiated many legal actions against nuclear power, sometimes with other organizations. The national organization of the Sierra Club, in conjunction with the Union of Concerned Scientists or the Natural Resources Defense Council, has on many occasions filed suits against federal agencies on issues ranging from prohibition of nuclear fuel sales to India to litigation that would require the Nuclear Regulatory Commission to consider alternative sources of energy available in an area before issuing a construction permit for a nuclear power plant.

The strip mining of coal has always been anathema to Sierra Club members. Thus, their opposition to nuclear power has been tempered by an awareness that heavy dependence on coal is extremely detrimental to the aesthetic beauty of the environment as well as to the quality of air. Smog in the Los Angeles region has reached such high levels as to require oxygen to be available to the public in airports. A major victory that can be attributed to the Sierra Club was defeat of the Kaiporowits project in southern Utah. Kaiporowits was to be the largest coal-fired electric generating plant in the world, supplying electricity for southern California. The success of the Sierra Club in defeating a multi-billion–dollar project, supported by some of the most powerful corporate and political leaders in the nation, is testimony to its power and prestige.

The Sierra Club is effective due to a large membership and access to considerable resources. Since the local units are autonomous, the Sierra Club has been a factor not only in the national struggle over nuclear energy but in innumerable local controversies. Without officially adopting a policy preference for solar energy or any other futuristic energy source, the Sierra Club is quick to oppose any energy source that will alter the environment in a detrimental way. Preservationist and conservationist ideology tends to run contrary to the liberal conception of technological progress. But the distinguishing characteristic of the Sierra Club is that its members have an orientation that is, in the terminology of the classical sociological theorist Max Weber, *wert-rational* ("value rational"). Preserving the natural environment is imperative for Sierra Club members, while the pragmatic consideration of conflicting social needs is largely irrelevant to realization of the primary goal. Essentially, there are no dilemmas in the value orientations of Sierra Club members, because all technological options for economic development that conflict with their preservationist ideal are foreclosed in a process of reaction formation.

Another major conservationist group, the Audubon Society, is organized in much the same way as the Sierra Club. While the Audubon Society has a smaller membership than the Sierra Club, it has a greater number of local affiliates in small communities throughout the nation. These affiliates are autonomous, thus freeing them for local initiative in the nuclear controversy.

A significant controversy over floating nuclear power plants brought the Florida state affiliate of the Audubon Society headlong into the antinuclear movement. Since the floating nuclear power plants were to be built in Florida and towed by barge to the Atlantic coast, where they would be anchored off the New Jersey shoreline, citizen groups in New Jersey as well as in Florida were drawn into the controversy. The Florida Audubon Society filed a complaint in 1973 against the Army Corps of Engineers in federal district court to prevent the dredging and filling of a marshy extension of the St. John's River near Jacksonville. This was to be an industrial site in the manufacture of floating nuclear power plants by the Westinghouse and Tenneco corporations. The fatal flaw in this $200 million project was its authorization by the now defunct Atomic Energy Commission before the commission had even approved the concept of floating nuclear power plants officially or conducted environmental impact studies.[10]

Since the feasibility of the concept was still open to question, and alternative sites, according to the Florida Audubon Society, had not been given sufficient consideration by the Army Corps of Engineers, the federal court issued a restraining order. The Florida Audubon Society presented as evidence in the complaint a study of the ecology of the St. John's estuary. This study, conducted by Dr. Edwards LaRoe, was based

on field observations, conservation measures taken, and review of aerial
photographs and other available data. Dr. LaRoe found that the marshes
formed an extremely rich and productive marine ecological system that

is very complex and depends for its fertility and continued viability on the
interplay between the marshland and the river; the tides and fresh-salt
water balance; water quality and runoff; the nutrient inflow and seasonal
or cyclical migrations of fauna and flora. Dredging, filling, pollution,
and water diversion all stress this system and decrease its productivity.[11]

However, the study produced by LaRoe was not accepted as legitimate
scientific evidence by the Army Corps of Engineers, which argued that
the observations LaRoe made could be discounted as casual and based on
hearsay evidence. Since scientific authority did not prevail in the situation, the nature of the conflict became purely political. Accusations of
unethical behavior and countercharges quickly undermined the role of
science in the matter. LaRoe suggested that Westinghouse and the Army
Corps of Engineers had deliberately kept the project a secret and then
rammed it through reviews and agency approvals. Furthermore, the
Florida Audubon Society argued that data prepared by consultants in
support of the project were not objective. The consultants had been hired
by the Jacksonville Port Authority, which had a vested interest in the
project.

The resource mobilization theory of social movements states that the
success of a movement often depends on how well contending groups
utilize external resources. In particular, the mass media will play an
important role in forming public opinion on an issue. The controversy
over Blount Island is the object of a study on mass media manipulation by
Sean Devereaux.[12] In the struggle over the Blount Island project, economic and political elites in Jacksonville were able to manipulate the
media to support their views. Florida Seaboard Coastline Industries of
Jacksonville was the potential recipient of railway business and land sales
should Blount Island become a reality. The company owns a local
newspaper, the *Florida Publico,* and publishes the *Times Union,* another
newspaper with a circulation of over 60,000. A committee was formed to
support Blount Island, and included in the committee were the Jacksonville Chamber of Commerce, the publisher of *Florida Publico,* and
eleven of the thirteen members of Offshore Power Systems, the Westinghouse–Tenneco project management organization.

News concerning Offshore Power Systems was evidently kept out of
the Jacksonville newspapers to avoid a premature announcement to

Portsmouth, Virginia, another potential site, of any local conflict over the project. Then the newspapers began a blitz in support of Blount Island, with large advertisements, over 146 stories, and sixteen editorials. The environmental impact of Blount Island on the ecology of the estuary was either overlooked or criticisms discredited. The newspapers did not publish a UPI story on biological hazards until an opposing article had been written. A local environmentalist leader was only mentioned once in two and one-half months, and pictures showed only supporters of the project.

How did the Florida Audubon Society respond to the argument that Offshore Power Systems represented a probable gain of 120,000 additional jobs in the Jacksonville area? There has always been a latent conflict between environmentalists and labor groups over questions such as this. The Audubon Society proposed that the floating nuclear plants should benefit their community of destination rather than the Jacksonville community which would gain the economic benefits from construction of the plants. If the plants operated off the coast, there would not be great employment opportunities, and New Jersey citizens would pay an even higher burden in taxes and utility bills to support the project. In addition, the Audubon Society questioned the military security of the plants in open seas.

In the end, Westinghouse agreed to purchase 1,000 acres of marshland and donate it to the public as compensation for the marshland lost in building a factory. This factory would mass produce a floating nuclear power plant in twenty-seven months. However, the battle over these plants had to be won in New Jersey rather than Florida.

The first four floating nuclear power plants were to be constructed for Public Service Electric and Gas Company (PSE&G) of Newark, New Jersey, with the first two to be sited off Little Egg Harbor in the Atlantic Ocean by the mid-1980s. But significant local opposition was spearheaded by the twenty-nine members of the Women's Club of Linwood, New Jersey. After hearing a local physician speak on nuclear poisons, the women formed a nuclear power study group, and then adopted a resolution to keep nuclear power plants out of New Jersey.[13]

The tactics of the women were fourfold: pressuring the city council to pass an antinuclear resolution, involving other organizations and the public in the opposition, insuring a negative vote in Linwood on an Atlantic County nuclear referendum, and securing signatures for the Clean Energy petition then being circulated by the Task Force Against Nuclear Pollution.

By showing up in full strength, the Linwood Women's Club was able to move the city council to officially oppose the location of any nuclear power plants off the New Jersey coast. The Women's Club produced literature focusing on moral issues and the dangers of plutonium. This literature was mailed to seventy-five other groups and organizations in the area. Other local groups such as Stop Nuclear Power, of Margate, New Jersey, joined in the campaign to bring voters to oppose floating nuclear power plants in a referendum. The eventual outcome in Atlantic County was 25,000 votes against nuclear power and 15,000 votes for the plants.

Citizen strength in local referenda will not alone decide the future of nuclear power. Court maneuvers by the nuclear industry negated the vote, but when the Nuclear Regulatory Commission published a report that indicated the risks associated with floating nuclear power plants were exceedingly small, citizens were helped by the state. The Department of Public Advocate intervened on behalf of an Atlantic County Citizens Council on the Environment because the federal agency had excluded them from hearings when an environmental impact statement was being made.

In this instance, the New Jersey Department of Public Advocate *funded* an independent study of the issue by the Center for Science in the Public Interest (CSPI) of Washington, D.C., an organization active in the antinuclear movement. The CSPI study concluded that in the event of a core meltdown, land–based nuclear plants could be surrounded by layers of sand, concrete, and gravel that would contain radioactive materials, but that a floating nuclear power plant would be surrounded by water, which, through tidal action and ocean currents, would transport the radioactive materials to the shore. Residents feared that just the thought of such a catastrophe would destroy the tourist trade on the New Jersey shore.

A federal hearing was then held in Atlantic City. While the citizens group had a local physician testify on potential radiation hazards, Westinghouse found support from the chamber of commerce, the National Association of Industrial Parks, and the New Jersey Industrial Development Association. The hearings were emotional. An antinuclear spokesman, for example, argued that

plans for evacuation in the event of accidental release of radiation are very vague. How are we going to get out? It is our lives you are dealing with, and by God, it's our ocean.[14]

A member of Stop Nuclear Power of Margate objected to citizens being guinea pigs. Israel Mossee, a black resident, added, "they plan to use the poor as guinea pigs in this highly experimental venture. They are saying to the poor and minorities: your lives have no value. I resent that!"

Perhaps human emotions and fears are often what drive citizens in local controversies, but for residents of urban areas there is a question of whether or not they could leave in time in the event of an accident because of the inadequacy of public transportation systems and emergency planning. In a state where mass panic was created years ago by the broadcast of Orson Welles's *War of the Worlds,* this might be a legitimate concern. In fact, one belief held by many opponents at these hearings was that a nuclear accident might create a tidal wave that would devastate the New Jersey coast. Moreover, a list of over 5,000 individuals who would not vacation in New Jersey if the floating nuclear power plants were built was also presented at the hearings. A few months later, demonstrations were held outside the courthouse.

Even with the escalation of the conflict over floating nuclear power plants in Atlantic County, neither legal tactics nor demonstrations were successful in ending the project. The end came almost a year and a half after the Three Mile Island accident. Since New Jersey utility companies were participating owners of the plant at Three Mile Island, New Jersey residents had to pay higher utility rates to help pay for the damage. Faced with renewed public opposition and lingering questions over the feasibility of the project, the floating nuclear power plant concept was finally abandoned.

Eschatological and Apocalyptic Environmentalists: Friends of the Earth and Environmental Alert

Eschatology is the religious doctrine or study of the last or final state of affairs, such as the end of the earth or resurrection. Apocalyptic outlooks are more concerned with prophetic revelations of impending doom. Groups with more secular goals often tend to have a fervor or outlook that gives their beliefs this same sort of religious intensity. Eschatological thinking in the environmental movement characterizes the Friends of the Earth, while the Environmental Alert Group in California is representative of apocalyptic environmental groups.

Friends of the Earth retains environmental lobbyists in the national capital who are experts in energy, wlidlife, air and water pollution, and wilderness or public lands issues. The organizational structure of the

Friends of the Earth is a key source of their strength. Field representatives in major cities direct activities on state issues, while sixty branches emphasize local issues and generate grassroots support for state and national activities of the organization. There are parallel organizations in England, France, Australia, New Zealand, Germany, Sweden, Yugoslavia, Ireland, and Guam.[15] The British representative of Friends of the Earth is Amory Lovins, one of the leading critics of nuclear power and an advocate of a nonnuclear future. Friends of the Earth estimate their membership at 23,000 persons. Moreover, they have an advisory council with such luminaries as Jacques Costeau, Linus Pauling, Konrad Lorenz, George Plimpton, C. P. Snow, George Wald, and Pete Seeger.

A major effort of the Friends of the Earth is the publishing of conservationist literature. Photographic studies of the most remote areas of wilderness in the world are combined with technical studies of "earth island." *Not Man Apart* is a newsletter on environmental and nuclear issues, while *Earth Law Journal* analyzes legal responses to environmental issues in different nations, including the socialist countries. The emphasis on conservation reflects the origins of Friends of the Earth. It was established by David Brower in New York City in 1969 as an alternative to the Sierra Club. Brower believed that traditional conservationist societies were not concerned with nuclear proliferation, the most serious environmental threat in both a military and ecological sense. Neither would the traditional organizations concern themselves with inflation, unemployment, or similar inequities that are often produced by environmental abuse.

The eschatological elements of the ideology of Friends of the Earth appear in the group's depiction of a single, all-encompassing and accelerating crisis that is the product of mindless technological and economic growth. The "California Tomorrow Plan" of Friends of the Earth envisages a utopian "California Two" that will be planned with intelligence in "post-industrial age earth," yet the ideology is tinged with romantic nostalgia:

If you think back no more than fifteen years ago, you know the loss as you remember how enjoyable breathing used to be, the taste of water, the sound of birdsong, or the renewal that could come safely from a walk in the city evening with stars in it, or on a lonely trail in the wilderness that ages have made perfect.[16]

Often using flamboyant tactics, Friends of the Earth has campaigned against the Boeing SST and the Concorde, the trans-Alaska pipeline, and the building of new towns on agricultural lands. Founded out of a concern for nuclear proliferation, Friends of the Earth was in large part responsible for the diffusion of the antinuclear movement to Europe. In one case, data provided by Friends of the Earth resulted in the British government's rejection of nuclear reactors manufactured in the United States.

Working with Senator Edward Kennedy, Friends of the Earth attempted to block passage of the Price-Anderson Act extension bill being debated by Congress. The Price-Anderson Act provides government insurance for owners and operators of nuclear reactors and was due to expire in 1977. Under pressure from antinuclear organizations such as Friends of the Earth, Congress attached an amendment to the extension bill that would invalidate Price-Anderson if the Rasmussen study on reactor safety were to produce disturbing results. This prompted President Ford to veto the extension, which was later passed again by Congress.

Defeat of Price-Anderson could have been a death blow to the nuclear industry, for without insurance the utilities could not afford nuclear energy. Although the insurance may protect the manufacturers and operators of nuclear power plants more than potential victims of a nuclear accident, Congress has continued to support government–backed insurance until it can be gradually phased out and replaced by private insurance pools.

Social movements often attract marginal "fringe groups" (sometimes derisively called the "lunatic fringe") whose doomsday prophecies seem to border on hysteria. Early in the evolution of the antinuclear movement Environmental Alert Group of California published pamphlets that may not have been so much emotional overreaction as scare tactics. Much of their propaganda was written by Dr. Douglas DeNike, who was also the vice-president of Zero Population Growth. Dr. DeNike was the alleged author of "a forthcoming book on radioactive crime and banditry."[17]

Environmental Alert Group in particular depicted the fast breeder reactor as a commercial doomsday machine that would produce plutonium in greater quantities. This raised the specter of the abridgement of civil liberties, as a federal security force would be needed to protect nuclear installations. Although the Nuclear Regulatory Commission is officially against creation of such a federal security force, fear exists that massive numbers of security clearances and investigators will eventually be needed. A newsletter of Environmental Alert Group reports that

the profliferation of nuclear materials opens wide the door to anarchy and chaos. Large regions, or any specific target within them, will be placed at the mercy of enemy spies, fanatic terrorists, criminal blackmailers, and deranged persons.[18]

Scare tactics, however, do not enter into the strategies of most antinuclear organizations despite the awareness of the dangers of radioactive wastes or nuclear accidents.

Chiliastic Environmentalists: Congresswatch and the Citizens Movement Against Nuclear Power

Chiliasm is actually the doctrine of the return of Christ to earth during the millenium. Used in the context of environmental ideology, chiliasm is a doctrine of the eventual restoration of the environment that will eradicate its present degradation. It is a belief that something can be done about environmental threats to humans.

The prime mover for the reassessment of nuclear power by environmentalists is Ralph Nader, also a consumer advocate. Nader sponsored a convention of nuclear power critics in Washington, D.C., ("Critical Mass'74") in order to coordinate antinuclear activities throughout the nation. Initially, Nader portrayed the emergence of a garrison state to protect plutonium. Only by not using fission power would this possibility be negated. The energy program advocated by Congresswatch, the Nader organization, in fact became federal energy policy during the administration of President Carter. Conservation and the use of coal, with environmental safeguards, were interim solutions, while in the latter part of the century solar, geothermal, and fusion power would be available.

Nader developed the strategy for nuclear lobbying to be implemented by Congresswatch. The chief lobbyist for Congresswatch was delegated the responsibility of meeting with other environmentalist groups to share intelligence information. Nader called for increased citizen intervention and joint activities among divergent groups, including those fighting utility rate structures. In the *Critical Mass* handbook, Nader wrote that

social movements need all the tactics and strategies they can muster. Thus, a coalition of these two movements is essential if either is to succeed. Citizens fighting utilities as nuclear proliferators need to understand the strategy of cutting off the flow of money to utilities for nuclear expansion—by entering rate fights, stockholder and mismanagement suits, etc.[19]

To survive this attack, the Atomic Industrial Forum launched its countermovement, approving a budget increase of over a million dollars. As Tahi Mottl argues, the specific tactics of countermovements respond to the range of tactics employed by the initial movement, even to the extent of adopting some of the initial movement's program.[20] The Atomic Industrial Forum fits this pattern, for it copied Congresswatch by giving its own press conferences, sponsored trips for reporters to nuclear facilities, taped messages for small town radio stations, and ghost wrote pronuclear articles on behalf of distinguished experts. The Forum also encouraged petitions, staged events, and direct article placement to minimize filtration by editors.

The counteroffensive of the Atomic Industrial Forum was aimed at decision makers in both the federal and state governments. Meanwhile, Congresswatch concentrated its lobbying efforts on blocking any legislation favorable to the nuclear industry, including the Price-Anderson act and fast breeder reactor research appropriations. Utility rate hikes related to the construction of nuclear power plants were opposed, and citizens were encouraged to participate in licensing proceedings for new plants and in nuclear referenda.

Nader's organization established a newsletter entitled "Critical Mass" to represent the Citizens Movement to Stop Nuclear Power. Many of the themes in this newsletter are centered around discrediting the nuclear industry by exposing powerful coalitions of financial and industrial interests, manipulation of the press, and biased government activity. One article, for example, uncovers alleged evidence that five banks—Morgan Guaranty, Chase Manhattan, Banker's Trust, Citibank, and Merrill Lynch—unduly influence the promotion, purchasing, financing, and insurance for the nuclear industry. These banks are all members of the Atomic Industrial Forum, are among the top ten stockholders of 74 percent of all utility companies, own almost 10 percent of General Electric stock and 11 percent of Westinghouse stock, and provide almost half of short-term loans to the nuclear industry. The inevitable conclusion: financial self-interest and government subsidies, rather than the stability of the nuclear industry, furthers the construction of nuclear power plants.

A second common theme of "Critical Mass" is that government agencies with functions of regulating the nuclear industry are staffed with persons who have a strong pronuclear bias. For example, the chief lobbyist, Jim Cubie, wrote that

almost thirty years of propaganda by the Atomic Energy Commission had convinced much of the public that atomic power was safe, cheap, and dependable. Thirty years of pork barrel patronage had placed nuclear facilities in a large number of Congressional districts, anesthetising otherwise skeptical members.[21]

Cubie argued that the Joint Committee on Atomic Energy refuses to listen to critics of safety regulations and to assess realistically the economic problems of the nuclear industry. Although the antinuclear movement was successful in getting Congress to abolish the Atomic Energy Commission and replace it with the Nuclear Regulatory Commission, no similar reorganization has been made for the Joint Committee on Atomic Energy.

A third theme in "Critical Mass" is that scientists cannot be objective on the nuclear issue because of their corporate affiliations. Ralph Nader reiterates this argument, pointing out that engineers who sign pronuclear statements are in organizations or corporations with a vested interest in nuclear power.[22]

Student Activism.   The Ralph Nader consumer and environmentalist organizations have an important influence on students in colleges and universities across the United States. Public Interest Research Group (PIRG) is a Nader organization with student affiliations in many major universities. National PIRG adopted an antinuclear program that called for the inclusion under the Price-Anderson Act of all segments of the nuclear fuel cycle, a moratorium on the recycling of plutonium, nonfunding for the breeder reactor, a ban on nuclear exports, and an end to government subsidies for the nuclear industry.

A new tactic introduced by PIRG organizations was the filing of show cause suits against utilities in New York and Maine to force them to produce evacuation plans in the event of a nuclear accident or close down their plants. In Maine, for example, PIRG found that evacuation plans in the event of a nuclear accident at Maine Yankee included the sounding in nearby towns of nonexistent sirens and the use of nonexistent hospital facilities for treating patients with radiation contamination. A similar petition was filed against Consolidated Edison in New York for having inadequate evacuation plans in the event of an accident at the Indian Point reactors near New York City.[23]

The students were successful in Maine, for Central Maine Power Company was required to disseminate information on evacuation plans each year to all of its customers within a forty–mile radius of Maine Yankee. With other groups, such as Safe Power for Maine in Stockton Springs, students blocked a proposed nuclear power plant at Sears Island and obtained the necessary 40,000 signatures for a seven–year moratorium on nuclear power in Maine.

One attitude toward the student activists was illustrated by an article in the *Portland Press Herald* that depicted Maine PIRG members as romanticists who, in the name of the public interest, were merely causing the public more expense. William Clark went on to write that "we will all pay to prove to this small group of prejudiced people that the leading scientists of this country and the specialists in nuclear power know what they are talking about."[24] The acting director of Maine PIRG responded that Mr. Clark was "hoisted by his own petard" and was a conservative afraid to challenge the rising cost of electricity. Rob Burgess asked, "Where would we be if Ralph Nader and his public spirited, public interest progeny were not with us?"[25]

Ralph Nader conceives of PIRG as a means for students to work within the system after a frustrating decade of activism in the 1960s. The organizational structure allows students to pool their monies together and hire a full-time professional staff under their control. PIRG organizations originated in Oregon and Minnesota and then spread to twenty-five states. PIRG allows students to research their own information needed to advocate a cause and bring it to public attention through an organization. Newsletters tie them together with the National PIRG in the capital, and funding is provided by an optional fee after a general petition among student bodies. The groups are multiple–issue oriented, but many sent representatives to the Critical Mass conferences held in Washington.

New Jersey provides good examples of PIRG structure. Major units of the organization exist at Seton Hall and Rutgers University, and at one time New Jersey PIRG had 20,000 fee-paying constituents in all on eight campuses in New Jersey. Their staff in 1976 received a basic salary of $5,200 and sometimes more, as determined by need. Nine professional staff members filled the positions of director, staff attorney, coordinator, researchers, and issues coordinator. Six of the nine had college degrees, and two had graduate or law degrees. The common denominator in the background of all these staff members was previous work for organizations including the National Organization of Women, the Movement for a New Congress, the American Civil Liberties Union, and the Sierra Club.[26]

New Jersey PIRG confronted a broad range of issues that included feminist concerns, tax reform, unemployment, and various higher education issues. As a consequence of PIRG activities, the New Jersey Environmental Protection Agency prohibited the use of plutonium in nuclear power plants in New Jersey and provided for the dismantling and restoration of the site of the Hope Creek power plant under construction in Salem County when its useful life has been exhausted.[27]

Although the National PIRG coordinates activities that require federal and statewide action, such as a nuclear moratorium, New Jersey PIRG cooperated with state affiliates of Common Cause, the League of Women Voters, and the United Auto Workers, among others, to develop an effective strategy on nuclear issues.

Nader: Chiliast or Charismatic Leader?   Ralph Nader exemplifies several types of leadership qualities: organizational skills, oratorical abilities, and ideological skill. A caustic attitude toward powerful establishment industrial and political leaders gives a charisma to his leadership. Appearing before the Joint Committee on Atomic Energy, Nader immediately launched into a condemnation of the committee for having a concentration of power contrary to the system of checks and balances and for failing in its oversight function of the nuclear industry. If arrogance before those who are in positions of authority is an element of charisma, then certainly Ralph Nader is a charismatic individual. He asserted that the Joint Committee only comes to a problem after others discover it, and then only to sweep it under the rug. It was the Union of Concerned Scientists who first raised questions about the effectiveness of reactor core cooling systems, environmentalists who discovered nuclear power plants were being built over geologic faults, and antinuclear groups who voiced objections to methods of waste disposal.[28]

During his appearance before the Joint Committee on Atomic Energy, Ralph Nader produced an internal memorandum that he claimed had been suppressed by the Atomic Energy Commission because it had concluded that safety problems were an "unanswerable question." Keeping up the attack, Nader asked why rural people were worth risking in plant siting, and then accused the Atomic Energy Commission of collusion with the nuclear industry. He depicted the Atomic Energy Commission and the Joint Committee on Atomic Energy as "Siamese twins" that have "condemned, bullied, or ridiculed citizens who tried to convey facts and concerns about nuclear power hazards and risks."[29]

According to Ralph Nader, he first inquired into nuclear power in 1963 and 1964 because he was worried about the export of nuclear power plants to countries with no technological expertise or nuclear infrastructure. Since that time, he has become one of the main catalysts of the antinuclear movement, providing incisive criticisms of nuclear power as well as the organizational structure with which to fight it.

Utilitarian Environmentalists: BPI and NRDC

Public sentiment often views professional and business people as being concerned only with their own interests and not at all with the public good. A Chicago–based organization, Businessmen and Professional People in the Public Interest (BPI), has attempted to reverse that image by becoming a public advocate. Its directors include the presidents of several Chicago–based corporations, lawyers, and college professors. Organized as a law firm and research center in 1969, BPI was defined as

a legal–oriented instrument for investigating and instituting action on behalf of the general public in such matters as safety and health, housing and discrimination, police procedures and public administration, favoritism in taxation, and conflict of interest in government.[30]

The environmental director of BPI became a national figure in the antinuclear movement. Originally, David Comey was a specialist in Soviet studies at Cornell University and was involved in the controversy over the proposed nuclear power plant at Cayuga Lake in New York. For his efforts to improve the safety of nuclear reactors, Comey received an Environmental Quality Award from the U.S. Environmental Protection Agency.

Comey argues that nuclear power plants have serious human error problems, for operators are poorly trained and often careless. His research has been aimed at showing that nuclear power plants are more expensive than coal-fired plants because of their low efficiency. This is because nuclear power plants operate at low percentages of their capacity, and are often shut down as a result of human errors, malfunctions, or refueling.

With an annual budget in excess of a quarter of a million dollars and volunteer assistance from lawyers in private practice or from law students, BPI has effectively confronted federal regulatory agencies for failure to abide by their own rules. When a fire closed down the Brown's Ferry nuclear reactors in Alabama, BPI petitioned the Nuclear Regulatory Commission to order an immediate closing of all nuclear power plants that did not meet the electrical safety standards for nuclear power plants established by the Institute for Electrical and Electronic Engineering. Another struggle was directed against the Zion reactor owned by Commonwealth Edison and located only forty-five miles north of Chicago. This reactor had one of the poorest safety records of all nuclear facilities, despite its location near a major metropolitan area.

Together with the Izaak Walton League, one of the oldest conservationist societies, BPI initiated a court battle to halt construction of a nuclear reactor in Bailly, Indiana. Bailly is one mile from the city of Portage on the southern shore of Lake Michigan. The court action was successful, marking the first time that a federal district court had blocked the construction of a nuclear power plant. The federal panel ruled that the Atomic Energy Commission had violated its own regulations by building a plant too close to a densely populated area. The utility company had only begun excavation of the site area, and was ordered to fill it in. However, several months later the United States Supreme Court reversed the lower court decision.

A second organization that is issue-specific and uses legal tactics after carefully researching technical problems is the Natural Resources Defense Council (NRDC), a nonprofit corporation with offices in Palo Alto (California), New York, and Washington, D.C. NRDC, with over 20,000 members, promotes intelligent environmental management of our natural resources. To accomplish this goal, NRDC monitors the activities of federal and state agencies and attempts to improve agency decisions that affect the environment by participating in administrative proceedings or by litigation. The organization frequently provides legal and technical assistance to individuals and organizations that are involved in confrontations with government agencies.

NRDC has a high–powered core staff that includes Arthur Tamblin, a biophysicist who was a key figure in the antinuclear episodes of the 1960s; Thomas Cochran, a nuclear physicist; Terry Lash, a microbiologist; Dean Abrahamsom, a former reactor designer at Babcock and

Wilcox; and attorney Gus Speth. With the Sierra Club, NRDC attempted to block the export of nuclear fuel to India by Edlow International Company. However, the two most important issues the organization has been involved in are radioactive waste disposal and the fast breeder reactor.

NRDC won a decision before the Court of Appeals in Washington in June 1973 requiring that the Atomic Energy Commission prepare an environmental impact study of the liquid metal fast breeder reactor. One major reason for their opposition to the breeder is that double systems failures are possible, for the emergency shutdown (SCRAM) system would have to operate in a few seconds. Human error under pressure might be sufficient to produce a core meltdown and possible core disassembly. The economics of the fast breeder reactor fare no better under NRDC scrutiny. They argue that learning curves, or decreasing costs per unit due to experience in manufacturing efficiency, would not actually occur because of unforeseen safety problems and increased construction costs. NRDC argues that only solar energy can benefit from a learning curve, and that hidden costs of the fast breeder reactor include safeguarding the plants.[31]

Conventional nuclear power plants cannot explode, although they can experience a loss-of-coolant accident. Breeder reactors, however, are susceptible to core disassembly if the sodium coolant is blocked from the core. The breeder would then reach a stage of "autocatalytic criticality," in which the fuel is compressed and collects on the walls of the reactor core, allowing a spontaneous and uncontrolled nuclear accident to take place. Dispersion of plutonium into the atmosphere would have far more serious consequences than a core meltdown in a conventional plant. The probabilities of core disassembly and the amount of property damage or number of fatalities have not even been calculated by a government agency.

NRDC reports that .0000001 of an ounce of plutonium causes cancers in dogs when inhaled as fine particles, and thus plutonium and other radioactive wastes are "the most fearsome products ever handled in quantity by man."[32] Fuel assemblies have begun to accumulate, for the West Valley, New York, reprocessing plant has been closed and federal funds provided for decommissioning the facility. The Barnwell Nuclear Fuels Reprocessing Plant in South Carolina was forbidden to operate by executive order of President Carter in 1978. Wastes are being stored at the site of nuclear power plants. The arguments made by NRDC almost seven years ago have been borne out: no satisfactory plan yet exists for even the interim storage of high–level radioactive wastes.

The Future of Environmentalism: The Burger Court

When a nuclear power plant has been proposed for construction, the Nuclear Regulatory Commission must prepare a draft environmental statement, which is followed by a final environmental statement after comments have been received. In one case, *Vermont Yankee Nuclear Power Corporation* v. *Natural Resources Defense Council,* a federal district court judge agreed with NRDC that Vermont Yankee could not be granted an operating license until the environmental impact of reprocessing spent fuel and disposing of the plant's nuclear wastes had been considered.[33] At first this was hailed as a major victory for the antinuclear movement as well as for environmentalism. But two years later, in 1978, the Supreme Court decided all issues in favor of the Nuclear Regulatory Commission. This decision has been damaging to environmentalists' strategy of pursuing litigation against utilities and nuclear power corporations under the National Environmental Policy Act of 1969. The Supreme Court viewed an environmental impact statement covering all phases of the nuclear fuel cycle to be speculative, reasoning that it would be better to prepare a study when reprocessing and waste disposal facilities were being considered for licensing. In addition, the Supreme Court ruled that courts may not demand procedures such as cross-examination in informal rulemaking procedures of the Nuclear Regulatory Commission. This has the effect of excluding public action groups from participating in subsequent proceedings to challenge findings made by the Nuclear Regulatory Commission in the environmental impact study. Thus, despite the *Calvert Cliffs* v. *Atomic Energy Commission* decision in 1971, requiring that the National Environmental Policy Act be complied with to the fullest extent possible, the 1978 decisions under the conservative Burger Court indicate that agencies will not be required to comply strictly with the act. As James F. Raymond concludes in his study of the Burger Court decisions, ''by minimizing NEPA's role in restraining agencies, and by holding sacrosanct agency discretion, the Court has dealt environmental law a severe blow.''[34]

Environmentalist groups may increasingly find that higher court decisions neutralize their success in changing government policy and environmental quality through litigation. Both the public and the government may now believe the myth that environmental quality must be forfeited in the name of economic efficiency in a depressed economy. An opposing view may be overlooked: if we had a genuine environmental consciousness, our society might realize that enormous savings result from controlling life–threatening byproducts of industrialism and economic growth, and that such control creates new opportunities for employment and investment.

Conclusion

Given the lessened effectiveness of legal tactics, the role of environmentalist groups in the antinuclear movement has waned, while direct–action antinuclear groups have become more successful. The technical advisory role of environmentalists has also declined with the emergence of independent scientist groups that advocate the public interest in matters of energy and the environment and in questions involving the proliferation of nuclear weapons. Although nuclear proliferation was a principal concern of environmentalist groups such as the Friends of the Earth, this was never translated into an effective strategy. With the nuclear issue becoming more international as dozens of societies acquire nuclear power plants and nuclear fuel, the expertise of scientists knowledgeable in the military implications of nuclear energy as well as the safety issues will become even more prominent in the antinuclear movement. In this sense, the movement in the 1980s may turn full circle back and become more linked with the peace movement, for scientist activists are internationalist in their outlooks.

Continued success for the environmentalist movement may well be contingent on the development of a wider social consciousness. Certain blue–collar workers are more likely to be victims of cancer than the general population, and the poor often receive inadequate medical treatment. Other pollutants affect age groups, as indicated by the respiratory diseases of the very young and the elderly. Although the problem of environmental toxins is one facing entire populations, epidemiologists do discover patterns that suggest specific age or class strata are more affected than others.[35]

Whether or not the diverse movements that have coalesced into the antinuclear movement will experience a basic change in formation and alliances may well depend on how environmentalist movement groups alter their strategy in the face of changing political conditions in the United States and the world political scene.

Notes and References

1. Rice Odell, *Environmental Awakening, The New Revolution to Protect the Earth* (Cambridge, Mass.: Ballinger Publishing Co., 1980), p. 3.

2. The future of coal in the 1980s and beyond is cogently presented in Mel Horwitch's "Coal: Constrained Abundance," in *Energy Future, Report of the Energy Project of the Harvard Business School,* ed. Robert Stobaugh and Daniel Yergin (New York: Ballantine Books, 1979), pp. 93–126.

3. Allan Schnaiberg, *The Environment: From Surplus to Scarcity* (New York: Oxford University Press, 1980), p. 367.

4. Hans Kruse, "Development and Environment: A Political Science Approach," in *The Politics of Environmental Policy,* ed. Lester W. Milbrath and Frederick R. Inscho (Beverly Hills: Sage Publications, 1975), p. 69.

5. These two dispositions in the environmentalist movement are discussed by Hans Kruse, "Development and the Environment:" p. 60–73.

6. See Lester W. Milbrath and Frederick R. Inscho, "The Environmental Problem as a Political Problem," in *The Politics of Environmental Policy,* pp. 7–34.

7. The typology of environmentalist groups is consistent with the social action approach to social movements that emphasizes the orientations of groups as they interact with the external world.

8. This position is taken by Allan Schnaiberg in *The Environment: From Surplus to Scarcity* (New York: Oxford University Press, 1980).

9. Michael McCloskey, "The Sierra Club and Nuclear Power" (San Francisco: Sierra Club, 1975).

10. This account is drawn from materials and legal briefs supplied by the Florida Audubon Society, particularly "Comments upon the Draft Environmental Impact Statement, Westinghouse–Tenneco Offshore Power Systems Development, Blount Island, Duval County, Florida," in Florida Audubon Society, Maitland, Florida, v. Howard Callaway, Secretary of the Army, civil no. CA-1692–73, 4 September 1973, before the United States District Court for the District of Columbia. Although the issue dates back to the early 1970s, it did not end until 1980.

11. Edward T. LaRoe, "Report to the Florida Audubon Society on the Blount Island Westinghouse-Tenneco Project." Naples, Fla.: Collier County Conservancy Inc. Mimeograph.

12. Sean Devereaux, "Slanting the News to Destroy a Marsh," *Audubon* 78 (May 1976): 135–37.

13. This controversy over nuclear power in New Jersey is documented by Laura J. Lewis and David Morell in "Nuclear Power and Its Opponents: A New Jersey Case Study," Center for Environmental Studies, Princeton University, 1977. Further accounts appear in the newsletter of the Center for Science and the Public Interest, *People and Energy–News of Citizen Action on Energy,* Vols. 1 and 2 (May 1975 to November 1976).

14. Accounts of this hearing in Atlantic City are from my own observations at the City Hall on March 29, 1976, and follow-up stories the next few days in the Newark *Star-Ledger.*

15. See publicity materials (1976) of the Friends of the Earth, San Francisco, California.

16. Ibid.

17. See various Public Interest Reports, Environmental Alert Group. ("Nuclear Terrorism;" "Commercial Doomsday Machines;" "Breeder Reactors and the Plutonium Economy;" "Nuclear Power Plants.")

18. Ibid.

19. Quoted in "Critical Mass—The Citizen Movement to Stop Nuclear Power," newsletter, volume 1: April 1975.

20. Tahi Mottl, "The Analysis of Counter-Movements," *Social Problems* 27, no. 5 (June 1980): 620–34.

21. See "Critical Mass—The Citizen Movement to Stop Nuclear Power."

22. Ralph Nader, "The Nuclear Advocates," letter to the editor, *New York Times,* 21 April, 1974, p. 38.

23. Maine PIRG, "News and Views," Augusta, Maine, vol. 1 (1975).

24. William Clark, "What's in a Name?" *Portland Press Herald,* (Portland, Maine), 18 August 1975.

25. Rob Burgess, "A Pricetag on the Constitution?" Maine PIRG *News and Views* 1, no. 1 (December 1975): 2.

26. New Jersey PIRG, "One Year in Review," Trenton, New Jersey, 1976.

27. New Jersey PIRG, "Everything You Wanted to Know About Nuclear Power But Were Afraid to Find Out," Trenton, New Jersey. (Unfortunately, Rutgers University students voted to discontinue supporting PIRG from student fees in 1977.)

28. U.S. Congress, Joint Committee on Atomic Energy, on the *Status of Nuclear Reactor Safety,* 93rd Congress, 2d session, 1975.

29. Ibid.

30. See annual reports (1971, 1973, 1975) of Business and Professional People in the Public Interest (BPI).

31. Thomas B. Cochran, *The Liquid Metal Fast Breeder Reactor,* (Baltimore: Johns Hopkins University Press, 1974).

32. Natural Resources Defense Council, "Can We Afford A Plutonium Economy?" NRDC newsletter 3, no. 2. See also, "Citizens Guide: The National Debate on the Handling of Radioactive Wastes" (1975).

33. This information is drawn from James F. Raymond, "A Vermont Yankee in King Burger's Court: Constraints on Judicial Review Under NEPA," *Boston College Environmental Affairs Law Review* 7, no. 4 (1979). 629–64.

34. Ibid, p. 664.

35. This conclusion is also reached by Allan Schnaiberg in *The Environment: From Surplus to Scarcity,* 418.

CHAPTER 3

The Intellectuals: Scientist Antinuclear Activists (and Comments on Moralist Views)

While many environmental associations such as the Natural Resources Defense Council have competent scientists on their staffs, the recognition given to scientists who conduct environmental impact studies, especially in nonacademic settings, is eclipsed by those who remain a part of the American scientific establishment. Among the most influential groups in the antinuclear movement, some count among their members individuals who are a part of the ultraelite in science, including several Nobel laureates and many nuclear physicists.[1]

The elite scientists sympathetic to the goals of the antinuclear movement have belonged primarily to three groups: the Union of Concerned Scientists in Cambridge, Massachusetts, the Federation of American Scientists, and the Committee for Nuclear Responsibility. The last organization is typical of several ad hoc committees that have been formed to articulate the interests of prestigious scientists and relatively well–known public servants. Some of these scientists have been involved in major policy decisions and have achieved recognition as "scientist statesmen" both in government and within their scientific disciplines.[2] They represent a higher echelon in science whose authority and opinion on matters of national policy and science affairs is respected and influential.

The normative structure of scientific institutions accords scientists the opportunity to engage in the disinterested and universalistic pursuit of truth. The product of their efforts is evaluated by peers who determine the originality and significance of the research for the advancement of human knowledge. Scientific institutions, however, are merged with and interdependent with the larger society. Thus, scientists may experience a role conflict when demands made on them by social collectivities external to scientific institutions lead scientists to be involved in political affairs.

For example, nuclear physicists became deeply involved in policy decisions regarding the uses of atomic energy during World War II, with the federal government creating roles of researcher, adviser, administrator, and diplomat for many scientists.[3] These scientists were not an apolitical elite. Their power in government policy decisions was increased when political leaders became indecisive or divided over how to control the awesome power of nuclear technology. Although the scientific achievements of nuclear physicists gives them authority to speak on matters of nuclear energy, their own nonscience views and assumptions can become integrated into the formulation of government policy. This presents a dilemma because the institutional nexus within which scientists operate and the norms of science are markedly different from the patterns of activity in political institutions.

During the 1950s, the scientist Edward Teller was an important influence on President Truman, who decided to proceed with development of the hydrogen bomb, an innovation in atomic warfare to a large extent based on the technical breakthroughs of Teller himself. While Edward Teller received a sympathetic hearing at the highest level of government, his scientist opponents in the Federation of Atomic Scientists were only able to express their opinions at the lower levels of the Truman administration. For this reason, one observer asserts that "the brief history of American nuclear policy does not encourage one to believe that depending upon a restricted intellectual elite is a sound practice in democracy."[4] The scientific revolution has fused together the private and public sectors of society, but for Don K. Price, the threat to democracy does not come from the secrecy of scientific advice to political leaders or from an excess of centralized authority. Instead, the real threat is from scientists who promise technological miracles when lobbying for research funds. Price claims that the powerful eminent scientists who are the *insiders* accept the subordination of science to government authority, while the independent critics are *outsiders* who see no necessity for science to be subordinated to a system of organized authority based on traditional views.[5] In a particularly caustic view, Price argues that scientists are capable of supporting any kind of authoritarian political theory, so that their attempts to guide political action are "little more than a rationalization of the will to power than a valid intellectual discipline."[6]

Scientists must also fear espionage trials, security clearance hearings, or other manifestations of the national phobias that have occurred in the past.[7] Daniel Bell has estimated the actual number of persons in the scientific elite at about 30,000, with over half in the physical sciences and with most concentrated in the elite universities.[8] However, these scientists divide ideologically on issues or align themselves with other elites. While modern technological systems have contributed to the centralization of political functions in society, the division of labor in science has tended to diffuse rather than concentrate authority.[9] The political elite is dependent on scientists because of their expertise in complex areas of science. Although scientists are competent in increasingly specialized areas of technology, we must ask if this assures their competence in making decisions that affect the lives of all members of society.

Scientists who are involved in the antinuclear movement represent a group of individuals who have not accepted government authority as irreproachable on matters of atomic energy. Some of this opposition is a continuity from the past, as in the Federation of American Scientists, while other efforts to challenge the government represent a new breed of scientists who are willing to adopt the role of advocate for the public interest. The technical objections to nuclear power raised by scientist antinuclear activists are parallelled by their concern for the arms race and proliferation of nuclear weapons. The fact of the participation of scientists in the political arena is perhaps more significant than their criticisms of technology and energy policy.

The Federation of American Scientists

The Federation of American Scientists began in 1945 as the Federation of Atomic Scientists, which was a lobby formed to facilitate civilian control of atomic energy. These efforts were symbolized by the struggles of J. Robert Oppenheimer with the government and the top military brass. Despite the tragic consequences for some of its members in security clearance hearings, the Federation of Atomic Scientists was successful and opened an office in the national capital for the purpose of educating the public on nuclear issues. The membership dropped from

3,000 in 1949 to a low of about 1,000, but revived when the organization broadened its scope of activities in 1969.

The new Federation of American Scientists grew from 1,500 members in 1970 to 2,300 in 1971 and gained prestigious sponsors. Among these supporters were Nobel laureates Hans Bethe and Harold Urey, ex-presidential science advisors George Kistiakowsky and Jerome Wiesner, and the economist and former ambassador to India, John Kenneth Galbraith. Many of the scientists in the organization have at one time or another been involved in the government of science or in secret defense policy committees. Their first goals after reorganization were to defeat development of the supersonic transporter (SST), fight against Congressional approval of the antiballistic missile (ABM), and generally work to stop the strategic arms race and to prevent the unemployment of scientists.

When President Richard Nixon abolished the White House Office of Science and Technology, the Federation of American Scientists fought unsuccessfully to have the decision reversed. Also during the Nixon Administration, the Federation of American Scientists urged the government to require cutbacks in the operating levels of nuclear reactors, to reorganize the federal government for management of the energy crisis, and to separate the promotional from the regulatory functions of the Atomic Energy Commission.

The Federation of American Scientists never officially announced support for a moratorium on nuclear energy, as the organization includes scientists who are pronuclear advocates, including Hans Bethe, who won a Nobel Prize in physics for his work on nuclear reactions and energy production in stars. As an organization of scientists, the Federation published newsletters discussing both pronuclear and antinuclear arguments. However, many of the sponsors of the Federation of American Scientists are also members of antinuclear organizations or have signed petitions indicating their support for a moratorium. Among these individual scientists are Carl Cori (Nobel laureate in medicine), Christian Afinsen (Nobel laureate in chemistry), John Edsall, Paul Ehrlich, Mark Kac (a scientist refugee from Poland during World War II), George Kistiakowsky, S. E. Luria (Nobel laureate in medicine), Roy Menninger, Severo Ochoa (Nobel laureate), Robert Merton (social theorist), Harold Urey (Nobel laureate in chemistry), Linus Pauling (Nobel laureate), David Riesman (sociologist at Harvard University), Albert Szent-Gyorgyi (Nobel laureate), Victor Weisskopf (Nobel laureate in physics), and Jerome Wiesner.

A nuclear policy ballot was conducted among its membership in 1975 by the Federation of American Scientists.[10] The ballot had four options for the future of nuclear power plants: rapid advance (10 percent growth rate); go slow (3 to 7 percent growth rate); moratorium (zero growth); and phase out. Only 10 percent of the membership responded, for the ballot was simply enclosed in a newsletter. The membership of the Federation of American Scientists is comprised of approximately 20 percent physicists, 16 percent medical scientists, 15 percent chemists, 15 percent biologists, 7 percent psychologists, 7 percent engineers, and the remaining 20 percent distributed among other disciplines. Of the respondents, 36 percent favored a moratorium and 26 percent a phase out, while only 16 percent chose rapid advance and 21 percent go slow.

The Federation of American Scientists is a professional association of scientists rather than an antinuclear group. The organization is a strong advocate of international freedom for scientists and intellectuals, particularly Jews in the Soviet Union. The influence and prestige of its membership on a wide range of social and scientific controversies has had a halo effect on its antinuclear activities, giving the Federation of American Scientists some prominence in the antinuclear movement despite a relatively low rate of participation on nuclear power plant issues in comparison to controversies surrounding the strategic arms race.

The Union of Concerned Scientists

The Union of Concerned Scientists is a coalition of about one hundred scientists, engineers, and other professionals concerned with the impact of advanced technology on society. This association is the most influential of all scientist antinuclear groups. Twenty to 30 percent of its membership is nontechnical, and the internal organization is made up of small study groups who have loosely structured ad hoc meetings. Only twelve to fifteen people work on the nuclear issue, and their activities are funded by members, the Sierra Club, and by other antinuclear groups when the Union of Concerned Scientists intervenes in federal hearings on nuclear power plants.

The organization is based in Cambridge, Massachusetts. During the last ten years, these scientists have conducted research on nuclear technology and government regulations over nuclear power plant safety and have concluded that nuclear technology poses a serious threat to the nation's safety, environment, and national security. The Union of Concerned Scientists is both an advocate and research organization. Its technical studies encompass the strategic arms race, air and water pollution, pesticide use, liquefied natural gas transport and storage hazards, and energy policy alternatives. Numerous volumes have been published on the technical inadequacies of the United States nuclear power program.

The Union of Concerned Scientists began as an informal faculty group at the Massachusetts Institute of Technology in 1969, growing out of the radical "March 4th" movement the previous year among graduate students at the institution. The goal of the March 4th movement was to stop all research activities at the Massachusetts Institute of Technology to bring pressure on the United States government for cessation of the Vietnam War. A joint faculty-student committee was formed, and 4 March 1969, was chosen for a symbolic one–day research stoppage.

Students and faculty were two distinct organizations, and the faculty organization became known as the Union of Concerned Scientists. Some of the major planks in the group's program were opposition to the antiballistic missile program and the promotion of civilian control of science. The student organization was more interested in direct confrontation with the political establishment rather than with the consensus politics of the Union of Concerned Scientists, but despite disagreement on tactics and strategy the research stoppage was held as scheduled.

Eventually, the more radical Scientists and Engineers for Social and Political Action (SESPA) denounced the Union of Concerned Scientists. The student organization went on to indict those who committed "crimes of science against the people," prompting Glenn Seaborg, the discoverer of plutonium and then chairman of the Atomic Energy Commission, to provide himself with five bodyguards. Edward Teller, who was crucial to the development of the hydrogen bomb, was given a "Dr. Strangelove Award" for being a "war criminal." The Union of Concerned Scientists responded to the extremism of radicals by affiliating with the Federation of American Scientists, stating that its goals were similar to that organization.[11]

The Union of Concerned Scientists has contributed to the antinuclear movement by providing technical analyses of the dangers of the nuclear fuel cycle, and on numerous occasions it has intervened in federal hearings on nuclear power plants and initiated a variety of legal actions to control nuclear energy in concert with other antinuclear groups. Three examples of their concerns are mining hazards in obtaining uranium for nuclear fuel, the safety of emergency core cooling systems in nuclear power plants, and the export of nuclear fuels to foreign countries that lack a developed technological infrastructure and also pose a threat to international military security.

Uranium Mining Hazards. Until 1949, uranium for American nuclear weapons came from a single mine in the Belgian Congo. When the Atomic Energy Commission realized the vulnerability of depending on a single source of uranium, domestic production of uranium was initiated with government price supports. The AEC made no special efforts to protect miners from radiation hazards, although in Europe it had long been established that this kind of mining was dangerous without proper ventilation.[12]

When adequate stockpiles of uranium for nuclear weapons had been accumulated, uranium mining activities were reduced. However, during this first period of intensive uranium mining in the southwestern United States, over six thousand miners were exposed to airborne radioactive gases in underground uranium mines. The Union of Concerned Scientists reports an excess of sixty-seven deaths over what normally would be expected from malignancies among white uranium miners, with an accumulated total of excess deaths among the six thousand miners estimated at between one and two hundred deaths. American Indian males had a significantly lower risk than white males.[13]

Radium and pitchblende miners suffered from epidemics of lung cancer in Europe because of poor ventilation in those mines. Airborne radon gas changes into radon daughters, which are responsible for the lung cancer. Although the Atomic Energy Commission was apparently aware of high levels of radioactivity in the uranium mines as early as 1947, no steps were taken to eliminate the danger.

Pitchblende miners in Germany also died in their middle years after working in mines for more than two years from what was then called *Berkrankheit* ("mountain sickness"). As far back as 1879 a researcher named Hesse had discovered that miners employed between 1869 and 1877 in Schneeberg, Germany, had an average life expectancy of less than twenty years after entering the mines.[14] Hesse diagnosed the cause of death as lung cancer in 75 percent of the deaths of these radium miners.

Also, in 1939 a scientist by the name of Peller found that radon entering
flurospar mines in ground water contributed to the deaths of twenty-six
out of twenty-nine miners. Excess cancer risk had also been demonstrated
in studies of British coal miners, American potash miners, and Russian
manganese miners.

Uranium mines had previously been mined for vanadium in the southwestern United States between 1930 and 1945, but monitoring of emissions and ventilation were not instituted until 1961. A U.S. Public Health
Service study predicted a significant mortality rate from lung cancer
among miners, and a follow-up study in 1962 found that deaths from
respiratory cancer were occurring at five times the normal rate. But
uniform standards were still not adopted until 1967, and then with
responsibility falling under state authority.

Uranium mining is the first stage of the nuclear fuel cycle. Natural
uranium is mined and then milled (crushed) to a concentrate containing
about 85 percent uranium oxide, a substance called "yellowcake." Since
uranium ore contains only about 1 percent of uranium, large amounts of
wastes accumulate, called tailings. These radioactive wastes discharge
radon-222 gas into the air, and the presence of thorium-230 makes the
tailings radioactive for thousands of years. The Environmental Protection
Agency estimates that individuals in the surrounding population receive
radioactive exposure to the lungs from the radon releases that are a hazard
to the health of miners. The mines are even more hazardous.[15] In the
United States, uranium mines are concentrated in the Wyoming Basin,
the Colorado Plateau, and the Gulf Plains, with the most recoverable
reserves in New Mexico, Wyoming, Texas, Utah, and Colorado. It has
been to the credit of the Union of Concerned Scientists that the issue of
uranium mining hazards did not escape the attention of antinuclear
groups.

The ECCS Controversy.   The accident at the Three Mile Island power
plant in Harrisburg, Pennsylvania, and a fire at the Brown's Ferry plant in
Alabama a few years earlier brought to public attention an issue that had
been a major focus of the Union of Concerned Scientists. The fear of a
catastrophic accident that would release large amounts of lethal radioactivity into the atmosphere is now impregnated into our consciousness.
Such an accident could occur if the emergency core cooling system
(ECCS) in a reactor did not function correctly during an emergency, such
as a pipe rupture causing a loss of normal cooling water. Although Three

Mile Island also demonstrated that the emergency backup systems do work, there is always a possiblity that a nuclear reactor could overheat, melt through its containment structure, and release radioactive poisons. There have been other near catastrophes in the history of nuclear power plants, and the ECCS systems tested by the Atomic Energy Commission have all failed.[16]

The Union of Concerned Scientists became involved in the controversy after discovering the Atomic Energy Commission report (WASH-740) that predicted an area as large as Pennsylvania being affected if an ECCS failure should occur. Ironically, Three Mile Island is located in Pennsylvania, and just before the accident *The China Syndrome,* a popular film depicting the occurrence of a similar accident, was released.

Conducting its own studies, the Union of Concerned Scientists concluded that emergency core cooling systems have design defects that may cause them to fail in an emergency, although it was believed this might occur more often from a pipe rupture than human error, as at Three Mile Island. Scientists working within the government had also complained of suppression of information on emergency core cooling systems. While the efforts of the Union of Concerned Scientists had no measurable impact on the United States government, the Reactor Safety Committee of the West German government recommended a moratorium on nuclear power until more research had been completed on emergency core cooling systems. Both the Federation of American Scientists and the RAND Corporation advised against further construction of nuclear power plants until the effectiveness of emergency core cooling systems could be resolved. Even the Atomic Energy Commission's Advisory Committee on Reactor Safeguards listed ECCS reliability as an unsolved reactor safety problem, and similar conclusions were reached by a working research group at the 1973 Pugwash Conference and by government scientists in Sweden.

The original Atomic Energy Commission report (WASH-740), released 1957, estimated that an upper limit of 3,400 persons would be killed in a nuclear accident and over 43,000 persons injured.[17] A 1965 update of WASH-740 was withheld from the public after these estimates were revised upwards. A major step forward for the antinuclear movement came when the Union of Concerned Scientists provided the technical and scientific support to a coalition of citizen groups intervening in federal hearings on the effectiveness of emergency core cooling systems. These technical studies suggest that radioactive gases released from a nuclear power plant could be lethal at a distance of one hundred miles, with health injuries occurring hundreds of miles away. As pointed out by the Union of Concerned Scientists, the Indian Point nuclear reactors in Westchester County, New York, are located only twenty-four miles from New York City. A temperature inversion at Indian Point could expose more than 100,000 persons to lethal or near-lethal radiation in just a two–mile–wide strip.

The WASH-740 update predicted 45,000 fatalities and tens of billions of dollars worth of damage in an accident. Conducted in 1965, the update was only released in June 1973 under a threat by the Union of Concerned Scientists to obtain it under the Freedom of Information Act. The update indicates a pipe rupture could cause a core meltdown in a nuclear reactor and that it would broach all manmade structures. The Union of Concerned Scientists estimates that a pipe rupture will occur approximately every seven years, although this does not mean that the emergency core cooling system would fail in every case. No deaths have ever been recorded in the commercial operation of nuclear power plants, but many accidents have occurred. The main casualties after Three Mile Island were the local residents who experienced severe psychological distress.

Pressure vessel ruptures are the most extreme case, because the ECCS would be rendered ineffective. If bolts ruptured that hold the main pressure vessel together, steam lines would be destroyed and disable the emergency core cooling system. Even minor accidents, however, can have devastating consequences. For example, an electrician working for the Tennessee Valley Authority held a lighted candle near insulation to determine the source of an air leak under the control room of a nuclear reactor at Brown's Ferry, Alabama. The fire that broke out decommissioned the reactor for several months, and destroyed the ECCS control cables, making them inoperative if the system had been needed.

Containment structures in nuclear reactors are capable of withstanding powerful impacts. If a plant reaches supercriticality, it cannot explode like an atomic bomb as some environmentalists once presumed. Bernard Cohen, a nuclear physicist at Stanford University, points out that there is a fail-safe mode in nuclear reactor operation—the control rods automatically go into the reactor core to stop the fission reaction if anything goes wrong. This process is enhanced by the "Doppler effect": a rise in temperature as water is converted into steam may cause a reactor to shut down as more neutrons are absorbed and the reaction becomes supercritical for a few thousandths of a second.[18]

A loss-of-coolant accident, known in the industry as a "LOCA," could be precipitated by a leak in the cooling system or a rupture in the reactor vessel. Pipes, thirty inches in diameter and made from two-inch–thick stainless steel, are monitored by radiographic, ultrasonic, and magnetic particle techniques. In an accident, the fuel pins would rise to a temperature of 2700 degrees Fahrenheit for four to five seconds in the pressurized water reactor type and in two to five minutes in the boiling water reactor type. Coolant would be useless at this point. Complete melting of the fuel would occur in thirty minutes in the pressurized water reactor and in two hours for the boiling water reactor. The reactor core would melt into the earth: this is the "China Syndrome."

The failure of ECCS tests in Idaho prompted the Union of Concerned Scientists to challenge the Atomic Energy Commission in federal court. Three workers died at the government test station in Idaho in 1961 when the experimental reactor went out of control. More tests were scheduled using a small fifty-five–megawatt reactor known as LOFT, but the results of these tests have not been publicized by the Nuclear Regulatory Commission.

After the Atomic Energy Commission was forced to disclose the revised version of WASH-740, a $3 million study headed by Professor Norman Rasmussen was conducted at the Massachusetts Institute of Technology. The Rasmussen Report, released in 1974, calculated that there is a one–in–17,000 chance for a core meltdown each reactor year, with one such accident occurring every 175 years. The probability of an accident with more than 1,000 fatalities would be one in a million years, the same probability of a large meteorite hitting a large city and causing 1,000 fatalities. The maximum damage would be $4–6 billion, and only one in ten meltdowns would have measurable health effects; that is, one disastrous accident in seventeen and one–half centuries.

The Rasmussen Report (WASH-1400) estimates that in the worst case an accident would cause 3,300 early fatalities, 45,000 cases of early illnesses, and $14 billion in property damage. The long-term health effects were estimated at 1,500 latent cancer fatalities per year, 8,000

thyroid nodules per year, and 170 genetic effects per year. The report did
not analyze the risks of breeder reactors, catastrophes from sabotage or
acts of war, or risks involved in other parts of the nuclear fuel cycle.

Critics of the Rasmussen Report asserted that its methodology, adapted
from the Apollo space and ballistic missile programs, was inadequate for
the purpose of evaluating nuclear power plant accidents. One failure per
10,000 missions was predicted in the Apollo program, but the lives of
three American astronauts were lost during a fire in an Apollo spacecraft.
The Union of Concerned Scientists criticized the Rasmussen estimates of
deaths as being at least sixteen times too low, primarily because assumptions were made that evacuation procedures could move people out of the
way of airborne radiation. A nuclear physicist, David Inglis, used the
same methodology to calculate the chances of a chain of seven safety
circuits and two backup circuits failing simultaneously, which were a
billion trillion. Nevertheless, human error accounted for a similar failure
in a Virginia nuclear power plant (which is now being considered for
conversion to coal).[19] The barrage of criticisms of the Rasmussen Report eventually resulted in its repudiation by the Nuclear Regulatory
Commission.

Export of Nuclear Fuels: The Tarapur Case.   New tactical ground
was broken in 1976 when the Union of Concerned Scientists, in conjunction with the Sierra Club and the Natural Resources Defense Council,
intervened in the application of Edlow International Company for a
license to export nuclear fuel for use in the Tarapur Atomic Power Station
in India. This was the first time that antinuclear groups had considered
employing legal tactics to control the international diffusion of nuclear
technology. Among the combined membership of over 175,000 persons
in the Sierra Club and Natural Resources Defense Council are citizens in
India and Pakistan. Because such legal cases usually require that the
petitioners themselves be threatened by specific actions, the organizations contended that some of their members who travel to India could be
exposed to radioactive risks. Without a review of the case by the Nuclear
Regulatory Commission, the ability of the petitioners to carry out their
function of disseminating information to the public concerning the environment and nuclear power would be impaired.

The real issue was that India, not a party to the Nuclear Nonproliferation Treaty, detonated a nuclear weapon in 1974 using nuclear fuel
supplied to them by Canada that was to be used only for peaceful

purposes. With the United States allowing the export of nuclear fuel to India, other nations might be encouraged to ignore the prohibition against nuclear weapons development. The United States failed to require India to meet safeguards and radioactive waste agreements. Therefore, the export of nuclear fuels to India would be a risk to the common defense and national security, as defined by the Atomic Energy Act of 1954, and inconsistent with the health and safety regulations of the National Environmental Policy Act of 1969.

General Electric manufactured the nuclear reactors at Tarapur, which constitute the largest nuclear complex in Asia. Paul Jacobs, an antinuclear activist until his death from cancer (perhaps the result of being forced to witness atomic bomb tests while in the military), reported that workers at Tarapur had been seen using bamboo poles to operate the reactors' radioactive waste disposal system. Jacobs investigated Tarapur after being informed of the situation by a disgruntled employee from the Bechtel Corporation. Writing in *Mother Jones,* Jacobs argued that the nuclear community had long been aware of the situation at Tarapur but said and did nothing because

the nuclear fraternity is a close one. Born so recently, shrouded for so long in military secrecy, this elite now numbers only a few thousand physicists and technicians. It has been likened to an ''old boy'' network of elite colleagues and, like other fraternities, it has bred close bonds of support and mutual protectiveness.[20]

Paul Jacobs argued that these bonds develop into symbiotic relationships between the nuclear industry and government. To support his contention that a closed elite chose to ignore Tarapur, Jacobs pointed out that the Bechtel Corporation has employed at one time or another the former Secretary of the Treasury under President Nixon, George Schultz; the former Secretary of Health, Education, and Welfare, Casper Weinberger (the Secretary of Defense in the Reagan administration); and the former general manager of the Atomic Energy Commission, R. Hollingsworth.

Some of Jacobs's contentions regarding a closed elite are supported by a study of stratification in American science by Harriet Zuckerman, a sociologist at Columbia University. Zuckerman finds that elite scientists are close to being a gerontocracy, in the sense that they have shared many common experiences in laboratories and in World War II. Long associations have created a strong sense of social solidarity in the group, as well as their similar commitments and interests.[21] However, no evidence is presented that suggests scientists would not be concerned with the misuse of nuclear technology. The existence of scientist groups such as the Union of Concerned Scientists contradicts the notion that government has total control over the scientific establishment. In the specific case of Tarapur, the efforts were largely unsuccessful because Congress voted to continue the shipment of nuclear fuel to India in 1980, overruling a decision by the Nuclear Regulatory Commission to prohibit such sales.

The Committee for Nuclear Responsibility

Founded in California by Lenore Marshall, the Committee for Nuclear Responsibility included on its board of directors several of the same scientists active in the Federation of American Scientists and in other ad hoc antinuclear groups. Four of these scientists are Nobel laureates: James D. Watson, for his work on DNA; George Wald, for work on chemical and physiological processes in the eye; Harold Urey, the discoverer of deuterium; and Linus Pauling, for his work on the forces that hold matter together.[22] The other scientists are Paul Ehrlich (biology), John Edsall (biochemistry), John Gofman (medical physics), and Robert Bellman (mathematics). The board of directors also includes writer Lewis Mumford, former United States Attorney General Ramsey Clark, architect Ian MacHarg, and Richard Max McCarthy, a former United States Congressman from New York State.

Of these scientists, Linus Pauling was an important figure in the antinuclear movement of the 1950s, when he was active in trying to stop atomic bomb testing because of the dangers of radioactive fallout. John Gofman was one of the early critics of commercial nuclear power in the antinuclear episodes of the 1960s. Paul Ehrlich gained a reputation somewhat as a doomsday prophet by popularizing an alarmist version of the Malthusian thesis of overpopulation. Ramsey Clark, George Wald, and James Watson were all critics of United States involvement in the Vietnamese War.

The affiliation of Lewis Mumford with an antinuclear organization provides a rare opportunity to compare the writings of a social theorist with his actual political activity. Mumford developed a philosophy of "basic communism" which he considered to be devoid of all the trappings of Karl Marx and his disciples. Mumford argued that with each phase of technical development in history, or with each technological complex, there corresponds a type of society and even a civilization.[23] Machines, the purpose of which is converting energy to work, now dominate modern civilization, according to Mumford. Perhaps the main contradiction in Mumford's advocacy of solar energy as a power source is that he theoretically establishes phases in the history of civilization that are each based on a specific means of utilizing and generating energy, and then argues for a return to the energy source of previous eras.

A more future oriented but pessimistic perspective is that of Nobel laureate James Watson:

When the history of this century is written, the greatest debacle will be seen not to be our tragic involvement in Southeast Asia, but our creation of vast armadas of plutonium whose safe containment will represent a major precondition for human survival, not for a few decades or hundreds of years, but for thousands of years more than human civilization has thus so far existed.[24]

On the other hand, Nobel laureate George Wald, while claiming objectivity for his own antinuclear views, argues that scientists who urge rapid expansion of nuclear power are doing so because of their affiliation with the energy corporations. Wald acknowledges that scientists on both sides of the nuclear controversy retreat to a mythology of objectivity, but that the pronuclear side has gone astray from the norms of the scientific community.[25]

The Committee for Nuclear Responsibility was formed as a political and educational organization to disseminate antinuclear views and information to the public. The goals of the organization were a moratorium on nuclear power and the development of alternative energy resources. Actor Jack Lemmon endorsed the goals of the Committee for Nuclear Responsibility with the statement that

nuclear power plants will introduce the age of private atom bombs. Nuclear power plants will put so much plutonium into commercial circulation that, sooner or later, terrorists will get hold of enough to make their own atom bombs. The moment they demonstrate their first explosion here, we can kiss our civil liberties goodbye. We can expect panic, and then martial law . . . indefinitely.[26]

The official spokesman for the Committee for Nuclear Responsibility, Ms. Egan O'Connor, had even more direct views. Before a group of religious leaders in Washington D.C., she said:

Ph.D.'s and other nuclear engineers have no special expertise in either common sense or morality. They are the wrong kind of experts to be making our country's energy policy—to be making a decision which will affect all men for all time.[27]

According to Egan O'Connor, both advocates and opponents of nuclear energy agree that it is an inherently dangerous technology, and that cancer and genetic mutations might some day nullify all the lifesaving efforts of modern medicine and social workers. She quotes former President Nixon, who once said:

all this business about breeder reactors and nuclear is over my head. That was one of my poorest subjects, science. . . . But it has always been fascinating to me that if a people are to be a great people, we must always explore the unknown.[28]

O'Connor calls the notion of safe nuclear power a fantasy, claiming that "a rapidly growing number of middle Americans are ready to revolt before they will make the habitability of this planet dependent on miracles in the nuclear power industry."[29] She argues that a sunshine economy instead of a radioactive one will have good effects for millenia.

The Moralists

Scientists active in social causes have something in common with those groups that base their opposition to nuclear power on moral principles. The scientist's justification for overstepping scientific neutrality is his or her moral responsibility to humanity. The debate between elite scientists is often colored, George Wald points out, by the biases of pronuclear scientists and engineers employed by energy corporations or the federal government. The essence of a moralist outlook is that the impact of nuclear technology on other generations or on underdeveloped societies is a problem that must be resolved by referring to moral standards.

Political action and religious organizations that attempt to bring morality to the arguments put forth by the antinuclear movement include Common Cause, the National Council of Churches, and the World Council of Churches. These organizations present a view that is not encumbered by analyses of technical or economic efficiency of nuclear technology.

Common Cause, for example, is an organization that attempts to redirect government policy on the basis of political and moral principles that are fundamental to the American system. It was founded in 1970 by John Gardner, the former Secretary of Health, Education, and Welfare, and grew into a national citizen organization with over 300,000 members. With an active core of about 30,000 persons and a professional staff of seventy in Washington, D.C., Common Cause lobbies the federal and state governments for reforms important to their nonpartisan ideology. Since its members ranked the energy crisis as one of their major concerns, Common Cause approved a statement in 1975 advocating a reduction in research commitments to nuclear fission power and an increase in funding for solar and geothermal energy projects, including the creation of a Solar Energy Research Institute.[30]

Another example of the moralist orientation is the National Council of Churches. Its Church and Society division, in response to requests from its members, commissioned anthropologists Margaret Mead and Rene Dubos to produce a report on nuclear power and plutonium wastes. Nuclear supporters were not asked to participate in the research committee because it was felt that a balanced report based on the principle of neutrality would be viewed as a tacit acceptance of nuclear power.

The research group felt that a lack of consensus on the nuclear power plant issue existed because the issues are really moral and ethical rather than scientific and technological. The moral dilemma is whether or not our descendants should be bequeathed with nuclear wastes that potentially cause cancers and genetic defects through exposure to plutonium. In addition, we must be willing to accept necessary changes in our material standard of living by redistributing resources and technology according to the principle of equity. The National Council of Churches statement also warned that "the more a society relies on complex technology, the more vulnerable it becomes to pathological behavior of a few, and to human errors which are bound to occur."[31] The National Council of Churches statement was endorsed by the Reverend David Eaton of All Souls Church in Washington, D.C., and by a number of well-known liberal social scientists. Endorsements came from sociologists Robert Merton and David Riesman, economist Robert Heilbroner, ecologist Barry Commoner (who founded the Citizens Party and ran for President of the United States in 1980), historian Barbara Ward, and environmental activist Amory Lovins. Many of the scientists active in other antinuclear organizations also endorsed the statement.

When the World Council of Churches convened in Sweden in 1975, they assembled nuclear physicists and scientists from sixteen nations to focus on the moral and ethical dilemmas presented by nuclear power. The proceedings of this conference raised important issues that had not really been considered by activist antinuclear organizations, such as the effect of the energy crisis on the gap between industrialized and developing nations and the role of nuclear technology in reducing this gap. These scientists recommended that the major industrial nations share nuclear technology with the developing nations and that the latter be free to make decisions regarding its use without interference from the advanced industrial nations or from multinational corporations. But they also urged that the siting of nuclear power plants not infringe on the rights of minorities and that safety precautions be improved for workers in nuclear industries.[32]

The scientists argued that it would be difficult to deny nations nuclear technology out of fear that it might be used for nuclear weapons development because the Nuclear Nonproliferation Treaty, already based on discrimination in favor of nations possessing nuclear power, is not sufficient to prevent arms proliferation. It is imperative that developing nations benefit from the peaceful application of nuclear energy without succumbing to technological domination by industrial nations. The problem of nuclear weapons proliferation is that the major industrial nations see it as indispensable for maintaining their power.

A consensus emerged among the scientists that social structures tend to conform to technological systems and that criteria must be established to decide the risks of technology to future generations and to distinguish actual needs from desires in societies. These scientists were willing to trust in humanity to master intellectually, morally, and spirtually the awesome potentialities of nuclear power to minimize the effects of human folly.

The closing statement of the World Council of Churches conference in Sweden cogently summarizes the argument of the scientists:

The nuclear situation deepens the questioning of the presuppositions and goals of contemporary technological civilization, and the dilemmas posed by its achievements and its weakness become inescapable. It also brings us to fundamental questions as: (1) How can men cope with their creativity? (2) How can they live together in their diverse societies in a tolerable harmony? (3) How far are they responsible for future generations? The Christian will want to seek help from his faith on these and other social issues. . . . But what precisely does this mean for human planning in the future? How far do recent scientific developments oblige us to reassess the whole scientific revolution from the seventeenth century out of which the harnessing of the powers of the universe which dominate our thoughts today have come? Is man playing God, or is he grasping creative techniques which God intends him to use responsibly? As humanity's scientific and technical capabilities increase, so do the stakes involved in its decisions become greater. The scale of success and failure becomes more dramatic. . . . The World Council of Churches is still just beginning to grasp the opportunity for probing the religious and ethical mysteries posed by the nuclear age. Attempting the challenge, in faith, they might still be a light to themselves and their world, which is in deep spiritual confusion.[33]

While the moralist perspective does not always fully support the views of the antinuclear movement, it certainly raises questions that scientists alone cannot answer. But the criticisms of nuclear energy by scientists and environmentalists all come into play when we consider the antinuclear groups on the front line of action. These are the groups that have mobilized mass support for the antinuclear cause and have directly confronted the nuclear establishment through the organization of referenda on nuclear power, demonstrations outside nuclear power plants, legal tactics, and integrating other movements into the antinuclear movement. In this sense, they are the real movement elite.

Notes and References

1. The term "ultraelite" is used by Harriet Zuckerman in her study of Nobel laureates, *Scientific Elite* (New York: Free Press, 1977), p. 11. Elite scientists are those who have been elected to membership in the National Academy of Scientists. I have used the term somewhat more loosely in this study.

2. This term is also used by Harriet Zuckerman in "Stratification in American Science," *Sociological Inquiry* 40 (Spring): 235–57.

3. See Robert Gilpin and Christopher Wright, *Scientists and National Policy Making* (New York: Columbia University Press, 1964).

4. Robert Gilpin, *American Scientists and Nuclear Weapons Policy,* (New York: Basic Books, 1962), p. 342.

5. Don K. Price, *The Scientific Estate* (Cambridge: Harvard University Press, 1965), p. 83.

6. Ibid., p. 271.

7. See Edward Shils, *The Torment of Secrecy* (New York: Free Press, 1956); and Michael Rogin, *The Intellectuals and McCarthy* (Cambridge: MIT Press, 1967) for documentation of this dark age for American scientists.

8. Daniel Bell, *The Coming of Post-Industrial Society* (New York: Basic Books, 1973), p. 229.

9. Fred Cottrell, *Energy and Society* (New York: McGraw-Hill, 1955), 207.

10. Federation of American Scientists, *Public Interest Report,* Special Issue with Nuclear Policy Ballot, Washington, D.C., 1975.

11. This history is drawn from Stuart S. Blume, *Toward A Political Sociology of Science* (New York: Free Press, 1974), pp. 160–65.

12. This account is drawn from Arell S. Schurgin and Thomas C. Hollocher, "Lung Cancer Among Uranium Mine Workers," in *The Nuclear Fuel Cycle,* ed. The Union of Concerned Scientists (San Francisco: Friends of the Earth, 1974), pp. 116–48.

13. Ibid., p. 129.

14. Ibid., p. 141.

15. United States Environmental Protection Agency, *Environmental Analysis of the Uranium Fuel Cycle,* 1. (Washington, D.C.: Office of Radiation Programs, 1973).

16. This account is drawn from Daniel F. Ford and Henry W. Kendall, "Catastrophic Nuclear Accidents," in *The Nuclear Fuel Cycle,* ed. The Union of Concerned Scientists (San Francisco: Friends of the Earth, 1974), pp. 75–91.

17. United States Atomic Energy Commission, "Theoretical Possibilities and Consequences of Major Accidents in Large Nuclear Power Plants (WASH-740)." (Washington D.C.: U.S. Government Printing Office, 1957).

18. Bernard J. Cohen, *Nuclear Science and Society* (New York: Doubleday, 1974).

19. David R. Inglis, "Sweet Voice of Reason," *Bulletin of the Atomic Scientists,* September 1974, pp. 50–52.

20. Paul Jacobs, "What You Don't Know May Hurt You," *Mother Jones* 1 (February–March 1976): 35–39.

21. Harriet Zuckerman, "Stratification in American Science," p. 239.

22. See the newsletter of the Committee for Nuclear Responsibility, "Common Sense" (1975). The information on the work of the Nobel laureates is from Zuckerman, *Scientific Elite,* pp. 282–90.

23. Lewis Mumford, *Technics and Civilization* (New York: Harper and Row, 1934), and "Technics and the Nature of Man," in *Technology and Culture,* ed. Melvin Kranzberg and William H. Davenport (New York: New American Library, 1972), pp. 200–215.

24. James D. Watson, letter to the *New York Times,* 11 October 1975.

25. George Wald, "The Nuclear Power Truth Maze," *New York Times,* 29 February 1976.

26. Committee for Nuclear Responsibility, "Letter from Jack Lemmon," 1975.

27. Egan O'Connor, "Remarks to a Gathering of Washington D.C. Religious Leaders," in U.S., Congress, Senate, *Congressional Record,* 94th Cong. 1st sess., 1975, 121, no. 124.

28. Ibid.

29. Ibid.

30. Common Cause, "Legislative Report," 1976.

31. National Council of the Churches of Christ, "The Plutonium Economy," 1975.

32. World Council of Churches, "Report on Nuclear Energy," *Anticipation* 21 (1975).

33. Ibid.

CHAPTER 4
The Movement Elite: Direct Action Groups

Social movements most often differ from voluntary associations or public interest groups in their tactics. The sit-in, mobilization of people for demonstrations and mass protest, and similar tactics usually begin to symbolize the cause of a social movement. At the vanguard of the antinuclear movement are the regionally based organizations such as the Clamshell Alliance in New England. Such groups do intervene legally in nuclear issues, but they have not confined themselves to the courthouse or federal agency hearings. They have taken their cause directly to the people, in the streets if necessary.

Some of these organizations have attempted to coordinate the antinuclear movement on a national scale much in the same way that the Nader organizations did. The Task Force Against Nuclear Pollution, Consolidated National Intervenors, and the Energy Action Committee are representative of groups that tried to transcend the often singular and disparate activities of antinuclear groups in local community controversies over nuclear power. Their efforts were mostly symbolic, for most of the discrete groups that make up the antinuclear movement rarely join in common action.

The regional direct action groups have generally been more successful in creating coalitions and alliances among antinuclear groups and defining the character of the movement through their distinctive tactics. These alliances and coalitions forged the social values that became constitutive of the movement as a whole. They also integrated the movement on a more cognitive and ideological level. As the struggle becomes more intense, theoretical and ideological doctrines evolve to justify the movement's goals and to provide a constant reference point from which to view changes in the career and direction of the movement. For example, the Environmentalists for Full Employment was an organization that began to link the antinuclear cause to the labor movement. Many of the antinuclear direct action groups represent linkages of diverse social movements that have been an important aspect of the American political system since the 1960s.

Expressive symbolization emerges in a social movement as a result of direct action. "Seabrook" became a symbol for the antinuclear movement across the country as the Clamshell Alliance persistently confronted the nuclear industry and the federal government with mass demonstrations outside the construction site of a nuclear power plant in this New Hampshire town. A more powerful form of expressive symbolization is created by martyrdom, for personal identification with a martyr merges the self with the community of the movement. The symbolic importance of Seabrook in creating a collective identity for the antinuclear movement was preceded by mass meetings in New York City and the national capital to bring attention to the death of Karen Silkwood. The National Organization of Women and a spinnoff group, the Supporters of Silkwood, helped to fuse together individuals from diverse organizations into a collective cause by focusing on the struggles and eventual death of Karen Silkwood. Since Silkwood was a labor activist, the issue brought both the women's and labor movements into the antinuclear movement.

National Coordination of the Movement

When the antinuclear movement was in its infancy, the Task Force Against Nuclear Pollution (TFNP) was instrumental in helping to coordinate the activities of emerging antinuclear groups by focusing its efforts on a specific task, the collection of signatures for the Clean Energy Petition. The petition states:

I, the undersigned, petition my representative in Government to sponsor and actively support legislation to: (1) develop safe, cost-competitive solar electricity and solar fuels within ten years or less, and (2) phase out the operation of nuclear power plants as quickly as possible.[1]

Collecting signatures facilitates group formation. The activity can commend national attention without offending or shocking the public. Tables set up near shopping centers or other busy pedestrian intersections attract signatures because people are willing to influence Congressional leaders in this accepted form of democratic political participation. Observing a group, mostly women, obtaining signatures for the Clean Energy Petition across the street from Princeton University, I found that few if any persons refused to sign the petition after reading it. Speaking with the group, I found that they stressed being polite but persistent and did not argue with those who refused to sign. None of the individuals were shabbily dressed, and none of the people at the table could be identified by appearance as a counterculture adherent. All the individuals took the petition seriously and believed that it was going to be effective.

When the petitions were signed, they were forwarded to TFNP in Washington, D.C. There, volunteers sorted the petitions by congressional district and added the names to a computerized mailing list. The petitions were then shown to members of Congress or used to influence state and local officials. In June 1974, TFNP had collected 80,527 signatures, which grew to 200,324 in May 1975, then to 306,241 by October 1975, and to 401,223 in June 1976.[2]

Part of the success of the Clean Energy Petition is that it had sponsorship in the political elite. Senator Mike Gravel of Alaska worked closely with TFNP, allowing TFNP to take advantage of some of the resources available to a United States Senator. Gravel also introduced the first nuclear moratorium bill in Congress after his involvement in the controversy over nuclear weapons testing on Amchitka Island. The strategy of TFNP was to show the public the link between the peaceful and military uses of nuclear power. Sentator Gravel perceptively outlined six reasons why he felt the nuclear issue would be a major focus in the 1976 presidential campaign:

(1) the local nature of the nuclear opposition would pressure Congress; (2) the exchange of antinuclear information was becoming more effective; (3) the issues and choices were becoming well defined, particularly with introduction of a five year moratorium bill into Congress; (4) the potential following of the antinuclear movement would be larger as more information was disseminated; (5) energy growth had begun to decline in the United States; and (6) the costs of nuclear power made it increasingly unattractive.[3]

These petition–gathering activities quickly subsided as more groups became involved in the antinuclear movement, changing the strategy and tactics of the movement. In the House of Representatives, the five–year moratorium bill was introduced by Hamilton Fish of New York, a Republican. The bill was entitled the Nuclear Energy Reappraisal Act (H. R. 4971) and would have directed the Nuclear Regulatory Commission to suspend the granting of construction licenses for new nuclear power plants pending a five–year independent study of the entire nuclear fuel cycle by the Office of Technology Assessment. Respresentative Fish argued that three tablespoons of plutonium was enough poison to give nine billion people lung cancer and that a "plutonium economy could instantly wipe out all the advances made in the field of human health in the last quarter of a century."[4]

H. R. 4971 became the focal point of TFNP. The bill provided for independent assessment of the effectiveness of all safety systems in fission power plants, determination that radioactive wastes can be stored or disposed of despite earthquakes, theft, sabotage, acts of war, or governmental and social instabilities; demonstration of the effectiveness of security systems throughout the nuclear fuel cycle; and analysis of all the safety, environmental, and economic consequences of nuclear energy to prove its superiority to other energy sources. The Office of Technology Assessment would also be required to study the short– and long–term genetic effects of low-level radiation, the economic implications of a plutonium economy (including the availability of raw materials and the potential for foreign uranium cartels), the cost of frequent shutdowns of nuclear plants, the hidden costs of government subsidies, and the question of nuclear weapons proliferation. Virtually none of the controversial questions surrounding nuclear energy as a source of electricity in our future was left untouched. The authorization of funds would be set at $15 million for each of the five years the moratorium would be in effect.

H. R. 4971 gained many sponsors in Congress but fell far short of the required number of supporters to pass it. The influence of TFNP in the antinuclear movement waned along with the bill. But Senator Gravel and the TFNP were the first influential opponents of nuclear power to define that opposition as being "the antinuclear movement," and the labelling of the nuclear opposition as such was taken up by the press in their articles on the controversy. Senator Gravel asserted that the antinuclear movement was not a response to technical or economic issues, but to moral concerns, and said that the most dedicated nuclear opponents see atomic energy as a fundamental antihuman technology, one that requires of mankind a perfection which he simply does not possess. In nuclear energy, the kinds of mistakes that we know we make—including mistakes of irrationality and malice—can lead to the most disastrous consequences. Nuclear supporters have acknowledged the danger when they have referred to atomic energy as a "Faustian bargain."[5]

The articulation of national goals for the antinuclear movement went a step further through the efforts of Consolidated National Intervenors, a coalition of environmentalist, consumer, and labor groups totalling nearly one hundred and fifty groups. While TFNP clarified the criticisms of nuclear power, Consolidated National Intervenors refined the ideas of the antinuclear movement on alternative energy sources. The antinuclear movement is unique in this sense, for many social movements are sharply critical of the social order without offering viable alternatives, while others simply become absorbed in their utopian goals. It is also unusual that each of the movement's various organizations seems to fulfill a specific function for the movement as a whole. This is a primary advantage of a loosely structured movement with many organizations that are not competing with one another for ideological leadership or power over the movement. In the socialist movement, for example, division over ideological leadership has always fragmented the movement, preventing the cooperation of competing factions or a consensus on the goals of the movement. The synthesis of varied organization goals in the antinuclear movement is one of its most distinctive features.

Consolidated National Intervenors began as a means to concentrate resources and talent in interventions during nuclear power plant licensing proceedings. But the organization gradually changed its goals to become almost exclusively concerned with generating support for solar energy legislation in Congress. Specifically, Consolidated National Intervenors supported solar energy legislation that would provide a solar tax incentive, along with low-interest loans for solar energy systems by the Small Business Administration, expansion of solar energy research funds, and prohibition of construction that would block sunlight necessary for heating and cooling systems. Other major goals were to require that buildings constructed with federal funds be equipped with solar energy systems where possible, and that a special administrative office be created for Solar and Geothermal Energy within the Energy Research and Development Administration (now the Department of Energy). The organization was remarkably successful, for Congress was amenable to all of these goals and went on to implement them in a number of legislative proposals.

The transformation of its organization goals also had the effect of removing Consolidated National Intervenors from the mainstream of the antinuclear movement. Its main function became the dissemination of information on solar energy, including guides to all state laws dealing with solar energy, test facilities, and information sources. However, the activities of the Consolidated National Intervenors are in large part duplicated by organizations such as the International Solar Energy Society in Maryland and by publications such as *Solar Times, Sun Times, Solar Life, Solar Energy Intelligence Report, Solar Energy News, Solar Energy Report,* and many more.[6] The organizations and research groups that advocate solar energy are so numerous that one could argue that the solar energy movement developed independently from the antinuclear movement, which was simultaneously attracting the participation of many traditional social movement groups.

Resentment against the large oil corporations was another trend in American society, particularly after the energy crisis of 1973–1974, which many believed to be in part engineered by the major oil companies. While the radical left in the United States has long been obsessed by the imperialistic and monopolistic practices of international oil companies, hostility to these companies surfaced among the public and among more elite groups. For example, the Energy Action Committee emerged concurrently with the antinuclear movement, and though not in the mainstream of the movement, the group tapped public sentiment on energy issues. The Energy Action Committee was formed by four wealthy Californians who each contributed $600,000 to fund its initial efforts. These individuals were Harold Willen, national chairman of the Businessmen's Educational Fund; Leo Wyler, chairman of the TRE Corporation; Miles Rubin, chairman of the board of Optical Systems Corporation; and actor Paul Newman. Two coordinators were hired: John Cabusi, a former campaign worker for Morris Udall, and Tom Girard, a former employee of Westinghouse Corporation. A staff of twelve persons was created with a suite of four offices in Washington, D.C. The central goal was to challenge the oil lobby. James Flug, an attorney who advised Senator Edward Kennedy for several years, stated that the Energy Action

Committee would have "energy policy made in Washington instead of the Houston Oil Club."[7]

The specific goals of the Energy Action Committee were the divestiture, of oil corporations, placing each phase of production (transportation, refining, and marketing) in the hands of a different company, and the retention of regulations on natural gas. A head-on attack was launched by the Energy Action Committee on the monopolistic practices of oil companies in order to make the industry more competitive. The slogan was "Get Mad." As actor Paul Newman said in an appeal for funds,

the giant oil monopolies are the most powerful corporations in the history of the world. To enter into the battle with them is no easy task. Their influence over our government and others is mighty. And to keep their power, they will continue to bribe and deceive just as they have bribed and deceived for three-quarters of a century to obtain that power.[8]

Kenneth Curtis, former governor of Maine and then United States Ambassador to Canada, joined in to give support of the group. Since the oil corporations are actually energy corporations with growing control over phases of the nuclear fuel cycle (for example, Exxon Nuclear), as well as coal resources and solar energy companies, the antinuclear movement must challenge the oil industry along with the nuclear industry.

The Task Force Against Nuclear Pollution, National Intervenors, and the Energy Action Committee were engaged in activities that, on a longitudinal basis, indicate the overall evolution of the ideology of the antinuclear movement. From the initial controversies raised over the safety and safeguards of nuclear power, groups went on to advocate that solar energy replace nuclear energy, and as the struggle intensified, the latent hostility to American business and industry in general that has always been a part of our political tradition began to surface. The most dramatic and significant confrontations occurred in New England and in California.

Regional Direct Action in the Movement

The New England Coalition on Nuclear Pollution and the Clamshell Alliance. Small groups of scientists and citizens from southern Vermont and western Massachusetts formed the New England Coalition on Nuclear Pollution (NECNP) to intervene in operator license proceedings for Vermont Yankee Nuclear Power Station, relying on public donations for legal retainer fees. This was the beginning of a regional direct action group that would eventually become the Clamshell Alliance, perhaps the most publicized of all antinuclear organizations. The scientists in the NECNP were affiliated with nearby universities and volunteered to review documents, write interrogatories, assist in policy formation, and educate activists on the technical problems of nuclear power plants. Despite their intervention, an operating license was issued to Vermont Yankee.

The NECNP persisted, gaining the cooperation of the Natural Resources Defense Council, and brought a lawsuit before a Court of Appeals, asking for a second review of Vermont Yankee on the grounds that plans for the transportation and permanent disposal of radioactive wastes had been excluded from the initial review. The outcome of this case was a court order requiring that Vermont Yankee construct cooling towers to prevent thermal pollution but circumventing the issue of radioactive waste disposal. With these lesser successes, the New England Coalition on Nuclear Pollution incorporated in 1971 as a voluntary, nonprofit organization with more than four hundred individual members and support from fifteen organizations in the New England area. It was governed by a twenty-seven-member board of trustees that met every month to establish policy and to decide what actions were to be taken to challenge nuclear power. The strength of the organization was its ability to get expert help from scientific advisors and legal counsel from specialists in nuclear power plant hearings and environmental law.

A major change in the organization came when it joined Consolidated Intervenors to participate in the Atomic Energy Commission hearings on the safety of the emergency core cooling systems of nuclear power plants. But the major shift in the strategy and tactics of the New England Coalition on Nuclear Pollution coincided with an increase in its membership. More sophisticated use of experts was made in intervention proceedings, and energy conservation lectures and public education seminars, debates, radio and television appearances, and energy conferences broadened the attack on nuclear power. An office with a library and part-time staff was maintained in Brattleboro, Vermont.

Strategic considerations governed the Coalition's call for a moratorium on any further construction and licensing of nuclear power plants, a gradual phasing out of all existing plants, and a national effort to develop nonradioactive and renewable energy options. As a president of the Coalition, Diana Sidebotham, observed, "this was an early and aggressive action in the national moratorium movement."[9] New Hampshire became the arena for the next confrontation with the Atomic Energy Commission over nuclear energy. Environmental groups had been fighting a utility company proposal to construct two large nuclear power plants on an estuary along the seacoast area at Seabrook, near Hampton. The New England Coalition on Nuclear Pollution assisted by initiating an intervention in the construction permit hearings for these proposed nuclear reactors. The case was strengthened because of the poor financial condition of the utility company (Public Service Company of New Hampshire), the seismic history of the area, and the summer resort nature of Hampton Beach, only two miles from the proposed site. This was followed by intervention in Massachusetts, where two plants were being proposed for construction in Montague, near Amherst. Sam Lovejoy, an environmental activist, received considerable publicity when he blew up a tower in protest of these plants.

In close to five years, the New England Coalition on Nuclear Pollution raised only about $125,000, spending the largest portion of this money on intervention proceedings rather than public education on the issue. By 1976, Seabrook was the primary interest of the organization. As Nathaniel Smith, also a former president of NECNP, argued, "powerful vested interests—the 'uranium lobby,' the reactor manufacturers, including General Electric and Westinghouse, the multi-billion dollar utility industry—are pushing the country towards an almost all–electric and almost all–nuclear energy economy."[10] During the Seabrook intervention, help came from the Audubon Society of New Hampshire, the Forest Society of New Hampshire, and the Seacoast Anti-Pollution League. Dr. James Nelson, an economics professor at Amherst College, testified that the utility industry could not generate enough capital internally to finance the construction of large nuclear power plants. Other expert witnesses on behalf of the intervenors were Carl Stein, an architect from New York City; Dr. Gordon J. MacDonald, professor of environmental policy at Dartmouth College; Dr. Alvin O. Converse, engineering professor at Dartmouth (testifying on the uses of solar energy); and Dr. Myrick Freeman, chairman of the economics department at Bowdoin College in Maine. The NECNP also enlisted the help of Dr. George Field, director of the Center of Astrophysics at Harvard University.[11]

Despite the highly credentialled expert testimony, the Nuclear Regulatory Commission issued the construction permit for the nuclear reactors at Seabrook. Shortly thereafter, the Clamshell Alliance formed to take direct action against building the reactors right at their site in Seabrook. A new stage of the antinuclear movement began, and civil disobedience became the major tactic. Arrests and mass demonstrations became commonplace at Seabrook for the next three years, although the demonstrations remained nonviolent.[12] The nonviolent tactics received tacit acceptance by Jimmy Carter, then campaigning in nearby Manchester. When asked about civil disobedience and nuclear power, Carter replied that

I've always felt that anybody who disagrees with the civil law in a matter of conscience has a right to openly express that disobedience. At the same time, under our societal structure it's necessary that they be willing to take the consequences of their disobedience.[13]

Although the Clamshell Alliance heralded a new stage of the antinuclear movement, we should be aware of the problems of creating oppositional organizations in the first place. Once established, such organizations experience a snowballing effect as more and more individuals are attracted to the movement. Decision making tactics consequently become more difficult. When 200,000 people rallied in New York City in 1979, many came for the music, to see Jane Fonda, and to relive the 1960s, as well as to protest nuclear power.

The stigma attached to those who begin small protest groups also becomes a hinderance. When Vermont Yankee was first proposed, the people in Vernon, a small town of about one thousand persons, were generally indifferent to the proposal. But in nearby Brattleboro, Mrs. Beatrice Brown, a former probate judge, began writing letters to the *Brattleboro Reformer* warning of the hazards of radioactivity. The following account of what happened after that is worth quoting at length:

As a result of her efforts, a small, informal antinuclear group grew up which sponsored a debate between two officials from Vermont Yankee and Larry Bogart, a one-man crusader against nuclear power from New Jersey.

Bogart had been director of Publications and Advertising for Allied Chemical but had no formal qualifications in the field of nuclear energy. He was branded in the Brattleboro newspaper as an "out of state propagandist" by a letter writer from Vernon, and the rumor circulated that he was an agent for the coal industry.

In August 1967, just a few weeks after the Bogart-Vermont Yankee debate, Mrs. Brown and five other area residents founded the Anti-Pollution League of the Connecticut River Valley.

The League's first order of business was to arouse public interest in nuclear power through meetings, letters to the editor, and conversations. Their enthusiasm for this work was so great that many readers of the Brattleboro newspapers soon tired of reading their letters. League members became thought of as well-intentioned but misguided do-gooders in the community.

Nevertheless, they raised enough unsettling questions that the Windham Regional Planning and Development Commission (WRC), composed of two representatives from most towns in southeastern Vermont, appointed a study group to investigate whether Vermont Yankee was in fact a hazard to the region as claimed by the Anti-Pollution League. The study group included a forester, a real estate salesman, a laboratory technician, the Director of WRC, two members of the Anti-Pollution League and three local scientists.

The report was accepted by the entire group except for the two members of the Anti-Pollution League. It was adopted by the full WRC in January 1968 without discussion and without a dissenting vote.

Rather than opening up a complex problem, the WRC report seemed to settle the issue in favor of nuclear power. Opinion leaders in the community who previously had given the appearance of neutrality could now climb off the fence on the pronuclear side.

The matter might have rested there except for Peter Strong, president of the Conservation Society of Southern Vermont (CSSV), who was disturbed by what he considered to be a gross oversimplification of a complex issue in Brattleboro. On his initiative, the CSSV sponsored a conference entitled "Nuclear Power and the Environment: An Inquiry," held at Stratton, Vermont, in September 1968.

Unlike the WRC group, the CSSV went beyond Vermont for expertise and brought to Vermont knowledgeable critics of nuclear power from the Scientists' Institute for Public Information.

An attempt was made to get the AEC to send debators, but the chairman of the AEC, Glenn Seaborg, declined, asking Strong on the phone if he was against progress and telling him that the meeting sponsors and participants were being investigated. Finally, the late Dr. Theos J. Thompson came to Vermont from the Nuclear Engineering Department of MIT to respresent the utility point of view.

The locus of the controversy now shifted from Brattleboro to Montpelier.[14]

In many ways, this account tells the story of the movement against nuclear power. A nuclear power plant is scheduled for construction in a remote, rural area whose residents accept it without question. A few individuals voice opposition, and they are labelled as propagandists or do-gooders. Nevertheless, local officials listen to the criticisms and then reject them, producing a reaction from other people interested in the issue. An outside expert is brought in, while the chairman of the Atomic Energy Commission (if we accept the validity of the account) suggests that the sponsors of the debate are against progress (rural ignorance?) and are being investigated (disloyal Americans?). But more people become interested, and the issue turns into a controversy. Should credit be given to Mrs. Beatrice Brown?

The Clamshell Alliance itself consists of small groups throughout New England. In Maine, they include the Downeast Alliance in Franklin, the Island Energy Coalition in Bar Harbor, and the Bluehill Mussels in Bluehill. Although the Clamshell Alliance has a coordinating committee, representatives from groups such as these are able to attend a "Clam Congress." But each small group has autonomy.[15]

During a 1979 demonstration at Seabrook, when the nuclear reactor core was being transported to the plant site, protestors were again arrested, although all demonstrators were supposed to carry certification that they had participated in a six–hour nonviolence workshop. While the resource mobilization perspective on social movements directs our attention to the level of internal resources available to movement groups or the nature of their outside support, we cannot overlook the importance of "positive solidarity" among members of movement groups. The bonds of solidarity among members of the social movement group allow members to attempt acts that as individuals they would never contemplate. As Mark Traugott explains:

In the case of failure, they enjoy a relative impunity that is no mere illusion because, acting as a collectivity, participants can neutralize the efficacy of social control by concentrating equal or superior forces. Similarly, their sense of power is realistic, based both on the strength of numbers and the opportunity to coordinate efforts of individuals joined by a sense of common destiny.[16]

Without this sense of positive solidarity, the hold of the movement on the individual is weakened. The Clamshell Alliance is comprised of small sects called "affinity groups," which in Maine have coalesced as MAGIC (Maine Affinity Group Information Committee). One member of the Clamshell Alliance in Maine observed that "the nature of this confrontation was different from earlier occupations. There wasn't the feeling of togetherness. There was more hostility, more confrontation. There wasn't something coming at us before. I think Seabrook 1977 showed how together we can be. Seabrook 1979 didn't work."[17] According to Jeanne Christie, MAGIC groups are also aware that many people are interested but view the affinity groups as associated with left–wing radicals. For this reason, MAGIC had a task force to look into "creative strategizing," meaning minimal commitment activities such as adding a dollar to your utility bill to be used for solar energy research.[18]

Despite the mass demonstrations in New Hampshire, Seabrook seemed destined to be the site of operating nuclear reactors sometime in the 1980s. It is likely that many of the antinuclear activists will become alienated from further demonstrations at Seabrook after five years of failure and will turn their attention more to solar energy and other alternative energy sources without completely giving up on the antinuclear struggle. In the 1980 Maine antinuclear referendum, many groups wavered on the issue. The Maine Audubon Society and the Maine Civil Liberties Union took no position on the referendum, while the Natural Resources Council, the state's largest environmental group, only opposed Maine Yankee after two heated debates among its board members.[19] At the same time, business associations were strongly pronuclear.

People for Proof, the Western Bloc, and the Abalone Alliance. The defeat of the Maine Nuclear Referendum and continued construction of the nuclear reactors at Seabrook were predictable if we compare the experiences of antinuclear groups in California to those in the New England area. Although the defeat of Proposition 15 in California in 1976 is now past history, there are aspects of that struggle which suggest the dimensions of the nuclear conflict. People for Proof, an organization based in San Francisco, coordinated the drive for an initiative on nuclear power in California. The California Nuclear Safeguards Initiative (Proposition 15) would have mandated a public review of the safety of nuclear power plants by shifting the burden of proof on the nuclear industry. Full compensation would have been given to all affected members of the public in the event of a nuclear accident, thereby removing federal liability limits on nuclear insurance. Proposition 15 also provided for the effectiveness of radioactive waste disposal systems to be demonstrated.

Although the initiative did not explicitly call for a moratorium on nuclear power, its effect would have been to prevent the construction of any new nuclear power plants in California. Supporters of the initiative included Ralph Nader, Jack Lemmon, Friends of the Earth, and various local citizens' groups. One highlight of the controversy was a debate between actor Robert Redford with former Governor Pat Brown, who argued that the initiative was a step backwards because clean burning nuclear fuels would be replaced with polluting fossil fuels.

While Governor Brown's attitudes might not find acceptance in West Virginia or eastern Kentucky among the United Mine Workers, his argument appeared legitimate. On the other side of the coin was the deep involvement of former Governor Brown with the pronuclear group called Citizens for Jobs and Energy. The pronuclear organization hired three public relations firms and received campaign funding from Pacific Gas and Electric, operator of the Humboldt nuclear reactor; Southern California Edison, operator of the controversial San Onofre reactor; and from Westinghouse Corporation and the Bechtel Corporation (the company involved in the Tarapur case). Over $2 million were invested by opponents of Proposition 15, including Exxon Nuclear, Atlantic Richfield, and more than thirty utility companies from all over the United States.[20]

People for Proof obtained the 500,000 signatures necessary to have the initiative placed on the June 1976 California ballot. Another regional organization was also formed called the Western Bloc. This organization was to be a coalition of independent and local community groups helping to coordinate initiative drives in nineteen states, particularly Oregon, Colorado, Montana, and Maine. The founder of Western Bloc was Edwin Koupal, who attended the Critical Mass '74 antinuclear conference sponsored by Ralph Nader. Koupal and his wife Joyce contributed $17,000 dollars to finance the Western Bloc.

Edwin Koupal died of cancer in 1976, but before his death, he wrote a masterful document entiled "The Nuclear Web," illustrating the quasi-conspiracies of government officials and private industry leaders in the pronuclear countermovement.[21] This document supports what many sociologists have always observed about the leadership of countermovements. For example, Tahi L. Mottl of Harvard University writes:

Countermovement leaders are elites within existing institutions who strongly oppose change; they perceive their power as threatened by change or augmented by their resistance to change. . . . Countermovements are frequently mobilized by elected officials and other elites in the name of their constituencies, whose perogatives are superseded by the success of the initial movement.[22]

Thus, as the initiative loomed closer, the California State Assembly began to consider bills that would bring a one–year moratorium on the construction of any new nuclear power plants pending a study of the feasibility of locating the plants underground and until the federal government had developed reprocessing and waste disposal systems for the California nuclear reactors to the satisfaction of the California legislature. This move by elected officials to forestall possible defeat by incorporating some of the goals of the antinuclear movement into legislation was supported by Governor Jerry Brown, then running as a candidate for President of the United States in the Maryland primary.

Edwin Koupal asserted that the nuclear web, which included Citizens for Jobs and Energy, was not created by design but "merely by the circumstances of finance and employment, and in some cases, marital and nepotistic ties."[23] The nuclear web in California included many persons who grew up in a governmental system that has "become contemptuous of the voters and disdainful of the public at large."[24] Campaign contributions, friendships, and party affiliation all might determine who is part of the web of influence that makes government seem inpenetrable to ordinary citizens.

Koupal presented impressive evidence that government agencies and officials in California worked in concert to discredit the People's Lobby. He concluded that

all it took was a simple phone call from a government official to get several agencies involved in an effort to discredit a citizens organization that challenged the way the business of government was being conducted.[25]

When the ballots were counted, the California Nuclear Safeguards Initiative had been defeated by a margin of two to one. The result of both the California initiative and the Maine Nuclear Referendum seem to bear out Koupal's warning to other activists that "chances are that you have your own nuclear web, and it reaches all the way to the White House, just like ours does. Many of the same corporate characters will be in it."[26]   One of the more interesting facets of the antinuclear movement was the resignation early in 1976 of three middle management engineers responsible for monitoring the performance of nuclear reactors from General Electric Corporation in order to participate in the antinuclear movement. These resignations brought the antinuclear movement to the center stage of the mass media. Dale Bridenbaugh, Gregory Minor, and Richard Hubbard all had well-paying positions and had families to support. All three engineers expressed concern over government plans to sell nuclear reactors to Egypt, Israel, and South Africa. As Gregory Minor said, "Nuclear reactors and nuclear weapons present a serious danger to the future of all life on the planet."[27] He also stated that the fire at the Brown's Ferry nuclear plant in Alabama had been influential in his decision.

It is almost axiomatic that the movement recruitment process is not just a matter of the sway the movement goals have for individuals (who may be psychologically predisposed to joining a movement), for individuals are drawn into movements through their associations with friends or other persons who are already a part of the movement.[28] These preexisting social networks provide an interpersonal tie for outsiders to a particular movement.[29] All three engineers had been members of the Creative Initiative Foundation, a two–thousand–member organization in California with the goal of exploring ethical and philosophical values. The Creative Initiative Foundation, in turn, had close ties with Project Survival, an antinuclear organization with approximately 7,000 members. This was apparently the social network of the three engineers that helped to create the motives for their eventual dramatic resignation from General Electric. To give an idea of the tenor of the Creative Initiative Foundation, the *New York Times* reported that at a meeting only a few days before the three resignations, a group leader had concluded a discussion of nuclear energy by saying, "God did not create plutonium and therefore it is evil."[30]

Dale Bridenbaugh mentioned uncertainty associated with human error and the potential genetic effects of radiation as reasons for his resignation, while Richard Hubbard stated that "you cannot continue to build plants and operate them without having an accident." Although we can assume that the membership of these engineers in the Creative Initiative Foundation provided the social support for entrance into the antinuclear movement, we could also assume that they were rational men whose decision to join the movement was facilitated by socially constructed motives in a group that offered an alternative view of reality. Sociology is replete with possible theoretical explanations of why and how people join social movements. The engineers might just as well have been experiencing a mid-life crisis involving alienation from their work. Gregory Minor reported a subjective experience that most of us could envision happening to ourselves. It almost appears to be a precipitious experience prior to a conversion to a different view of reality. Minor reported that just before his resignation he viewed the blue radiation given off by some plutonium in a tank of water at a government facility in Hanford, Washington:

I looked through that ten or fifteen feet of water, the life–saving shield between me and that fuel, and I knew that if any one of those elements were to come up and hit me, that I was dead, just like that. And I got the feeling right there of the precarious balance we have between radioactive materials in a safe state and radioactive materials in an unsafe state, and the dangers to life are that close.[31]

We cannot dismiss the testimony of an intelligent person who reacts to an advanced technology and a dangerous substance such as plutonium as the mere product of differential social experiences. Nor can we exclude the possibility that the engineers would *seek out* groups such as the Creative Initiative Foundation as a means to express a perspective on life, or, in this case, on advanced nuclear technology. Appearing before the Joint Committee on Atomic Energy, Gregory Minor observed that

the nuclear industry has developed to become an industry of narrow specialists, each promoting and refining a fragment of the technology, with little comprehension of the total impact of our world system.[32]

Again we have the insight of someone reflecting on his occupational rather than personal experiences. Only a few days after the three resignations, Robert Pollard, a federal safety engineer for nuclear reactors at Indian Point in New York and a project manager for the Nuclear Regulatory Commission, also resigned because he believed that the plants were unsafe and posed the danger of a major catastrophe. The Union of Concerned Scientists made him their Washington, D.C., representative at a salary of $20,000 a year. In his statement before the Joint Committee on Atomic Energy, Pollard said the Indian Point nuclear station constitutes an unconscionable threat to the health and safety of the millions of people who live in the metropolitan New York City area. The Indian Point plants have been badly designed and constructed and are susceptible to accidents that could cause large–scale loss of life and other radiation injuries, such as cancers and birth defects. The magnitude of these hazards associated with these plants have been suppressed by the government because the release of such information might cause great public opposition to their operation.[33]

The symbolic impact of defections from nuclear establishment cannot be underestimated, nor can the personal courage of the engineers be denied. At a time when the nuclear issue was being coopted by the Democratic party in the presidential campaign of Jimmy Carter, these resignations signified that opposition to nuclear power was deep enough for three individuals to risk their financial security and substantial careers to bring changes to energy policy that they believed to be in serious error.

Expressive Symbolization: The Silkwood Case

The case of Karen Silkwood was dramatic enough to give her the status of martyr for the antinuclear movement, Karen Silkwood left her supporters with a memory that helps to explain why the antinuclear movement continues to struggle.

Martyrdom is an important feature of social movements. Martyrs create solidarity within the movement and reinforce commitment to the movement's goals. Identification with those who have made a great sacrifice, often of their lives, as did Karen Silkwood, confirms that the sacrifice the individual is making is small in contrast to that made by the martyr. Mythological consciousness arises through such identification with an individual who has experienced intensive suffering as a consequence of his or her beliefs and activities. This is as powerful as religious sentiment and often plays an essential role in eliciting mass commitment to a faith, as martyrdom did for the Catholic Church during the Middle ages.

The feeling toward martyrs, however, may be ambiguous, for the actions may be viewed as suicidal, as an escape leaving the survivors of society to cope with its problems. The human foibles or weaknesses of martyrs become acutely significant. The opposition can point to those weaknesses as vices that discredit the martyr, but a character defect only shows followers that the martyr was redeemed in the face of a struggle.

Karen Silkwood became a martyr for the antinuclear movement even though her death may have been accidental. It occurred in the midst of an important labor struggle involving the safety of workers at a plutonium reprocessing plant in Oklahoma. Silkwood obtained a position at the Kerr-McGee plant as a laboratory assistant. Soon she was on the picket line with strikers. Within the next two years, she was exposed to plutonium on three occasions as a result of what appeared to be company negligence, prompting her to become a part of the Steering Committee of the local unit of the Oil, Chemical, and Automic Worker's Union. She was documenting grievances on safety abuses for the union when she discovered in November 1974 that she had been exposed to high levels of plutonium and that her apartment—including food in a refrigerator—was also contaminated. After undergoing decontamination procedures in Los Alamos, New Mexico, she arranged a meeting with a reporter from the *New York Times* and a labor union official to deliver more evidence of safety infractions that her investigation had uncovered.

While driving to the meeting, Karen Silkwood had a fatal automobile accident. Although the police report indicated that she had fallen asleep at the wheel, a private investigation firm hired by the union found evidence that the car had been struck from behind by another vehicle. The safety abuse documents were missing. The Federal Bureau of Investigation collaborated in the police report but did not release its own report. A few months later, however, *Time* magazine (24 May 1976) revealed that an informer for the Federal Bureau of Investigation, Jacque Srouji, had been given access to over one thousand pages of bureau documents on the Silkwood case in exchange for information about radical groups. The documents gave an unflattering view of the drug habits and sexual life of Karen Silkwood.[34]

The cause of Karen Silkwood was taken up by the National Organization of Women (NOW). NOW president Karen DeCrow headed a delegation that met with Justice Department officials to discuss the circumstances of her death. The organization awarded Karen Silkwood honorary membership and on 13 November 1975, one year after her death, NOW observed a Silkwood Memorial Day. Four nights later, following the Critical Mass '75 antinuclear conference, a candlelight vigil was held at the national capital, and Representative Bella Abzug of New York called for a congressional investigation of the case. Bella Abzug illustrated the mood of Silkwood supporters when she remarked at the Critical

Mass rally that "as society grows larger and more impersonal, we must depend on courageous individuals . . . to expose and challenge unsafe conditions. These issues often seem technical and complex, but become very concrete when viewed through the life of Karen Silkwood."[35] The Critical Mass newsletter that quoted Abzug also commented that

the activities and reactions of the Kerr-McGee company in the Karen Silkwood case exposed many of the deficiencies of the nuclear power industry: careless safety procedures; violent corporate reaction to critical appraisal; worker harassment; intimidation of dissenters; ruthless support of corporate goals; arrogant corporate indifference toward neighboring communities; extreme secrecy and coverup of federal and state law violations.[36]

A second delegation, headed by the National Organization of Women, with representatives from the Coalition of Labor Union Women, Environmental Policy Center, Critical Mass, the United Auto Workers, and including Karen Silkwood's parents, presented a petition of seven thousand signatures asking Senator Lee Metcalf, with the consent of Senator Abraham Ribicoff, to reopen the investigation of her death. National Public Radio had already filed a suit against the Justice Department seeking details of its investigation under the Freedom of Information Act.

In the months following, Kerr-McGee was unable to account for at least forty pounds of plutonium and shut down the plant in order to administer lie detector tests. Questions were reportedly designed to determine management loyalty, and two of Silkwood's coworkers in the plant who aided in her investigation of safety procedures were either transferred or fired. A spinoff group from NOW, called the Supporters of Silkwood, emerged with a coordinator from NOW and a staff of five that created a division of labor of communications, community organizing, legal issues, and financing. The Supporters of Silkwood concentrated on the labor issues that involved the Oil, Chemical, and Atomic Workers International Union with the management of Kerr-McGee. Along with the traditional labor issues of scab labor, health and safety conditions, and management intimidation, several mishaps at Kerr-McGee had resulted in worker contamination cases. Soon after Karen Silkwood was contaminated with plutonium, Kerr-McGee was accused of falsifying quality control and health records. Since the documents of safety violations that

Silkwood had compiled were missing after her fatal automobile accident, one NOW member went so far as to say in the Supporters of Silkwood newsletter that

Karen's allegiance was to her sisters and brothers in the plant and to the American people, not to bulging bank accounts and/or corporate power at any price. Karen was silenced because she was an effective fighter for her constituency and a standard bearer of all women.[37]

In April 1976, the Congressional investigation into the death of Karen Silkwood ended. Senator Metcalf, according to a Supporters of Silkwood newsletter, was reported to have said that the Oil, Chemical, and Atomic Workers International Union was satisfied with the original Oklahoma police report, although the union president denied this. The Supporters of Silkwood argued that political pressure from the president of Kerr-McGee and other members of the Senate abrogated the investigation.[38] Three years later, an Oklahoma City jury awarded the estate of Karen Silkwood $10.5 million in damages, and the judge ruled that the doctrine of "absolute liability" applied to Kerr-McGee Corporation; that is, the company was fully responsible for radiation damages even to people outside of the plant, whether or not government safety standards were met or negligence occurred.[39]

The spirit of martyrdom was best expressed in an essay printed in the first newsletter of the Supporters of Silkwood entitled "Who is Karen Silkwood?" The excerpts below from this essay show the personal meaning that the death of Karen Silkwood had for social activists:

Who was Karen Silkwood? What is her relevance to us as women? As union members? Karen Silkwood was a working woman, a union member, a rank and file union activist, a believer, a fighter. She was made of the raw material that built the American labor movement. Our history, that of the labor movement and women's contribution to it, is not the story of a few charismatic leaders; it is rather the history of thousands of quiet, responsible, committed union members, and Karen Silkwood was one of these.

Karen's story was most like those of other unionists who over the past two hundred years have fought to preserve the dignity of the worker by seeking to achieve decent hours, fair wages, and humane working conditions. These gains have been made, not by the hotheaded orator of the soapbox, but by thousands of individual workers and their families. They committed themselves not to personal gain, not to their own pleasure, but to struggle, self-sacrifice, and sometimes physical danger, imprisonment, and even death. So many of the martyrs who fought for the eight-hour day, for a fair day's wage for a fair day's work, to end the oppression of child labor have gone unmourned and unsung by their sisters and brothers. These women and men whose lifeblood gave us the legal rights to have a voice on workplace issues affecting our health and well-being were the building blocks of the growing labor movement.

Karen Silkwood is such a martyr. She saw the problem—saw the dangerous working conditions she and her fellow workers faced daily. She struggled and fought, she organized other union activists to overcome these threats to their health. Karen didn't lead a demonstration; she kept scrupulous records. She didn't seek personal notoriety; she worked to develop a strong, courageous shop committee. The very last meeting Karen had was with her fellow union members to map out last–minute strategy exposing the hazards and unsafe working conditions at Kerr-McGee facility. Then she was off, to meet with a representative from her International and a *New York Times* reporter. Karen Silkwood's work ended that night as her car went off the road. Yet she left us—women and trade unionists—a burden and a legacy.

Karen left us the burden of finishing the work she set out to do—the work of securing the rights of workers who deal with radioactive substances to rigorous job safety controls; the work of assuring that workers fighting for health and safety conditions on the job need never again fear the harassment Karen suffered; the work of investigating the conditions surrounding Karen Silkwood's contamination with radioactive materials during the last few days of her life and the "mysterious" accident which caused her death.

Her legacy is one of conviction, courage, and heroic determination; the legacy of one human life invested in the battle to defend the rights of all workers to work in dignity; the legacy of a woman who took the cause of worker safety and health forward and made it a rally cry for her survivors.

This is who Karen Silkwood is to us—the sisters and brothers who never knew her in life—who in her death must carry the burden of her work and preserve the legacy of her life for those who follow us.[40]

Cognitive Symbolization: Environmentalists for Full Employment

Many social movements evolve a consistent body of theoretical doctrines that amount to an ideology. Theory emerges at a distinct phase of the movement. Internal division or uncertainty within the movement may necessitate the formulation of ideological doctrine, usually at a time when conflict becomes more focused, and growth of the movement may suffer.

The only group to have developed an incipient theoretical doctrine of the antinuclear group has been Environmentalists for Full Employment. This organization was created in response to conflict between environmentalist and labor movement factions within the movement (or to forestall such conflicts), and to conformations between antinuclear activists and workers in nuclear power plants. At the site of the Indian Point reactors in New York, Representative Bella Abzug was jeered after speaking in favor of antinuclear groups demonstrating outside the plant. At Seabrook, construction workers participated in counterdemonstrations that supported nuclear power. Ideological rationalizations of a movement's goals are born out of such conflicts. When the group formed in 1976, it appealed to Leonard Woodcock, President of the AFL-CIO, to unite these two factions, arguing that "both the environmentalist and the labor movement must keep in mind the ecological principle that there can be no division between the natural and social environment."[41]

Organized labor in general and the construction unions in particular support nuclear power. Both the Teamsters and the United Mine Workers, the latter in order to protect the coal industry, are pronuclear. Unions that support the construction of nuclear power plants have worked with the utilities to help defeat the California Nuclear Safeguards Initiative and to mobilize pronuclear demonstrations at Seabrook in New Hampshire. But gradually more labor union locals have sided with antinuclear groups and have opposed nuclear power projects at Barnwell, South Carolina; Bailly, Indiana; and at the Clinch River breeder reactor project in Tennessee.[42] Groups such as the Clamshell Alliance have endorsed resolutions that express their solidarity with the labor movement.[43]

While antinuclear groups are open to the labor issues of worker safety in nuclear facilities, they have not overtly adopted left-wing views on capitalism in general. For groups such as the Clamshell Alliances, refusal to condemn capitalism reflects a strategic consideration as well as the existence of competing points of view among their affinity groups. Most of the activists had no desire to broaden the nuclear issue to an attack on corporate capitalism with the advocacy of socialism, as this would alienate the public and the government.[44]

Environmentalist or ecology–oriented groups tend not to recruit from the working class, appealing instead to the college educated and upper–middle–class social stratum.[45] Ironically, the U.S. Labor Party, a

Marxist-Leninist group, views "Naderism" as the ideological enemy in the nuclear controversy. In their publication, *Stop Ralph Nader, The Nuclear Saboteur,* the U.S. Labor Party asserts that banks are trying to increase the cost of raw materials and energy in order to generate capital to amortize debts. These banks supposedly are funding the environmentalist movement in order to hold back technological progress and economic growth, including the denial of nuclear power plants and technical assistance to the Third World.[46]

The U.S. Labor Party may not accurately reflect the views of the American left wing, but it has been one of the more visible leftist groups in the controversy. At one time, travelers at La Guardia or the other major airports were often urged by members of the Fusion Energy Foundation to subscribe to a magazine entitled *Fusion* at extraordinarily high prices. This group seems to be ideologically affiliated with the U.S. Labor Party and propounds a view that nuclear fission power is a necessary transition to nuclear fusion power and a growth economy. Radical left groups as such have not gained any prominence in the antinuclear movement, although it has attracted many individuals with radical left views.

Another irony in the nuclear controversy is the contention that the federal government is actually a major funder of antinuclear and antiutility direct action groups. In two articles entitled "Where Do the Antis Get Their Money?" H.A. Cavanaugh asserts that the public interest groups that are attacking investor-owned electric utilities, nuclear power, oil companies, banks, and corporations are funded by government grants which total over $2.5 billion.[47] Cavanaugh claims that one of the three major antinuclear intervenors in the Seabrook controversy, National Consumer Law Center, was supported by grants both from the Department of Energy and the Federal Trade Commission. Some of the success of the antinuclear movement must therefore be attributed to their access to external resources from factions within the political elite. According to Cavanaugh, many of the government administrators are actually recruits from Ralph Nader and other environmental or antinuclear organizations.[48]

Conclusion

The antinuclear movement has remained a loosely organized movement despite the efforts by a few national organizations to coordinate the activities of diverse local and regional groups. The regional direct action organizations have provided the movement with symbols, especially in the struggle against the Seabrook, New Hampshire, siting of nuclear reactors. The Karen Silkwood case was extremely important to the movement because it offered a martyr and widened the spectrum of the movement's ideology to include issues important to the women's and labor movements. As conflict intensified, antinuclear movement groups have gravitated more to the labor movement as a source of cognitive symbolization or ideological rationalization of the movement's struggle. All of these efforts were both hindered and aided by the federal government.

The dual role of the federal government in the nuclear controversy is the key element in the assessment of the consequences of the antinuclear movement, for the government has been a critical factor in defining both the successes and failures of the movement. The exercise of social control over the movement's activities has been limited because antinuclear activists have been a vital element in the policy–making process as the bureaucratic apparatus struggles to cope with a generalized crisis in industrial society brought on by a growing scarcity of energy resources.

Notes and References

1. See the bimonthly "Progress Reports" of the Task Force Against Nuclear Pollution, September 1974 to September 1975.

2. Ibid.

3. Mike Gravel, "The Anti-Nuclear Movement." Testimony before the House Energy and Environment Subcommittee, 28 April 1975. *Congressional Record* 121, no. 75: 107–9.

4. Hamilton Fish, "Nuclear Powerplant Construction Ban," *Congressional Review* 121, no. 75: 42.

5. Gravel, "The Anti-Nuclear Movement," p. 107.

6. Information on these newsletters is available from most state energy agencies. This sampling came from "Solar Two," a publication of the Maine Office of Energy Resources, Augusta, Maine.

7. Energy Action Committee, "Oil Industry Profits Sky Rocket Since 1972," news release, 6 March 1976.

8. Letter appealing for funds, sent with Energy Action Committee news release (see note 7 above).

9. Diana Sidebotham, "History and Comments by President of the NECNP, in the newsletter of the New England Coalition on Nuclear Pollution, Brattleboro, Vermont.

10. Nathaniel Smith, "NECNP gives Support to Nuclear Moratorium," *Recorder* (Greenfield, Massachusetts), 7 December 1974.

11. New England Coalition on Nuclear Pollution, "Testimony at Seabrook Construction License Hearings," Brattleboro, Vermont.

12. An excellent case study of the multitude of federal hearings on the Seabrook controversy is now available. See Donald W. Stever, Jr., *Seabrook and the Nuclear Regulatory Commission* (Hanover, University Press of New England, 1980). The book deals primarily with the licensing procedures of the Nuclear Regulatory Commission. See also Steven E. Barkkan, "Strategic, Tactical, and Organizational Dilemmas of the Protest Movement Against Nuclear Power," *Social Problems* 27, no. 1 (October 1979): 19–37.

13. Quoted in Harvey Wasserman, "Showdown at Seabrook," *Nation 223:* (September 1976): 203–205.

14. This account is quoted from Larry Gay, "History of Nuke Plant Birth in Rural Vermont," *Recorder* (Greenfield, Massachusetts), 18 January 1973.

15. Jeanne Christie, "Maine Clamshell Alliance Groups Would Rather Stay Home and Develop Options," *Ellsworth American* (Ellsworth, Maine), 15 March 1979.

16. Mark Traugott, "Reconceiving Social Movements," *Social Problems* 26, no. 1 (October 1978): 38–49.

17. Jeanne Christie, "Violence Mars Clamshell Demonstration," *Ellsworth American* (Ellsworth, Maine), 15 March 1979.

18. Ibid.

19. David Platt, "Self-interest Sparks N-position," *Bangor Daily News,* 17 September 1980, p. 25.

20. "The Vote for Nuclear Power," *New York Times,* 23 May 1976, p.1.

21. Edwin Koupal, "The Nuclear Web," in the newsletter of the Western Bloc, 1976.

22. Tahi L. Mottl, "The Analysis of Counter-Movements," *Social Problems* 27, no. 5 (June 1980): 620–35.

23. Edwin Koupal, "The Nuclear Web."

24. Ibid.

25. Edwin A. Koupal, "California Government Agencies v. People's Lobby: A Study in the Abuse of Power," in the newsletter of the Western Bloc, November 1975, Los Angeles, California.

26. Edwin Koupal, "The Nuclear Web."

27. "Three Engineers Quit G. E. Reactor Division and Volunteer in Anti-Nuclear Movement," quoted in the *New York Times,* 3 February 1976, p. 12.

28. This notion contradicts the idea that persons who have no social ties are the ones most susceptible to the appeals of a social movement.

29. See David A. Snow, Louis A. Zurcher, and Sheldon Ekland-Olson, "Social Networks and Social Movements," *American Sociological Review* 45 (October 1980): 787–801.

30. "Three Engineers Quit G. E. Reactor Division and Volunteer in Anti-Nuclear Movement," *New York Times,* 3 February 1976, p. 12.

31. U.S., Congress, Joint Committee on Atomic Energy, "Investigation of Charges Related to Nuclear Safety, 94th Cong., 2d sess., 1976, p. 2.

32. Ibid.

33. Ibid., p. 97.

34. The book by Jacque Srouji, eventually published as *Critical Mass* (Nashville, Tenn.: Aurora Publishers, 1977), also dwells on the alleged use of drugs by Karen Silkwood.

35. See vol. 1 (November 1975) of the newsletter of Critical Mass—The Citizens Movement to Stop Nuclear Power.

36. Ibid.

37. Supporters of Silkwood newsletter, no. 1, 1976.

38. The most detailed accounts of this sequence of events I have found is Howard Kohn, "Malignant Giant—The Nuclear Industry's Terrible Power and How It Silenced Karen Silkwood," *Rolling Stone* 27 March 1975; and *Organizer* 1, no. 1 (November 1975), an issue prepared by Sara Nelson, National Coordinator for the Labor Task Force of the National Organization of Women.

39. "The cost of Karen Silkwood," *Economist,* 26 May 1979, p. 57. The settlement in federal appeals court was later reduced to a smaller sum.

40. Susan Holleran, "Who Is Karen Silkwood?," in the newsletter of Supporters of Silkwood, 1976.

41. Environmentalists for Full Employment, *Jobs & Energy,* no. 1 (1976).

42. See Rebecca Logan and Dorothy Nelkin, "Labor and Nuclear Power," *Environment* 22, no. 2 (March 1980): 6–12.

43. Ibid.

44. Steven E. Barkan, "Strategic and Tactical and Organizational Dilemmas," pp. 24–25.

45. See W. B. Devall, "Conservation: An Upper–Middle–Class Social Movement," *Journal of Leisure Research* 2: 123–26.

46. U.S. Labor Party, "Stop Ralph Nader—The Nuclear Saboteur," (New York: Campaigner Publishers, 1977).

47. H. A. Cavanaugh, "Where Do the Antis Get Their Money?," *Electrical World,* 15 April 1980 and 1 May 1980.

48. Ibid.

CHAPTER 5

Consequences of the Antinuclear Movement

The success of a social movement is defined by the outcomes of the controversy. A complete moratorium on nuclear power development would have signified total success for the antinuclear movement, but this has not occurred. Of all the differing theoretical schools of thought on social movements, the resource mobilization theory of social movements is most concerned with how and why a movement succeeds or fails:

The resource mobilization approach emphasizes both societal support and constraint of social movement phenomena. It examines the variety of resources that must be mobilized, the linkages of social movements to other groups, the dependence of the movement on third parties for success, and the tactics used by authorities to control or incorporate the movement.[1]

In practice, resource mobilization theory must assume that the movement obtains resources and leadership from political elites in order to succeed. But division among political elites must also be assumed, for while some elite factions may help to sponsor the movement, others will attempt to suppress it or neutralize the movement by incorporating some of its goals into government policy. The antinuclear movement has had a significant impact on government policy concerning both the allocation of energy resources and the problems of nuclear proliferation and nuclear terrorism. It has also had dramatic effects on public opinion. However, it would be misleading to overstate how much power the antinuclear movement has. We must keep in mind the keen observation of David Lilienthal, the first chairman of the Atomic Energy Commission:

It is a formidable army that marches under the banner of *status quo atomicus*. If the controversy over the future of nuclear power were to be decided by a trial of political strength, there would be no contest. The pronuclear interests are immeasurably the more powerful. The protest marches, sit-ins, and environmental lawsuits are a nuisance to them, but once they rally their forces, there will be little doubt as to the outcome.[2]

I have discerned three key areas in which the antinuclear movement has had an impact on attitudes or policies. The first area is that of electoral politics: during the 1976 presidential campaign, nuclear energy was the most important issue on which Democrats were able to capitalize to regain the presidency. The antinuclear movement had a lesser but still discernible effect on the presidential electoral campaign of 1980 that put Ronald Reagan into the White House. The second area of impact has to do with the actual policies of the Carter administration on nuclear energy, which have set the tone for the debate over nuclear power for the coming decade. These policies deal with the recycling of plutonium, the fast breeder reactor, priorities to alternative energy technologies, the potential for nuclear terrorism, and the more general problem of nuclear proliferation in a world wide arms race. A third arena of impact has been public opinion: every movement attempts to influence the public as well as the government elite.

There are perhaps other ways to measure the success of the antinuclear movement. One could look at the percentage of voters opposing nuclear power development in various initiatives or referenda, the growing number of people at mass demonstrations and protests, the diffusion of opposition to larger political arenas (as in Europe), the cancellations of nuclear power plant projects (more frequently due to economic costs), or the improved safety conditions at nuclear power plants. The impact of the movement on political parties, public opinion, and government policy, however, indicates both the general and specific impact of the movement.

Presidential Politics and the Antinuclear Movement

The success of a social movement in the United States is intrinsically related to its impact on the major political parties.[3] Traditionally, the Democratic party has been the most receptive to demands made by aggrieved groups and social movements. However, a basic condition affecting this receptiveness has to do with which political party is

TABLE 1

PROJECT INDEPENDENCE SCENARIOS*

Historical Growth	**Technical Fix**	**Zero Energy Growth**
1. High oil price	1. Less capital requirements	1. Land use problems
2. Less emphasis on environmental concerns	2. Minimize demand on environmentally controversial sources of energy	2. Offshore oil and gas drilling
3. Stockpiling of resources	3. Change rail regulations to promote recycling	3. Mining of Western coal and oil shale
4. Offshore oil and gas exploration	4. More efficient automobiles	4. Change public attitudes on value of growth
5. Fast breeder reactor	5. More efficient heating and cooling systems	5. Decentralize technology
6. Synthetic fuel from coal and oil shale	6. More efficiency in steam generation	6. Energy sales tax, reduction of tax for low income groups
7. Capital formation problem (25% of all plant and capital equipment for energy)	7. Restrict nuclear exports	7. No nuclear expansion
		8. Increase energy efficiency
		9. Import natural gas from Canada

*Adapted from *A Time to Choose*, Final Report of the Energy Policy Project of the Ford Foundation, 1974.

currently in power. The antinuclear movement began to attract national attention at a time when the Republican party controlled the White House while the Democrats had control of the legislative branch. This is a classic situation in American politics that frequently immobilizes the executive branch of government.

The Republicans did attempt to change government policy to adapt to the crisis in energy resources, but the response to this crisis was not very flexible. The framework for a national energy policy that emphasized nuclear fission as a source of electricity was Project Independence, developed by the Federal Energy Administration and the Energy Policy Project of the Ford Foundation. The Project Independence blueprint was an analysis of alternative courses of action according to three different scenarios of energy growth.[4]

One scenario, that of historical growth, assumes that the increase in energy use would continue at the rate of 7 percent a year, with high oil prices and the OPEC cartel necessitating a lesser emphasis on environmental problems in order to stimulate offshore oil and gas exploration, commercial operation of the liquid metal fast breeder reactor, development of synthetic fuels, and channelling of public funds to assist industry in their capital formation problem.

On the other hand, the technical fix scenario emphasizes research into energy conservation, such as more efficient automobiles, heating and cooling systems, recycling of resources, and co–generation. Less capital investments would be required, and nuclear power growth would be minimized, in part through a restriction on nuclear exports. Finally, the zero energy growth scenario stresses no nuclear expansion, the decentralization of energy technology, changing the public attitude on the value of growth, and resolving problems of efficient land use. Social policy measures to reduce the impact of energy shortages on the populace would also be a part of the zero energy growth scenario. The historical growth scenario was accepted by the Republican leadership, but largely rejected by Democrats, who proposed a plethora of policies based on combined aspects of the technical fix and zero energy growth scenarios.

Since the historical growth scenario would require up to 25 percent of all capital formation in the United States for investment into energy industries if energy self-sufficiency were to be obtained, the Republicans championed the proposal of late Vice-President Nelson Rockefeller that an Energy Independence Authority be created to make $100 billion of public funds available for energy loans to private industry. This proposal was never implemented into public policy, but the budget for the Energy Research and Development Administration (an agency that briefly preceded the Department of Energy), clearly indicated where priorities in energy policy were being placed by the Republican administration. Fifty-four percent of the 1976 energy budget went for nuclear fission and fusion development, 11 percent to fossil fuels, 1 percent to energy conservation, and less than 4 percent to solar, geothermal, and advanced energy systems research. The amount of dollars actually budgeted to nuclear energy was absolutely enormous if defense and space nuclear systems are included, for even larger sums were spent on these programs.

From the outset of the energy crisis, the Democratic party leadership was fundamentally opposed to the Republican program, believing that it was neither an equitable nor a comprehensive energy policy. Some Democrats supported the emphasis on nuclear power, but most favored increasing research expenditures for alternative energy technologies and redistributing income to compensate poor families for the increased burden of energy costs. Modest federal and state government subsidies for the energy needs of poor families now exist. Two contenders for the Democratic presidential nomination pledged support for a moratorium on nuclear power and divestiture of the holdings of oil corporations. Neither of these two candidates, Senator Fred Harris of Oklahoma and Representative Morris Udall of Arizona, could mount a sustained campaign for the nomination. Governor Jimmy Carter of Georgia, on the other hand, was more moderate in his appraisal of policy changes that would be needed for energy security.

Jimmy Carter chose the nuclear power controversy as the topic for his first major policy speech, given before a United Nations conference on Nuclear Energy and World Order in New York City in May 1976. Carter emphasized his background in nuclear engineering and his work on Admiral Rickover's nuclear submarine program after his graduation from the Naval Academy. Prior to this speech before the United Nations, Carter had told the Washington Press Club that a disastrous nuclear accident would be more devastating than a total Middle East oil embargo, necessitating the underground location of nuclear power plants. Now Carter proposed that the United States shift from oil to coal as its main source of energy, maintain strict energy conservation, derive renewable energy from the sun, and keep dependence on nuclear power to a minimum. Specifically, this would involve a voluntary moratorium on the sale of uranium enrichment facilities and nuclear fuels reprocessing plants, and a world energy conference to control the spread of a dangerous technology. Carter would keep these promises when he went to the White House, and his ideas reflected the sentiment of the antinuclear movement:

Power reactors may malfunction and cause widespread radiological damage unless stringent safety requirements are met. Radioactive wastes may be a menace to the future generations and civilizations unless they are effectively isolated in the biosphere forever. And terrorists or other criminals may steal plutonium and make weapons to threaten society or its political leaders with nuclear violence unless strict security measures are developed and implemented to prevent nuclear theft. By 1999, the developing nations alone will produce enough plutonium to build 3000 Hiroshima–size bombs a year.[5]

When Jimmy Carter became President Carter, it seemed as if the goals of the antinuclear movement had been realized despite the defeat of six antinuclear initiatives or referenda in the November 1976 election. A national commitment was made to energy conservation, the development of coal resources, and research into solar energy. The liquid metal fast breeder reactor demonstration project at Clinch River, Tennessee, was cut back when President Carter vetoed appropriations, but Congress attached a rider to a different bill to continue funding of the project.

At no time was there any indication that President Carter supported the abandonment of conventional light water nuclear reactors. His policies were actually geared to facilitate their construction by blocking the multiple access to the legal system that antinuclear groups had successfully utilized to forestall the licensing and construction of nuclear power plants. For example, President Carter supported standardized designs for nuclear power plants that required only one hearing on each design.

In a televised address to the nation on 18 April 1977, President Carter outlined a comprehensive energy policy which he termed the "moral equivalent of war."[6] The short–term strategy of this energy program was to reduce dependence on foreign oil supply by implementing a conservation program and converting industries and utilitites from oil and natural gas to coal. The long–term goals were to develop alternative sources of energy, including solar, geothermal, and hydroelectric power. It was in this address that President Carter reiterated his campaign promise to avoid a "plutonium economy" by abandoning the liquid metal fast breeder reactor project in Tennessee and deferring opening of the nuclear fuels reprocessing plant in Barnwell County, South Carolina. However, the conventional light water nuclear fission plants would still be built, but on a lesser scale than that suggested by President Ford.

Further policy decisions made by the Carter administration were to avoid the horizontal or vertical divestiture of holdings of large oil corporations, nor would corporations be required to share in the expense of research and development from which they gain large profits. Generally, the Carter plan was to maintain centralization in both the private and public sectors. This included the creation of a super agency, the Department of Energy. These changes in the direction of energy policy were supported by Congress and followed later by a windfall profits tax on the oil corporations to be used for research into synthetic fuels development. The move to synthetic fuels marked a major shift in energy policy with a crash program to produce synfuel from coal liquids and gases and oil shale. Congress responded by creating the Synthetic Fuels Corporation in June 1980.

In contrast to the heavy expenditures on nuclear energy in fiscal year 1976 (54 percent of the energy budget), only 34.6 percent of the 1979 budget (if expenditures for the strategic petroleum reserve are excluded) went to nuclear energy, as well as an additional 6.6 percent for the administrative expenses of the Nuclear Regulatory Commission. Authorizations for solar and alternative energy sources rose enormously: together they accounted for over one-fifth of the 1979 energy budget, compared to less than 4 percent in 1976. Energy conservation experienced the greatest increase, from 1 percent in 1976 to over 12 percent of the energy budget in 1979. The proportion spent on fossil fuels was only slightly changed, from 11 to 15 percent. These figures, as summarized in Table 2, indicate the change in government priorities during the administration of President Jimmy Carter.

The major change to coal and synthetic fuels may have been a victory for the antinuclear movement, but not for its environmentalist segment. Coal mining has been estimated to cost the lives of 250 miners each year, and air pollution from coal-fired electric generating plants was once estimated to contribute to the deaths of 20,000 Americans each year.[7] In addition there are problems involving reclamation of land after strip mining, acid rain, black lung disease, sludge byproducts, and railway transportation. The Sierra Club has already filed suit to force a better

TABLE 2
1979 FEDERAL BUDGET FOR ENERGY

Program	Authorization (in millions)	Percent of Total*
ENERGY RESEARCH & DEVELOPMENT	3547	71.9
Solar	514	10.4
Other renewable sources	541	11.0
Fossil	784	15.9
Nuclear fission	1218	24.7
Other nuclear technology	490	9.9
ENERGY CONSERVATION	611	12.3
Technology development	229	4.6
Conservation grants	377	7.6
Public Information	5	.1
STRATEGIC PETROLEUM RESERVES	3008	n.a.
ENERGY INFORMATION & POLICY	82	1.7
ADMINISTRATIVE AND REGULATORY EXPENSES	695	14.1
Department of Energy (DOE)	215	4.4
Nuclear Regulatory Commission (NRC)	327	6.6
Other	153	3.1
	7,382**	100.0%

*Excludes deductions made for offsetting receipts from direct energy production and expenditures for the strategic petroleum reserve in order to get a better comparison.

**Includes adjustment for offsetting receipts as well as expenditures for the strategic petroleum reserve. Percentages are based on total of $4935 million.

Source: *The Budget for Fiscal Year 1981* (Washington D.C.: U.S. Government Printing Office). Since the 1981 budget included a controversial temporary deficit of $17 billion for synthetic fuels and 1980 figures were only estimated expenses, the 1979 budget was used for a comparison of research and development on alternative energy technologies.

environmental review of the impact of shipping coal from the Wyoming reserves,[8] and previously was instrumental in preventing the multi-billion–dollar Kaiporowits coal-fired plant in southern Utah from ever being built.

The federal government actually owns one-half of all potential energy resources in the United States. With the exception of the Tennessee Valley Authority, the government does not develop the resources but leases federal lands to private industry. When we consider that energy costs consume about 15 percent of a poor family's budget, and that the energy crisis of 1973–1974 contributed to the unemployment of 535,000 persons, the government's role in land-use decisions is extremely controversial.[9] To what extent are federal lands and national resources to be used for profit-making ventures by private industry? Without nationalizing the energy corporations, public lands could be used to provide cheaper energy for the populace as a whole rather than to subsidize large corporations.

With respect to government policy, the generalization of new social values to political elites was a primary success of the antinuclear movement. The movement exerted pressure on these elites to pursue alternative sources of energy, commit the nation to conservation as a way of life, and to consider the effects energy production has on the environment and health and safety of the population. The gradual institutionalization of these new social values into national policy in the Carter administration was more important than the specific success or failure of movement goals as a consequence of government action.

The most specific success of the antinuclear movement in terms of its consequences on government policy was the passage of the 1978 Nuclear Nonproliferation Act by Congress. The issue of safeguards on nuclear material to prevent further proliferation of nuclear weapons was as important to the antinuclear movement as the issues of nuclear reactor safety or radioactive waste disposal. Several events made the safeguards issue all the more acute. India detonated a nuclear device in 1974 by obtaining plutonium from a reactor supplied to them by Canada in the 1950s, while West Germany sold an entire nuclear fuel cycle to Brazil. In the coming decade, it is likely that Brazil, Taiwan, South Korea, South Africa, Pakistan, and Argentina may all have nuclear weapons.[10]

Former Secretary of State Henry Kissinger once called transfers of nuclear technology the greatest single danger of unrestrained nuclear proliferation. Egypt, Argentina, Brazil, China, France, India, Israel, Pakistan, South Africa, and Spain have not signed or ratified the Nuclear Nonproliferation Treaty of 1968. This 1968 treaty pledged nations that did not have nuclear weapons never to develop them. Some of these nations, such as Brazil and Argentina, have publicly stated intent to manufacture nuclear weapons.[11] Others have engaged in clandestine activities that suggest they will soon possess nuclear weapons.

Intrigue and clandestine activities are one of the most interesting aspects of the international uranium and nuclear reactor markets. The Central Intelligence Agency uncovered a patent filed in West Germany by two Israeli scientists who claimed their process could hypothetically enrich seven grams of uranium to weapons-grade material in twenty-four hours. South Africa developed an enrichment process with secret technical assistance from West Germany. This discovery came from documents stolen from the South African embassy in Bonn by an opposition group called the African National Congress. The files indicated illegal nuclear cooperation by the West German government-owned Gesellschaft für Kernforschung in Karlsruhe with South African scientists.[12] Among other possibilities, South Africa could use low–yield nuclear weapons against black insurgents to preserve apartheid policies.

All the other nations that have not signed the Nuclear Nonproliferation Treaty have similar reasons to join the nuclear club. Israel has long been thought to possess nuclear weapons that were developed with French technical assistance.[13] Pakistan, a rival of India, has been the subject of much controversy, including speculation of their planting a spy in a Dutch nuclear project and being the recipient of stolen nuclear material from India. Italy provided Iraq with the two nuclear laboratories that were destroyed in an Israeli raid.

Under the Ford Administration, steps were taken to prevent this proliferation of nuclear material. Although Ford supported private control of uranium enrichment facilities in the United States, the major nuclear suppliers met in conference and agreed to prevent nuclear material from being used for weapons development. This agreement among the London Suppliers Group became in part the basis for the 1978 Nuclear Nonproliferation Act, which gives the Nuclear Regulatory Commission power to prohibit the export of nuclear fuel to nations suspected of using the material for nuclear weapons and mandates a ban on nuclear exports to nations that aid others in nuclear weapons development.

The nuclear industry believes these policies will harm the export market and enable West Germany, France, Britain, and Japan to control the international market. International competition is misleading, for American companies frequently have licensing agreements with foreign companies to provide them with steam supply systems or electric turbines and even invest in foreign companies or participate in consortiums with them. This participation, however, enables the foreign companies to gain experience with the technology and later build their own nuclear reactors without having to depend on American corporations.

Amory Lovins, a prominent antinuclear activist, takes a different position. Lovins argues that it is impossible to prevent the proliferation of nuclear bombs through government policy as long as we have nuclear power.[14] Institutional arrangements for nuclear safeguards will never be adequate to prevent diversion of nuclear materials for military purposes. Therefore, national efforts to displace oil with nuclear power are the source of the problem of nuclear proliferation.

The export of nuclear technology to developing nations is much more complex, however, than the problem of nuclear proliferation suggests. On the one hand, developing nations lack the technological infrastructure to support nuclear power systems, and the need for technological elites and nuclear materials might mean further domination by the advanced nations. Nuclear accidents might also be more likely. But on the other hand, it is discriminatory to developing nations to prohibit nuclear exports to them. The high cost of oil has dealt a severe blow to the economies of the developing nations as well as to the industrialized world.

Although the 1978 Nuclear Nonproliferation Act represented a response to the safeguards issue, its credibility was undermined when President Carter issued an executive order approving shipment of nuclear fuel to India. Critics in Congress argued that the uranium shipment made a mockery out of American efforts to prevent the proliferation of nuclear weapons. Senator William Cohen of Maine said the decision "will be perceived as once again raising the white flag of impotence."[15]

As the nuclear controversy spills more into a problem of international politics and foreign policy, the role of the antinuclear movement in affecting government policy may diminish. Since a near moratorium on nuclear power already exists, due to the cancellations of orders by utilities for new plants, criticisms of nuclear power for reasons of safety or environmental impact are becoming moot. This may signal the onset of opposition to nuclear power based more on the values of the peace movement than those of environmentalists.

Nonetheless, public sentiment was forcible enough in 1980 for the Democratic party to adopt officially the position of a phaseout of nuclear power, a platform accepted by President Carter despite his pronuclear policies. But the Republican party platform advocated accelerated use of nuclear power, storage of radioactive wastes in underground sites, and reprocessing of spent nuclear reactor fuel.[16] Ronald Reagan also opposes the windfall profits tax on oil companies that is being used to develop synthetic fuels, and advocates abolishment of the Department of Energy. Thus, the return of the Republican party to political power portends dramatic changes in energy policy and potential new directions in the strategy and tactics, as well as the basic ideology, of antinuclear groups.

Terrorism and Nuclear Power

Would a terrorist group be able to attack a nuclear installation or steal nuclear materials? Early in the antinuclear movement, this became one of the most emotional and symbolic issues. The emphasis on nuclear reactor safety and proliferation of weapons through governments acquiring control of nuclear technology displaced the issue of nuclear terrorism, but the rise in international terrorism was certainly a factor in the passage of the 1978 Nuclear Nonproliferation Act. The initial warnings of a possible danger to societies from terrorists who might acquire nuclear weapons came from Theodore Taylor and Mason Willrich.[17] In their study of the issue, they also warned of nuclear theft by criminal organizations for blackmail or sabotage and of diversion of materials from within the nuclear industry.

Michael Flood cogently presented an argument of why terrorists will turn to nuclear power.[18] Nuclear installations are attractive targets because the fear of radioactivity adds a new dimension to terror. Since terrorist violence is violence for effect, nuclear facilities are prime targets. Any event involving "atomic terror" would make world headlines. In the developing nations, nuclear power plants may become symbols of imperialism to leftist groups who have the sophisticated weapons to launch an attack that might lead to a core meltdown. Soviet-made missiles were used in an attack on the construction site of the

Super-Phenix breeder reactor in France by an unknown group in 1981. Although the missiles could not penetrate the containment shelter being built, such an attack is not beyond the resources of violent groups.

On the other hand, it could be argued that terrorist groups would never develop a nuclear weapon because the theft of nuclear materials involves such a high death risk. Terrorists have many options to realize their goals more easily, as a complex technological society is vulnerable in many different ways. In fact, a study by the BDM Corporation of the threat to nuclear installations found that most attacks have come from dissident employees or psychologically disturbed individuals.[19] Few terrorist groups have the organization and skilled personnel for an attack on a nuclear site or the technical knowledge to steal nuclear materials without exposing themselves to lethal radiation. Terrorists also tend to refrain from malevolent acts that bring mass casualties because this mobilizes public opinion against them.

However, the BDM Corporation report documented seventy-seven terrorist attacks against nuclear facilities during the time period between 1966 and 1975. The major left-wing incident came with the takeover of a nuclear power plant under construction at Atucha in Argentina by a guerilla band of fifteen men. On the radical right, eight people were arrested in plot to poison a water supply in Italy with stolen uranium. Fuel rods have been stolen from nuclear power stations in France and Germany, and plutonium has been reported missing at plants in the United States. Some of the incidents in the United States since 1969 include a pipe bomb found in the reactor building of the Illinois Institute of Technology, dynamite found at the site of a Michigan reactor, a break-in at a fuel storage facility in North Carolina, detonation of an incendiary device near the Pilgrim reactor outside of Boston, and arson attempts in New York and California.

Table 3 shows how the BDM Corporation report conceives the potential source of nuclear terrorism, according to whether the behavior is in the private or public sphere of society, the source of stimulus to the act (external or internal), and the degree of rationality or emotionality found in the act. In the public sphere are terrorists, protestors, sociopaths, and paramilitary groups. In the private sphere are criminals, avengers, psychopaths, and vigilantes. The range of objectives for each subtype is also indicated.

TABLE 3

POTENTIAL SOURCES OF NUCLEAR TERRORISM

SOCIAL STIMULUS	PRIVATE OBJECTIVES	PUBLIC OBJECTIVES
Rational-Internal	CRIMINALS Financial gain Extortion Mercenary sales Ransom	TERRORISTS Bargaining Publicity Social paralysis Mass casualties
Rational-External	VIGILANTES Restoration of a social order Protection of public from danger	PARAMILITARY Adventurism of a local commander Restoration of a social order
Emotional-Internal	PSYCHOPATHS Nuclear mystique Ego gratification Pyromania	SOCIOPATHS Vandalism Subculture of violence
Emotional-External	AVENGERS Revenge Retribution Dissident employee Labor dispute	PROTESTORS Exhibitionism Political statement Confrontation

Source: Adapted from ''Analysis of the Terrorist Threat to the Commercial Nuclear Industry,'' BDM Corporation (1975), pp. 33, D-5.

According to the BDM Corporation, outside assistance to terrorist activity, such as Cuban support of Latin American guerillas, or the training of Mexican guerillas and the Japanese Red Army by North Korea, is becoming more common. The Palestine Liberation Organization is reported to have had liasons with the Irish Republican Army, the Basque separatists, and with French terrorists. Thus, international cooperation among terrorists might make an attack on a nuclear installation possible.

Should a terrorist group ever acquire nuclear materials, the technical expertise to fashion a weapon might be within their grasp. Mason Willrich and Theodore Taylor estimated that between ten and twenty-four skilled scientists with several thousand dollars worth of equipment could fabricate a crude nuclear bomb. To obtain materials, they could engage in armed attacks, bombing, hijacking, and kidnapping.[20] A television documentary produced by Public Broadcasting Systems entitled "The Plutonium Connection" followed the progress of an undergraduate chemistry major at the Massachusetts Institute of Technology after he was asked to design a bomb using only publicly available materials. The task was accomplished in five weeks.

The Nuclear Regulatory Commission responded to this issue in 1976 by requesting that Congress allow a special Army unit to be trained in the event of an emergency, rather than by trying to protect the entire nuclear fuel cycle from terrorists or saboteurs. This action did not allay fears of antinuclear activists that a garrison state might be needed to protect the nuclear fuel cycle. The most commonly advocated safeguard now is the underground location of nuclear facilities. The BDM Corporation report attributes the mystique of nuclear energy and the fear of it as the most effective deterrents to theft or nuclear terror. Nuclear energy frightens the terrorist as much as it does the public.

Public Opinion and Nuclear Power

Public opinion is a measure of the success or failure of a social movement. Among the various public opinion polls of attitudes toward nuclear power, we find an indication of not only who is more likely to oppose nuclear power plants, but of how the antinuclear movement has influenced public opinion. Surveys of attitudes give some knowledge of which social categories are the support base of the antinuclear movement.

Two of the most comprehensive surveys of public opinion were conducted by Lou Harris and Associates in April 1975 and August 1976 for

Ebasco Services Incorporated, a company that supplies technical services to the nuclear industry.[21] The methodology followed and the questions asked do not suggest any systematic bias or deliberate distortion in the surveys. Although these two surveys are not recent, they do show the wellsprings of antinuclear sentiment. The year between the two surveys was one of the most intensive in the movement, so the latter survey is a good measure of shifts in public attitudes toward nuclear power that may in part be attributed to the antinuclear movement.

These public opinion surveys should probably be divided into pre- and post-Three Mile Island, an event that was a "Watergate" in the nuclear controversy. Although Three Mile Island did have an effect on public sentiment toward nuclear power, a survey by ABC News two weeks after Three Mile Island showed that 47 percent of the public still favored the construction of new nuclear power plants, while 45 percent were opposed. Eighty percent of the public rejected the idea of a permanent shutdown of all power plants, while 71 percent wanted more nuclear power plants *with stricter government supervision.* However, a majority of persons opposed the location of nuclear power plants in their local community. These data do not tell us if there were many crossovers after Three Mile Island other than among those who were predisposed against nuclear power before the accident and whose opposition became active as a result of the accident.[22]

Table 4 indicates two dimensions of public opposition to nuclear power in the United States. First, the percentage of those who opposed nuclear power among subgroups defined by such criteria as age, income, sex, and race are given. The second column shows the percentage of all persons in each of the subgroups who opposed nuclear power. For example, opposition was concentrated in the East, with 40 percent of all those who opposed nuclear power living in that region, although only 29 percent of all Easterners were opposed to nuclear power development. In the South, there was only a small minority of nuclear opponents, and moderate levels of opposition in the West and Midwest. Most opposition came from those living in urban areas, while in the rural areas (where most nuclear power plants are sited) there was little opposition. Persons over fifty years of age were the least likely to be opposed to nuclear power, and most who were opposed had some college but were not college graduates (although college graduates were more likely to be opposed to nuclear power). Scarcely any opposition came from blacks, and women were much more likely to be opposed than men.

TABLE 4

NUCLEAR POWER OPPOSITION IN THE UNITED STATES

	Percentage of those opposing nuclear power in each subgroup	Percentage of each subgroup who oppose nuclear power
Region		
East	40	29
Midwest	25	19
South	15	14
West	20	25
Residence		
Cities	43	29
Suburbs	27	22
Rural	18	18
Small towns	22	18
Age		
18–29	35	27
30–49	37	24
50 plus	28	17
Education		
Some high school	24	18
Some college	48	21
College grad	27	31
Income		
Under $5,000	16	22
$5,000–9,000	24	25
$10,000–14,999	21	23
$15,000 plus	—	19
Sex		
Male	41*	19
Female	59*	25
Race		
White	85	19
Black	8	22

*Approximate percentage

Source: 1976 Harris Survey, p. 100.

What were the major problems with nuclear power plants perceived by the public? Radioactive waste disposal was the main concern of all groups, particularly college graduates, while those with some college were more concerned with radioactive discharges into the atmosphere or theft of plutonium by revolutionaries. There was a pattern to these beliefs: Easterners, the young, and those who opposed nuclear power were more likely to identify major problems.[23] People express concern about hazardous problems but frequently draw the conclusion that nuclear power plants are safe. In 1976, solid majorities believed that nuclear power plants were either very safe or somewhat safe, while only about one-fourth of the public believed that they are unsafe or dangerous. In the one year between the two surveys, the number of people opposing nuclear power grew by about 8 percent among college graduates and among those living in the West or Midwest. Support for nuclear power lost ground among urban dwellers and the young, while slight increases in support for nuclear power occurred among rural dwellers, southerners, blacks, and those with low incomes.[24] Although women were more likely than men to be opposed to nuclear power, the percentage difference between the sexes was affected by the fact that twice as many women as men were not sure about their attitudes toward nuclear power.

The Lou Harris survey also measured the confidence that members of the public have in various individuals or groups concerning nuclear power. The most trusted were scientists, with 58 percent of respondents having a great deal of confidence in scientists in both surveys. The credibility of environmentalists grew by 12 percent to 34 percent in 1976, while about 40 percent had confidence in the Nuclear Regulatory Commission. Slightly more than one-fifth of the public expressed confidence in Ralph Nader, and even fewer had confidence in elected officials, the nuclear industry, utilities, or in newspaper commentators.[25]

A 1976 Gallup public opinion survey includes social characteristics of respondents ignored in the Harris surveys: political affiliation, religion, occupation, and number of people following the discussion about nuclear power. As Table 5 shows, Republicans were somewhat more likely to be receptive toward a plant being located in their neighborhood than Democrats, and Protestants were more receptive than Catholics. Those in the lower–middle–class occupations of clerical and sales work were much more likely to oppose a nuclear power plant than those who are either professionals or manual laborers. This is consistent with the Harris data,

TABLE 5

RECEPTIVITY TOWARD A
NUCLEAR PLANT IN NEIGHBORHOOD*

POLITICS	Favor	Oppose	No Opinion
Republican	48%	43%	9%
Democrat	38	47	15
Southern Democrat	43	38	15
Independent	45	45	10
RELIGION			
Protestant	45	42	13
Catholic	39	51	10
OCCUPATION			
Professional and business	50	43	7
Clerical and sales	32	59	9
Manual workers	45	42	13
Nonlabor force	41	43	16
FOLLOWED DISCUSSIONS	46	46	8
HAVEN'T FOLLOWED	29	71	Under 1%

*Source: 1976 Gallup Poll, p. 99.

for those with only some college were generally opposed to nuclear power and also were most concerned with the emotional issue of the theft of plutonium by radical groups. High levels of knowledge are not associated with opposition to nuclear power; 71 percent of those who opposed a nuclear power plant being located in their neighborhood did not follow discussions about nuclear power.[26]

All the surveys taken on attitudes toward nuclear power demonstrate that opposition increases if the nuclear power plant is going to be located in the vicinity of one's own neighborhood. A government study of the attitudes of residents in Hartsville, Tennessee, where a power plant was actually going to be located, found that those who were less favorable to the proposed plant emphasized potential hazards, while those who favored it were interested in the economic benefits that would accrue to the community. Again, people in the business professions and laborers were most favorable, and women were the most adamant opponents, along with a small majority of farmers. Opponents placed a high value on the way of life that presently characterized Hartsville and were concerned with how the plant would affect noise levels, traffic congestion, crime rates, school overcrowding, the number of taverns and bars, and drug problems. They were also concerned about water and air pollution, radiation, accidents, and sabotage of the plant. Nevertheless, over 60 percent of the Hartsville community surveyed favored the construction of the proposed nuclear power plant.[27]

The cumulative effect of the antinuclear movement on public opinion cannot be precisely determined by these surveys, but trends are apparent. The three-to-one margin of those favoring nuclear power development in the early 1970s had dropped considerably by 1979. Although many of the beliefs of the antinuclear movement have become incorporated into public opinion, such as agreement that conservation and development of alternative energy sources are needed, the public view that nuclear power plants may be a necessary evil still prevails by a small margin. Surveys do not always discover the underlying reasons for attitudes. Consider, for example, the views of David Lilienthal, first chairman of the Atomic Energy Commission:

The citizen protest against atomic energy plants here and abroad was not raised against nuclear hazards alone. Nor would it be satisfied if all nuclear plants were to be closed tomorrow. To a large extent, it has been a protest against the misuse of science, the misdirection of enormous forces that human ingenuity has brought into being. It is a protest against the abuses of industrial technology that poison the land instead of nurturing it, that sour the air and foul the water, that devour marsh and woodland and make hazardous to health and peace of mind the cities and factories in which people live and work. It is a protest against governments—all governments—that spend billions in an endless, insane atomic arms race that consumes the cream of the world's resources and much of its brightest talent. It is a protest against the uses of science and technology that are antihuman and antilife.[28]

The public opinion surveys do not concern themselves with associating antinuclear sentiments with basic attitudes toward the environment, science and technology, or governments. There are vicissitudes of public opinion related to contemporary events. A major accident such as that at Three Mile Island would seem to be the most important activator of broader citizen participation in the movement and less favorable attitudes toward nuclear power. Nonetheless, the omnipresent reality of dependence on Arab oil, which only increases in cost, is an important counterbalance to negative attitudes toward nuclear energy. Much of the antinuclear literature argues that nuclear power is acutally the most expensive form of energy, and that it is heavily dependent on government subsidies. Amory Lovins, for example, argues that nuclear power programs provide a disincentive to replace oil with alternative energy sources, and that nuclear energy does not even result in a saving of oil. As Lovins says, "Further confirming the loose coupling between nuclear output and oil saving, between 1978 and 1979 the United States reduced by 16 percent the amount of oil used to make electricity, while U.S. nuclear output simultaneously fell by 8 percent: the oil saving came instead from conservation and coal and gas substitution."[29] In other words, many of the basic arguments of antinuclear activists have not yet filtered into the public mind.

Neither has there been a determination of the effect on public opinion of subsequent events such as the Soviet invasion of Afghanistan, the Iranian hostage crisis, or the Israeli attack on an Iraqi nuclear reactor. Although these foreign policy issues diverted mass media attention away from the commercial use of nuclear power, it is probable that the American public is even more aware of the tenuousness of energy security. The war between Iran and Iraq also severed oil supply to other western nations. However, the 1980 presidential election focused on the SALT treaty, the military strength of the United States and the Soviet Union, and the potential for nuclear warfare. Thus, a continuing concern over nuclear proliferation keeps alive issues important to the antinuclear movement, for a main source of nuclear weapons proliferation is the diffusion of nuclear technology throughout the world. Reprocessing technology, which enables a nation to obtain weapons–grade nuclear material, was once considered a monopoly of the United States but is now available to Western Europe and Japan. The world market for nuclear fuels reprocessing technology will probably mean further diffusion of nuclear weapons potential to a number of countries, including Brazil, India, Pakistan, and South Africa.[30] All of these more recent events may have a cumulative effect that involves a rethinking of nuclear energy policy.

Conclusion

The success of the antinuclear movement lies more in the realm of pressures exerted upon the government to redefine and enforce safety regulations concerning the safety and safeguards of nuclear power plants than to completely revamp energy policy. The greatly increased number of government regulations has made nuclear power more expensive and less desirable to the utilities industry.

During 1976 the nuclear issue helped to propel Jimmy Carter into the White House. Since Carter had credibility as an expert in the field of nuclear energy, it was advantageous to his campaign and to the Democratic party to capitalize on the issue. Many of the goals of the antinuclear movement were realized: government reorganization, including the abolishment of the Atomic Energy Commission; a slowdown of research into the liquid metal fast breeder reactor program; a temporary moratorium on plutonium recycling and nuclear fuels reprocessing; international efforts to control nuclear technology and nuclear weapons proliferation; increased government regulation over the safety of nuclear power plants; steps taken to protect the nuclear fuel cycle from terrorists; increased funding for solar and other advanced energy systems; and incorporation of public opinion into energy policy decisions rather than a strict reliance on scientific, military, and industrial elites.

Despite all these accomplishments, the Carter energy policy represented appeasement of antinuclear sentiment and not a basic redirection of energy policy. The Carter administration never formulated a comprehensive energy policy that was to rely on alternative energy sources. In fact, the decisions of the Carter administration accomodated the demands of antinuclear groups while retaining a basic commitment to the construction of light water nuclear power plants. Some of the failure of the Carter administration to control the diffusion of nuclear technology throughout the industrial and developing world must be attributed to events not completely in the control of the United States government. A sixty–nation, two–year conference called the International Nuclear Fuel Cycle Evaluation (INFCE), initiated by President Carter, indicated deep international rifts over the question of nuclear power. The conclusion of this conference gave international support to the development of the fast breeder reactor and international reprocessing of nuclear fuel.[31] West Germany, France, Great Britain, the Soviet Union, and Japan will all have fast breeder reactors in operation during the 1980s. Both Great Britain and France have nuclear fuels reprocessing plants in operation, and Japan will soon have facilities available. These nations are also prepared to take a sizeable share of the world nuclear reactor export market. Even if agreement existed among the United States and its Western European and Japanese allies to halt this expansion of the nuclear fuel cycle, clandestine proliferation of nuclear technology into nations such as Pakistan and South Africa would most likely continue.

The antinuclear movement has had an effect on foreign governments. The opening of a reprocessing plant was suspended in West Germany under pressure of environmental groups. But all the major issues still remain unresolved. However, the antinuclear movement has been a major factor in the stalemate in the nuclear technology market that exists in the world today. As Pierre Lellouche points out:

To be sure, the political uncertainty resulting from the nonproliferation controversy of the past six years has certainly contributed to the slow-down of most nuclear programs around the world. It is also true that the proliferation argument has come to be used increasingly by antinuclear movements, particularly in Western countries. However, the main causes of the nuclear recession lie elsewhere: societal problems, particularly after the Three Mile Island accident, have increased dramatically in recent years, reaching even developing countries committed to nuclear energy, such as Brazil. Environmental issues, combined with the eroding competiveness of atomic energy, and the overall reduction in demand arising from continuing worldwide economic recession, have drastically reduced the pace of atomic energy growth throughout the world.[32]

Finally, we must consider that the issue of radioactive wastes, perhaps the most important to the antinuclear movement in the United States, must be increasingly linked to the production of nuclear materials for our weapons systems. Now that the public is convinced of the danger of radioactive wastes, how will this affect attitudes to wastes produced for military purposes? Can the two issues be separated?

While the public has been informed of the drawbacks of commercial nuclear power plants by the antinuclear movement, it has not been convinced that the goals of the antinuclear movement are viable ones. With the gradual convergence of two nuclear issues, one involving commercial nuclear power plants and the other questioning a nuclear arms race throughout the world, the controversy has become more complex. The linkage of military and civilian sides of the nuclear issue could forseeably strengthen pronuclear attitudes among a conservative electorate. Conceivably, an entirely new form of radical opposition to nuclear power could also develop in the 1980s.

Notes and References

1. Mayer Zald and John D. McCarthy, eds., *The Dynamics of Social Movements* (Cambridge: Winthrop Publishers, 1979), p. 1.

2. David Lilienthal, *Atomic Energy, A New Start* (New York: Harper & Row, 1980), p. 31.

3. Rudolph Heberle, *Social Movements* (New York: Appelton-Century-Crofts, 1951). Heberle argues that movements are not restricted to a national society or state as are political parties, and that they are bound together more by ideologies. Unlike the resource mobilization school, Heberle considers the relationship between political parties and social movements to be a major focus of investigations into the impact of movements.

4. The Ford Foundation, *A Time to Choose* (Cambridge: Ballinger, 1974).

5. Jimmy Carter, "Three Steps Toward Nuclear Responsibility," *Bulletin of the Atomic Scientists,* October 1976, pp. 8–14.

6. I have analyzed this television address in "Dilemmas of Energy Policy in the Carter Administration," Rutgers Graduate Student Colloquia, New Brunswick, New Jersey, 1977.

7. Bernard J. Cohen, *Nuclear Science and Society* (New York: Doubleday, 1974), pp. 139, 143.

8. Mel Horwitch, "Coal: Constrained Abundance," in *Energy Future*, ed. Robert Stobaugh and Daniel Yergin (New York: Ballantine, 1979), p. 103.

9. Federal Energy Administration, *Project Independence* (Washington D.C.: U.S. Government Printing Office, 1974).

10. Congressional Quarterly, *U.S. Defense Policy*, 2d ed. (Washington D.C.; Congressional Quarterly, Inc., 1980) pp. 37–44.

11. John R. Redich, *Military Potential of Latin American Nuclear Energy Programs* (Beverly Hills: Sage Publications, 1972). For an analysis of possible nuclear proliferation in the Middle East, see Robert J. Pranger and Dale R. Tahtinen, *Nuclear Threat in the Middle East* (Washington D. C.: American Enterprise Institute, 1975). A basic primer on this subject is Henry A. Kissinger, *Nuclear Weapons and Foreign Policy* (New York: W.W. Norton Co., 1969).

12. See Barbara Rodgers and Zdenek Cervenka, *The Nuclear Axis: Secret Collaboration Between West Germany and South Africa* (New York: Times Books, 1978).

13. See Robert Tucker, "Israel and the United States: From Dependence to Nuclear Weapons?" *Commentary* 60 (November 1975): 29–43.

14. Amory B. Lovins, L. Hunter Lovins, and Leonard Ross, "Nuclear Power and Nuclear Bombs," *Foreign Affairs* 38, no. 5 (Summer 1980): 1137–77.

15. Quoted in Congressional Quarterly, "Fuel Sale to India Tests Nuclear Policy," in *U.S. Defense Policy,* p. 46.

16. Marsha Dubrow, "The Candidates on Energy," *Boston Globe,* 12 October 1980, p. 9.

17. Mason Willrich and Theodore B. Taylor, *Nuclear Theft: Risks and Safeguards* (Cambridge: Ballinger, 1974). See also John McPhee, *The Curve of Binding Energy* (New York: Ballantine, 1973).

18. Michael Flood, "Nuclear Sabotage," *Bulletin of the Atomic Scientists,* October 1976, pp. 29–35.

19. Braddock, Dunn & McDonald, Inc. (BDM), "Analysis of the Terrorist Threat to the Commercial Nuclear Industry," report submitted to the Nuclear Regulatory Commission (Washington D.C., 1975).

20. Willrich and Taylor, *Nuclear Theft,* p. 51.

21. Ebasco Services Incorporated, "A Survey of Public and Leadership Attitudes Toward Nuclear Power Development in the United States" (New York: Ebasco Services, 1975), and "A Second Survey of Public and Leadership Attitudes Toward Nuclear Power Development in the United States" (New York: Ebasco Services, 1976).

22. W. P. Hoar, "Independence for America—Energy," *American Opinion* 22 (May 1979): 5–10.

23. Ebasco Services survey (1975), p. 58.

24. Ebasco Services survey (1976), pp. 69, 95.

25. Ibid., p. 131.

26. George Gallup, *Opinion Index,* report no. 134, September 1976, pp. 12–16, 99.

27. Oak Ridge National Laboratory, "Executive Summary of ORNL-5124," Oak Ridge, Tenn. 1976.

28. David Lilienthal, *Atomic Energy,* pp. 109–10.

29. Amory B. Lovins et al., "Nuclear Power," p. 1150.

30. This market, however, is bottoming out. See "Nuclear businessmen Fight to Survive the 1980s," *Economist* 274 (23 February 1980): 73–74.

31. See Stephen Salaff, "The Plutonium Connection: Energy and Arms," *Bulletin of the Atomic Scientists* 36, no. 7 (September 1980): 18–23.

32. Pierre Lellouche, "International Nuclear Politics," *Foreign Affairs* 58, no. 2 (Winter 1979–80): 343–44.

CHAPTER 6
The Antinuclear Movement in Perspective

The antinuclear movement is one of the most significant social movements ever to emerge in the United States. Why? The movement has raised issues of a scope that emcompasses the gravest problems yet faced by human societies: how to control the spread of nuclear weapons, how to prevent lethal radioactive materials from ever afflicting large populations, and how to provide energy that is crucial to the survival of society.

Social movements are groups of people involved in the process of social change. The egalitarian goals of modern social movements are frequently a response to large-scale changes in the social order brought about by technological innovations, for these changes are rarely even or constant in their impact on society. However, the antinuclear movement is not basically an antitechnology movement, no matter how much the ideology of particular groups questions the value of technological progress. How a society is to be organized for the production and distribution of social wealth is central to the ideology of many social movements.

Energy, the ability to do work, is the basis of all surplus wealth in a society. Relatively inexpensive sources of energy greatly magnified the surplus wealth produced by industrial societies, but this era of abundance is quickly becoming one of scarcity as developing nations attempt to control their own depleting natural resources. Governments must emphasize conservation not only as an energy policy but as a way of preventing instability and gradual erosion of social institutions under the pressures of scarcity. On the other hand, nuclear technology is a technological innovation that could insure continued high levels of energy production.

Anthropologist Leslie White believed that the culture or civilization of mankind could be regarded as an organization of energy. He developed the law of cultural evolution, which asserts:

Culture develops when the amount of energy harnessed by man per capita per year is increased; or as the efficiency of the technological means of putting this energy to work is increased; or, as both factors are simultaneously increased.[1]

This is a succinct statement of an underlying problem of nuclear power. Faced with dwindling supplies of fossil fuels, advanced societies must implement efficient and new means of producing energy. White argued that social evolution is a consequence of technological evolution, and that the social system may retard progress if it resists new technologies. Either the technology or the social institutions must give way. Thirty years ago he warned of the depletion of fossil fuels and speculated about the potential of both nuclear and solar energy, quoting a research associate in physics as having said that with atomic energy,

the face of the earth will be changed. . . . Privilege and class distinctions . . . will become relics because things that made up the good life will be so abundant and inexpensive. War will become obsolete because of the disappearance of the economic stresses that immemorially have caused it. . . . The kind of civilization we might expect . . . is so different from anything we know that even guesses about it are futile.[2]

In retrospect, these views must appear as wishful thinking, for nuclear technology has not made war obsolete but more probable, while economic stresses in societies have intensified. If nuclear power is a step forward in technological evolution, then it must accelerate changes taking place in the social and political structure of both modern and developing societies. A complex technology forces the creation of an infrastructure that allows people to adapt to the technology. Nuclear power demands greater structural differentiation in the institutions of societies. Specialized occupations emerge at all levels dealing with the technology, bringing new problems of social organization. Increased safety precautions must be taken to protect workers, who, like Karen Silkwood, may risk their lives in plants and factories. Technicians and plant operators have to be better trained to prevent accidents such as those at Three Mile Island and Brown's Ferry. Along with the growing complexity of the social organization that accompanies the technology, political structures of control must become more centralized. This enforces elitism and powerful bureaucracies in both scientific and political institutions.

From the perspective of positivism, the belief in evolutionary progress, societies must make these kinds of adaptions in order to gain the benefits from a new technology. When sociology first developed from the positivism of Auguste Comte, social phenomena were interpreted through the laws of natural science. One branch of positivism was the school of thought that has been dubbed social energetics.[3] Man and society were viewed as energy apparatuses, with their history subject to the processes of the transformation of energy: culture was thought to progress through the transformation of crude energy into useful energy, while society was viewed as an arrangement for the better utilization of energy.

As documented by Pitirim Sorokin, the social energetics school attempted to explain the social phenomena of change, differentiation, equalization, domination, and general historical progress through the basic laws of thermodynamics. These theorists predicted a trend toward social entropy that would be manifested in egalitarian and socialistic movements. Although Sorokin believed these assertions were unscientific extrapolations that represented a caricature of scientific law and disguised the meaning of social facts, social energetics contributed to positivism by arguing that science could reconstruct society if the state or policy were to guarantee the efficient use of maximum energy.[4]

The positivist view suggests then that nuclear technology is perhaps the epitome of technological evolution. With all of its problems, nuclear energy represents historical progress in science and an enormous potential for resolving the crisis of energy resources. It is the role of government to assure the implementation of a technological system that can bring continued survival to societies that exist primarily to create surpluses through the efficient use of energy. There is no alternative to nuclear power.

Alvin M. Weinberg, a senior nuclear scientist at Oak Ridge National Laboratory, is an articulate advocate of continued reliance on nuclear energy.[5] Weinberg argues that the need for fission depends on the availability of alternative sources of energy, of which coal is the only abundant alternative. Since solar technologies have not yet proved feasible on a large scale and oil is scarce, we must rely on either nuclear fission or coal or a combination of both. Technological innovations such as the electric car and the heat pump may further increase the demand for electricity. However, Weinberg points out, coal still has serious environmental drawbacks and is not readily available to the rest of the world. Characterizing coal as a "sword of Damocles" because the burning of it results in carbon dioxide emissions into the atmosphere that could one day lead to an ice-free Arctic and change the world's climate, Weinberg says that we should resort to nuclear fission and fusion energy, including even the fast breeder reactor, and work toward reducing the probability of accidents through technical improvements.[6]

The positivist view is also present in the arguments of antinuclear activists. Amory Lovins, also a physicist, asserts that we can resolve the energy crisis by making more efficient use of existing sources of energy other than nuclear, including coal, which can be made environmentally safe through technical improvements and does not bring the threat of atomic warfare.[7]

By opposing nuclear power plants, have antinuclear groups accepted a negative view of evolutionary processes? The destructive consequences of modern technology are all too apparent, including the automobile, chemical wastes, and the burning of fossil fuels. The antinuclear movement resists technological evolution in terms of large-scale, centralized nuclear power stations, but affirms the belief in creative innovation and evolutionary change by seeking progress in solar energy and a more decentralized social structure. At present, solar energy is only an intermediate technology not suitable for the large-scale demands of industrial societies. The use of solar energy would necessitate the reorganization of social institutions so that energy is not wasted and the kind of communal cooperation that existed in frontier society. Is this a utopian and visionary ideal that can never be realized, or does it represent the direction societies must take as we enter an era of scarcity with ever increasing populations? The use of alternative sources of energy such as solar, hydroelectric, and geothermal systems seems to depend on changes in other spheres of the social order to be completely viable. Population growth must be slowed. Consumer patterns must drastically change so that expanding economic growth is not seen as a necessity. New directions in the use of leisure time must be forged, and productive activities found for those dependent on energy-intensive industries. Conservation and self-reliance must become a way of life, while cooperative societies assure that the basic needs of all humans are met. Public transportation systems must replace the extensive use of the private automobile. Most importantly, government must change to prevent new forms of inequity from emerging, and when economic surpluses decrease, war, revolution, and enslavement must be avoided.

Who Will Make the Decisions?

In the eyes of its participants, the antinuclear movement functions in the public interest. Social action is justified in the name of the people. Although public opposition to nuclear power does not appear to include a majority of the American or Western European populace, activists persist in identifying the interests of the nuclear industry, oil corporations, and government agencies as private interests. Antinuclear groups do not desire state control of energy production if that means that private interests prevail in decision-making. The role of large energy corporations in formulating energy policy must be minimized, while the public role should be expanded. Citizen participation has already brought an end to secrecy in matters concerning nuclear power development, and the inability of political elites to develop a policy assuring a continued supply of safe energy has helped the antinuclear movement to prepare the way for creative adaptation to a precarious situation.

The antinuclear movement should be evaluated in terms of the crucial options that it has introduced for the survival of societies. The energy crisis created a generalized societal crisis that demanded new values to guide political action; that is, to give direction to energy policy, to order our priorities, and to bring public participation and support for new alternatives.

Government policy on energy was characterized by a bureaucratic commitment to nuclear power. The antinuclear movement must be given credit for pressuring the government to consider the viability of a nonnuclear future through greater use of coal, solar energy, geothermal energy, synthetic fuels, and through conservation. These alternative energy technologies also mean the diffusion of social control and the decentralization of energy production. Nuclear power and the complex nuclear fuel are a technology demanding centralization of productive and political functions. The dangerous implications of large-scale use of nuclear power place a greater responsibility on the state for providing both the military and operational security for nuclear power plants. Centralization of state control over the nuclear fuel cycle is also necessary to assure the safety of citizens from the dangers of radioactive wastes, nuclear accidents, and safeguards problems. Will this lead to the abuse of government power and the deprivation of civil liberties for citizens? Consider these comments by antinuclear activists on the proposed final environmental statement on the liquid metal fast breeder reactor:

Intolerance of minorities, pervasive domestic intelligence, centralization, technological priesthoods, human engineering, specialization, inequity, epidemic paranoia, and dilemmas already stressing the institutions of a disoriented society: nuclear technology will affect these dilemmas, and if effects compound the stressed to some ultimate threshold, then the apocalyptic means of resolution will bear no resemblance to the arid bureaucratic cant that appears in the draft statement.

Sabotage is a terrifying prospect where we may be creating a quasi-military private army system under government directives, which may be impossible to totally monitor.[8]

Government must be involved actively in coordinating efforts to implement diverse sources of energy and in funding the necessary scientific and technological research. Capital expenditures are so great that social resources must be distributed to meet these efforts. However, if citizens are not involved in this decision–making process, by default they may contribute to the creation of a leviathan state that has enormously increased power over its populace.

Nuclear technology is proof that science does not produce perfect systems, but public confidence in scientific authority remains high. Thorstein Veblen, a maverick theorist in the development of American sociology, once observed that scientists now have the ultimate answers to questions that once had their grounds of finality with other types of social authority.[9] When scientists break from the cryptic barriers of rationalization and become prophets or social activists, they open themselves up to criticism that they have gone beyond their areas of competence. For example, Talcott Parsons writes that

professional authority, like other elements of the professional pattern, is characterized by "specificity of function." The technical competence which is one of the principal defining characteristics of the professional status and role is always limited to a particular "field" of knowledge and skill.[10]

Thus, charges of irresponsibility often face scientists who are social activists. In one instance, Richard Wilson, a professor of physics at Harvard University, wrote to Representative Hosmer of the Joint Committee on Atomic Energy and asserted that Linus Pauling had exaggerated the cancer hazard associated with nuclear power—"scared the living daylights out of people"—and that this same exaggeration "is now plaguing the peaceful application of nuclear energy."[11]

In the public view, a Nobel laureate who warns of the danger of nuclear power has a great deal of credibility. Within the sciences, an unknown technician may have greater knowledge and experience with nuclear power than the Nobel laureate. It is true that some antinuclear scientists make judgments outside of their technical sphere of competence. Nuclear engineers, on the other hand, are usually more likely to be pronuclear, and they have competence over specific aspects of nuclear technology. The engineer, however, may have a narrow perspective that goes along with his narrow speciality, and he is often not free to adopt a critical role without jeopardizing his career. Scientist activists may sometimes be regarded by their peers as misrepresenting scientific authority for other social rewards, but these activists are free from many of the social constraints placed on scientific elites. Nor could we deny the fact that scientists, by virtue of their education, are likely to be highly informed on issues and thus have difficulty in segregating their roles as citizen and scientist. None of these criticisms, however, would seem to apply to groups such as the Union of Concerned Scientists, who combined political activism with exceptional technical criticisms of nuclear power. Nuclear engineers may have an intrinsic interest in the status quo. As Amory Lovins points out, nuclear power is "a highly bureaucratized high technology that must be permanently run by a self-perpetuating (and probably paramilitary) technical elite, likely to be remote from their clientele."[12]

On What Basis Will Decisions Be Made?

Will the economics of nuclear power eventually decide its future? Capital investment in nuclear power plants is already astronomical, and it requires heavy government subsidies. The government and the nuclear industry would have to amortize billions of dollars worth of debts if the nuclear power program came to a complete halt. The nuclear industry already faces a crisis because it prepared for a market that does not now seem to exist. However, the market has not disappeared, and one reason is the interest of developing nations in the technology.

Energy shortages are particularly acute in the Third World. These nations invest considerable proportions of their gross national income in oil exports. As Dennis Goulet observes, in many of these nations intermediate energy technologies would be more useful in helping to alleviate unemployment and poverty, but investments are being made into nuclear technology for the military and political status that it may give them.[13] Third World nations lack the technical infrastructure to adapt to nuclear power and must rely on the developed nations. Global cooperation must involve consideration of the needs of nations for which a major investment in nuclear power is not wise or necessary.

Although some labor unions oppose nuclear power, most are supportive, including the United Auto Workers, the United Steel Workers, and the International Brotherhood of Electric Workers. The nuclear industry has argued that over 200,000 jobs will be lost if the current pattern of nuclear power plant construction continues. While nuclear power plants have encountered significant opposition in local communities, many welcome the jobs, the increased property tax base, and the general contribution of the nuclear power plant to community interests.

Thus, any decision involving the future of nuclear power must take into account the needs of the developing nations and the effect that it will have on local communities and labor. Opponents of nuclear power also assert that the future of light water reactors cannot be considered independently of fast breeder reactors and the recycling of plutonium, as the government has done. The Reagan administration will have the responsibility deciding whether or not to continue with development of the fast breeder reactor, for if the nuclear option is going to be viable it must be tied to recognition that at least some nations are committed to the breeder as a way of assuring that they will not be victims of a depletion of uranium reserves. Similarily, if radioactive wastes continue to accumulate at the site of nuclear power plants, steps should be taken to begin providing for their permanent disposal underground. Finally, if the United States is going to participate with other nations in agreements to control nuclear power, decisions must be made as to whether or not this will include making American nuclear fuels reprocessing plants available to these nations. The trend in the 1980s and 1990s is toward an international fuel cycle, which may provide governments with a basis of cooperation in political spheres other than that involving nuclear power.

If the United States does abandon nuclear power, then the problem is still with us. Radioactive wastes are produced in the manufacture of nuclear weapons, and, more importantly, Pandora's box has been opened, for no one nation has a monopoly over nuclear energy anymore. We must resist a Manichean world view, in which nuclear energy is inherently evil, while solar and alternative sources are inherently good. Solar energy, hydroelectric power, and geothermal energy may not be the panacea to energy problems. Neither may conservation. As Gerald Garvey of Princeton University writes, "despite exhortations to conserve energy, the logic of modern American history points in the opposite direction—that is the dominating fact of energy planning today."[14]

As religious leaders and organizations have shown us, nuclear energy is a moral dilemma that individuals must confront. The ultimate moral question raised by the antinuclear movement is whether or not succeeding generations should be saddled with the problems created by the present generation. Radioactive wastes remain lethal for centuries and might afflict people in nations without nuclear power plants. Bequeathing a future generation with the technological means of total destruction is hardly a positive contribution from the moral perspective. The Right Reverend Mortimer, bishop of Exeter, observes that

new scientific discoveries and advances increase human power and, therefore, moral responsibility. . . . The ability to employ nuclear energy is an immense advance in human power to control and adapt man's environment and an immense increase, therefore, in human responsibility.[15]

On the other hand, excessive moralism can retard the progress of society. Moral absolutism threatens the existence of a social system because the society is compared to its own standards, which are never perfectly fulfilled. The Italian political theorist Gaetano Mosca once argued that the individual of average morality was better adapted for the struggle for existence than the morally deficient or the individual with an unusually delicate moral sense.[16] We must at least give the succeeding generation the means to control nuclear energy if not abandon it altogether.

In the final analysis, it is up to individuals to decide our energy future and to take social responsibility for that future through actions as mundane as installing wood–burning heaters or solar panels or walking instead of driving whenever possible. Political action might take the form of a letter to one's congressman or the president of the United States, or it might involve chaining oneself to the gate of a nuclear power plant. Expressing an opinion is better than allowing someone else to make the decisions by default. This is the responsibility of being a member of society. As the eminent historian and social philosopher, Barrington Moore, Jr., writes:

If human society is noxious for anybody, why then does it exist? The obvious and banal answer is that by means of the division of labor, possible only in and through society, human beings enormously enhance their capacity to adapt to and control their environment. And even if it is obvious and banal, it is true. Without the invention of human society, *Homo sapiens* might well have become extinct long, long ago.[17]

Notes and References

1. Leslie White, "Energy and the Evolution of Culture," *American Anthropologist* 45 (1943): 338.
2. Ibid., p. 251.
3. Pitirim A. Sorokin, *Contemporary Sociological Theories* (New York: Harper & Row, 1928).
4. Ibid., pp. 23–25.
5. Alvin M. Weinberg, "Is Nuclear Energy Necessary?" *Bulletin of the Atomic Scientists* 36, no. 3 (March 1980); 31–35.
6. Ibid., p. 33.
7. Amory B. Lovins, L. Hunter Lovins, and Leonard Ross, "Nuclear Power and Nuclear Bombs," *Foreign Affairs* 58, no. 5 (Summer 1980): 1137–77.
8. Energy Research and Development Administration (Department of Energy), *Proposed Final Environmental Impact Statement on the Liquid Metal Fast Breeder Reactor*, vol. 5 (Washington D.C.: U.S. Government Printing Office, 1974). pp. 3–4.
9. Thorstein Veblen, *The Place of Science* (New York: Russell & Russell, 1961).
10. Talcott Parsons, *Essays in Sociological Theory* (New York: Free Press, 1949), p. 38.
11. Richard Wilson, letter in *Proposed Final Environmental Impact Statement on the Liquid Metal Fast Breeder Reactor*.
12. Amory B. Lovins and John H. Price, *Non-Nuclear Futures* (New York: Harper Colophon, 1975), 6.
13. Dennis Goulet, "The Paradox of Technology Transfer," *Bulletin of the Atomic Scientists* 31 (June 1975): 39–46.
14. Gerald Garvey, "The Potential of Energy Remodeling," in *The Northeastern States Confront the Energy Crisis*, ed. Jay Rolison (Washington D.C.: National Science Foundation, 1975), p. 195. Also see Gerald Garvey, *Nuclear Power and Social Planning: The City of the Second Sun* (Lexington, Mass.: Lexington Books, 1977).

15. The Right Reverend Mortimer, bishop of Exeter, "The Moral Aspects," in *Economic and Social Consequences of Nuclear Energy,* ed. Lord Sherfield (London: Oxford University Press, 1972), 69.

16. Gaetano Mosca, *The Ruling Class* (New York: McGraw-Hill, 1939), pp. 121–22.

17. Barrington Moore, Jr., *Injustice: The Social Bases of Obedience and Revolt* (White Plains, N.Y.: M. E. Sharpe, 1978), 8.

APPENDIX A

The Antinuclear Movement and Sociological Theory

Whom are we to believe in the controversy over nuclear power? While most of the public is willing to trust the trained judgment of scientists, there is notable disagreement in the scientific community as to whether or not nuclear power is a safe technology. The political system is not structured to ensure that the views of scientists are not distorted for political ends, either by supporters or by opponents of nuclear energy.

Despite a burgeoning literature on the subject of energy, only a few social scientists have studied the citizen action groups concerned with nuclear issues. In the late 1960s, scientists and citizens opposed the construction of a nuclear power station on the shore of Lake Cayuga in New York State. Dorothy Nelkin documented the conflict between those who recognized a need for growth in the electric power industry and those who opposed construction of the plant out of belief that it would damage the ecology of Lake Cayuga.[1] Nelkin's case study demonstrated the difficulty of attaining consensus in a local controversy when disagreement existed among scientists as to the extent of ecological harm that might ensue from operation of a nuclear power plant. The study was prophetic in that the role of the scientific community in the public controversy over nuclear energy is as critical now as it was in the late 1960s.

The role of experts and the use of scientific and technical information in nuclear power plant licensing hearings before the now defunct Atomic

153

Energy Commission was the focus of analysis of two political scientists. During their months as participant observers in hearings in Michigan and Vermont, Steven Ebbin and Raphael Kasper examined the roles of the conflicting parties in these hearings, concluding that licensing the process

is neither fair nor expeditious nor democratic in any substantive or meaningful way. It is marked by manipulation of scientific information by all parties in order to substantiate their predetermined points of view. It is a system evidently designed for lawyers for the consideration of legal issues and as such does not resolve important issues of science and technology and human and physical ecology which are likely to accompany the construction and operation of nuclear power plants.[2]

Distortion of fact is commonplace among politicians. Consider the statement of the presidential nominee of the Republican party in his 1980 acceptance speech on the subject of nuclear energy: "It must not be thwarted by a tiny minority opposed to economic growth which often finds friendly ears in regulatory agencies for its obstructionist campaigns."[3] What are the underlying assumptions in such statements? Are antinuclear activists opposed to economic growth or to nuclear power (or both?) Are they obstructionist or do they present viable alternatives to energy policy? Are they a tiny minority or are their views actually representative of a substantial part of the electorate? Political statements will often raise more questions than they answer and take us away from a factual consideration of the issues.

Social scientists have the role of presenting balanced and objective analyses of political and social problems in order that those who have the responsibility for making decisions will be better informed on the issues. In a democracy, it is important that the public, and in particular the voting public, be as informed as those elected to public office.

By understanding the antinuclear movement as a social movement, the entire panoply of issues raised by opponents to nuclear power should be more clear. The case studies by Nelkin and Ebbin and Kasper of controversies in the Northeast over nuclear power were written before the energy crisis of the early 1970s enabled the antinuclear groups and organizations to coalesce into a movement.

Social movements are collective attempts by groups and organizations to change an aspect of society or the state. They are among the more difficult phenomena to explain by social scientists, for movements have complex organizational structures and often complex ideologies or justifications of the changes the movement seeks. In the discipline of sociology, there are many competing theoretical explanations of why movements emerge.

Resource Mobilization and Social Action Theory

A recent theoretical perspective in sociology is known as the resource mobilization school.[4] This school of thought is concerned with what makes a social movement succeed or fail. The main thesis of these theorists is that organizations in a social movement must gain access to external resources in society such as mass media publicity, economic sponsorship of their activities, or legitimation of their symbolic worth in order to succeed. Most social movements are not loosely structured associations of discontented individuals, as was once assumed, but are comprised of organizations that do many of the same things that all organizations do in order to survive. The main difference is that social movement organizations frequently choose dramatic and unconventional means of gaining attention to their cause.

Although social movement organizations always seek to maximize their use of resources available in society, they may also have varying levels of internal resources. Some movements may have leaders that give extraordinary strength to them, as did Martin Luther King, Jr. to the civil rights movement. One of the internal resources of the antinuclear movement that gives it strength is the cadre of scientists who have devoted a substantial part of their personal and professional lives to the movement.

The resource mobilization perspective enables the researcher to specify the conditions that lead to the successful organization of a social movement. The strategy and tactics used by movement groups as they attempt to gain power in the political arena are in large part determined by the need to coordinate and unify the various groups that are in the movement, and also are affected by the reaction of those in positions of formal authority to the movement.

A more general approach to the antinuclear movement is through social action theory.[5] The basic tenet of action theory is that behavior is purposive and motivated and that it is guided by symbolic processes.[6] From this perspective we examine the orientations of groups or collectivities as they interact with the external world. The resource mobilization school correctly points to the need to discover the mode of support that a movement is able to obtain, but social action theory focuses on the values and beliefs that bind members of a social movement group together as an entity.

The first sociologist to apply social action theory to the study of social movements was Rudolph Heberle.[7] This work emphasized that although movements have organizations within them, they are not the conventional organizations with roles that are independent of individuals and social relationships that are merely functional. Heberle observed that social movements require a similarity of sentiments and a sense of group solidarity and identity among members. Social movements have "constitutive values," or ideas and beliefs that form the spiritual–intellectual foundation of group cohesion and solidarity.[8] As we saw in chapter 1, the ideology of the movement includes its goals as well as alternative conceptualizations of the direction social change might take. The ideology of the movement includes core beliefs and values that unite diverse antinuclear groups.

These values and beliefs of a movement define the general direction that collective action will take. In a large nation such as the United States it is difficult to understand how a movement could really occur. When antinuclear activists are arrested during a demonstration outside a nuclear power plant in Seabrook, New Hampshire, what impact will this have on movement groups in California or Tennessee? Since *events* are the substance of movements, the actions of a group in one part of the nation become significant to groups in another part. The need to identify with other activists and to have a sense of solidarity with them is characteristic of people in social movements. If the core values of the movement have diffused sufficiently throughout the country, then the movement is more integrated despite geographical separation.

Antinuclear groups and organizations are extremely diverse, ranging from the voluntary associations in local communities, such as the Women's Club in Linwood, New Jersey, to Friends of the Earth in California. There must be constitutive values that have symbolic importance in integrating and maintaining cohesion within the movement.

Social movements are often a means through which a society makes a transition from traditional modes of organization to a new social order. The version of social action theory propounded by Neil Smelser suggests that persons who are attracted to social movements have been dislodged from traditional social ties but are not yet integrated into a new social order.[9] These people feel psychological strain and are susceptible to the appeals of the social movement. Social movements give them an opportunity to define new social norms and values. The energy crisis contributed to basic alterations of American social structure. How do people cope with fundamental changes in their economic situation? One way is to redefine individual goals and to change collective social values. A simple act such as walking may take on new significance in everyday life, and people who purchase large automobiles may find themselves to be the object of social criticism rather than envy. Instead of feeling that it is important to vacation in Hawaii, the national park a few hundred miles away looks more appealing. Conservation if resources at both the individual and societal level becomes a more desired state of affairs.

Individual Motivations to Participate

The argument that social movements appeal to people who are experiencing psychological strain and individual discontent has always been one of the more controversial themes in social science. For example, a recent study of the Boston antibusing movement found that social cohesion increased protest against busing among Boston residents, but that discontented individuals were more likely to protest than others.[10] These contradictory findings in one study are characteristic of the uncertainty in social science as to why certain individuals will be motivated to participate in social protest or in a social movement.

When an individual joins a movement, his motivation may be intentionally concealed or even unknown to him. Rather than argue vaguely that individuals who are frustrated or under stress are the ones who join, Heberle simply constructs four types of motivation out of the complexity of individual motives.[11] These are based on the typology of orientations to social action developed by the classical social theorist Max Weber. The *emotional–affectual* orientation emerges when an individual has experiences that arouse his or her emotions against the persons or conditions that the movement attacks, or when he or she has affection for the leaders and followers of the movement. The *value–rational* orientation holds the goal of the movement to be desirable: the success of the movement is desirable for the sake of the cause that it advocates. In the *purposive–rational* orientation, the individual has expectations of personal advantage, and in the *traditional* orientation, the status characteristics of the individual (such as social class or ethnicity) give the motivation for participation in the movement.

Groups in social movements involve the individual in a more intensive way than do formal organizations. If the movement is a rebellion against social conditions, then individuals who break from established cultural traditions are often more prone to alienation and anomy, although new support groups develop to lessen the negative effects of their deviance. At one extreme, the individual's identity becomes almost totally dependent on the social movement group.

The emergence of a common set of values that sets participants in a social movement apart from the mainstream of social life is, perhaps, a necessary condition of movement formation. Although the individual's motives for "conversion" to the movement may be too complex to determine accurately, the basis of collective social action are the values and orientations of groups in the movement.

There is a strong tendency to impute motivations to social activists. This is often done by opponents of the movement who wish to discredit the leaders by questioning their moral character. Such a Machiavellian perspective is characteristic of the historical sociology tradition exemplified by the late Hans Gerth and C. Wright Mills.[12] Although they were social action theorists (and Mills a radical activist), these sociologists looked for "inner" motivations of historical figures that varied from their publicly revealed motives. Motivations, they argued, are to be found in the psychic structure of individuals as social action is ultimately subjective in nature. Thus, they did not accept the idea that common value orientations are necessary for the formation of a movement, asserting instead that individuals have various motivations that may converge or coincide with the movement's direction.[13]

The fact that there may be as many motives to join a movement as individuals who actually join suggests that the stated ideology of activists is not necessarily the reason for their participation in the movement. Ideology supplies the beliefs that integrate events and goals of movement activists into comprehensive explanatory schemes that can help to mobilize groups into collective action.[14] Possibly, people do have distinct motivations for participating at various stages in the life span of a social movement. For example, Heberle suggests that at the beginning, the movement attracts men and women who are devoted to the goals of the movement and who are often original and idealistic thinkers.[15] As the movement gains power, ambitious and careerist individuals join, at which point the moral and intellectual caliber of the movement may begin to deteriorate. The ideology of the movement will also be affected by the political experiences of a generation. The general conditions of life in an historical period such as war or peace, prosperity or depression, will have a particular impact on movement activists.

Sequential Stages in Social Movements

The idea that social movements go through stages is one of the main characteristics of theories and models of movements. For example, movements may have *careers* that pass through stages such as social unrest, popular excitement, formalization, and institutionalization.[16] During the stage of social unrest agitators emerge who then begin to develop an esprit de corps and a supportive morale. It is at this point that an ideology forms and strategy and tactics of the movement take shape. The agitation phase has the function of dislodging people from traditional ways of life, liberating them for movement in new directions. Leaders have different roles during the course of the movement. The role of agitator is usually associated with the stage of social unrest and that of the prophet with popular excitement. When the movement becomes more organized and formal, leaders must become statesmen. At the final stage, social movement organizations may become institutionalized, and their leaders are then administrators of the organization. The history of the NAACP, for example, supports this notion.

Another widely accepted model of the stages of social movements sets forth six determinants that explain the development of social movements.[17] These determinants proceed in sequence. The first stage is that of structural conduciveness. For instance, one of the reasons the antinuclear movement emerged was the failure of the political elite to formulate a comprehensive energy plan. Beginning with the administration of President Richard Nixon, the need to do something about the energy crisis and the high cost of oil made nuclear energy appear to be the most feasible alternative. There were also a number of environmental voluntary associations with access to government channels of communication. Thus, these groups were well aware of some of the risks of nuclear energy that were not known to the public.

There is a vagueness and generality to the concept of structural conduciveness, for innumerable conditions could be specified that created situations conducive to the emergence of the antinuclear movement. The second state is that of structural strain. There must be some sort of disturbance in the social system that contributes to psychological strain on the part of affected people. The energy crisis contributed to severe economic hardship for large numbers of Americans, although these people were not necessarily the ones who became antinuclear activists. However, groups with members who held ecological values did perceive other forms of energy technology, such as solar energy, to be less threatening and dangerous than nuclear power. We could, therefore, say that conditions of structural strain existed.

The next stage is the growth and spread of a generalized belief. This is the most critical stage if the social movement is to develop. The concept of generalized belief pertains to social psychology. At the common sense level, we could simply say that activist groups came to believe that nuclear power was not safe as a form of energy and that it produced harmful radioactive byproducts, while solar energy was a safe, plentiful, and clean form of energy. These beliefs, however, involve the totality of the wishes and desires of individuals and their perception of relevant situations that make them redefine the direction of their activities. The content of generalized beliefs assume that there are extraordinary, threatening, and conspiratorial forces at work in the universe. In this sense, there is a psychological element involved in generalized beliefs. It is true that some antinuclear activists believe that plutonium is the ultimate evil creation of man or that nuclear power plants will explode like nuclear bombs or that people who live next to a nuclear power plant will probably die of cancer. On the other hand, many antinuclear groups, such as the Union of Concerned Scientists, have high levels of knowledge and information about nuclear technology and radiation, and their opposition is based on that knowledge as well as their social values.

Precipitating factors follow the spread of a generalized belief. Events such as the nuclear accident at Three Mile Island in Pennsylvania or the fire at the Brown's Ferry nuclear power plant in Alabama crystallize beliefs into action. The movement is now under way as precipitating events lead to the mobilization of participants for action. Groups form, leaders emerge, coalitions and mergers of organizations take place, demonstrations or other forms of tactical action occur. It is at this stage that the mobilization of external resources—finances, mass media attention, defection of members of the opposition, public support—becomes critically important to the movement. The final stage is the operation of social control. As dissent magnifies, those in positions of formal political authority must act. The National Guard may be called out to arrest demonstrators, concessions will usually be made, government agencies may be reorganized, and leaders of the movement may themselves become more moderate. Dissent between moderates and radicals may splinter and weaken the movement, or drastic tactics, particularly if they are violent, may turn away public support from the movement.

The core assumption of this six–stage theory of collective behavior is, however, the idea that conditions of social strain create ambiguous and difficult situations for individuals. Generalized beliefs restructure and redefine these ambiguous situations through a psychological process that provides simple answers to a complex situation—a type of short–circuiting process that reduces the stress of ambiguity.

Generalized beliefs help maintain group solidarity for those in the movement. If the "enemy" is regarded as diabolically powerful and threatening to movement activists, the sense of persecution and apprehension will bring solidarity to the movement.[18] The belief that the nuclear industry is engaged in conspiracies may give its representatives the face of a superhuman enemy against which drastic measures must be taken. Some observers claim that Manichaeism, a view of the world in terms of saints and sinners or good and evil, gives members of a movement a sense of elite status.[19] This is particularly the case when members feel that organization becomes a social constraint that is contrary to the spirit of change. Social movement organizations have a management function, for their members must identify with the movement or they will leave. Unlike conventional organizations, members are not dependent on the movement for an economic livelihood and are free to leave with no adverse consequences. There are of course exceptions, as many leaders are professional social movement entrepreneurs,[20] and in some cults desertion may even bring death, as in the case of the people who lived in Jonestown.

Psychologists have also developed theories stressing the idea that individuals have a frame of reference, or a generalized point of view, that determines their specific attitudes and psychological motivations.[21] A frame of reference is learned as a normal part of the socialization or learning process and defines the meaning an individual will give to his or her life. When the individual is presented with a chaotic external environment that is difficult to interpret, he or she becomes highly sug-. gestible. Leaders of social movements are able to exploit slogans and symbols to stimulate individuals to perceive their experiences in a new way without being critical. Thus, the psychology of suggestibility explains why people join a movement.

In a similar vein, some argue that social movements draw people from the ranks of those who have personal problems and are therefore predisposed to the movement.[22] Susceptibility to the appeals made by the social movement increases if such a person believes that he or she must take action to solve the problems. Personal resentments may be exploited by movement leaders.

People may turn to illusory solutions to their personal problems in dead-end situations, becoming paranoid or perhaps searching for a sense of community. Eric Hoffer notes that a "full-blown mass movement is a ruthless affair, and its management gives an appearance of spontaneity to consent obtained by coercion."[23] In other words, the movement may exploit the individual, by indoctrinating someone who is in a dependency situation.

When an individual undergoes conversion to a movement, the process of "seeing the light," he or she usually has had a precipitating experience.[24] The convert is a disillusioned person whose conversion is the result of a discrepancy between his or her conventional beliefs and psychological realities. This theory is anathema to informed political activists, for they do not wish to believe that their activities are the result of a distorted view of social reality or of frustrated personal needs. In addition, psychological theories are generally held in some disrepute by sociologists, who are more interested in external social events or conditions that produce an activist response.

The motivation of individual members to join a social movement is also important to the organizational structure of the movement. All groups and organizations must have some division of labor, even if it emerges spontaneously with tacit agreement among members on what their role is in the group. Some of the major problems are the nature of the relationship between leaders and followers, the interrelationship between different movement organizations, and the relationship of the movement to political parties.

The Social Organization of Movements

Inevitably, a status hierarchy will develop in a movement organization, usually in the nucleus of the group and among the core members. As rules and regulations develop and leadership roles become more formal, the organization increasingly devotes time to maintaining itself rather than acting on the goals of the movement.[25] As an aspect of this transformation of the organization, one can distinguish between centripetal forces, through which groups begin to coalesce while keeping their local autonomy, and centrifugal transformations, in which a small group gathers around a charismatic leader and then other groups spin off as the movement expands.

Social competition for leadership is endemic to social movements, and this often creates diversion from unified action. Charismatic leaders may be a source of membership gratification and identification, but eventually more bureaucratically oriented leaders begin to dominate the organization. The resource mobilization school in particular emphasizes the organized nature of social movements. However, movements vary greatly as to the degree of organization or centralization. Herbert Blumer distinguishes three different types of movements.[26] In the general social movement, the collective efforts to change aspects of society are uncoordinated, episodic, formless in organization, and often inarticulate. This type of social movement is merely an aggregation of individual activities. On the other hand, specific social movements have a definite organization and structure. Finally, the expressive social movement does not seek changes in institutions but has profound effects on the persons involved. We could think of the labor and peace movements as general social movements, from which more specific movements emerge. The antinuclear movement would be a specific social movement in this typology. Hippies, on the other hand, were part of an expressive social movement that sought changes in the life–styles of individuals rather than specific changes in societal institutions. To some extent, the antinuclear movement would also be an expressive movement, for many groups desire not only the abandonment of the nuclear power program but an entire new way of life based on alternative social values.

The leadership of the antinuclear movement is diffused throughout the movement in a kind of "acephalous" (headless) leadership structure. To some extent Ralph Nader is recognized as a charismatic leader, and the Nader organizations have taken the "lead" role in many phases of the movement. But generally the antinuclear movement has involved so many diverse groups and organizations that it is almost impossible to ascertain which groups are the most important.

Strategy and tactics are the core activity of social movement organizations. A study of the strategy and tactics of antinuclear groups, primarily in New England, found that the main problem perceived by antinuclear groups was how to win publicity for their cause.[27] This need resulted in the decision of some groups to maintain a single-issue orientation rather than broaden the focus to an attack on capitalism or to include other issues such as disarmament or gay rights as part of the strategy of the movement. For much the same reason, civil disobedience and nonviolent action had to be carefully defined by activists in their protest against the Seabrook, New Hampshire, nuclear power plant and other nuclear installations.

Tactical action is extremely important to a movement in forming its public image and identity. Since movements turn to noninstitutionalized means of advocating a cause, the tactics chosen can very easily determine success or failure. Initially antinuclear activities were restricted to intervention in nuclear power plant licensing hearings, but as the movement grew and more diverse groups became involved, tactics began to change. Tactics will diffuse throughout the movement if they are successful, but they must advance the goals of the movement without causing splits.[28] Therefore they must be flexible and innovative. In some cases, however, the tactics of the movement may be more important than the goal, as is often the case with boycotts and strikes in the labor movement. At other times, the tactics serve the expressive needs of group members.

The interrelationship between movement organizations is a problem that is especially important to the antinuclear movement. The coordination of activities among diverse groups is rare at the national level. Only a few demonstrations in Washington, D.C., pulled together the wide range of groups involved. One of the more interesting characteristics of the antinuclear movement is that it is an amalgamation of several social movements, including the environmentalist movement and segments of the labor, peace, women's, and gay rights movements. In addition, many of the groups that were established during the decade of activism of the 1960s found new life in the antinuclear movement. Many counterculture figures became involved, and well-known music groups such as Peter, Paul, and Mary devoted their talents to the new cause. There has not been, however, any noticeable competition among these movement groups for leadership of the antinuclear movement. There has been, in the last several years, a substantial countermovement inspired by corporate elites and their political friends to block the efforts of antinuclear activists.[29]

Of specific interest to an analysis of the antinuclear movement is its relationship to the major political parties, particularly to the Democratic party. As Heberle observes, "In order to enter into political action, social movements must, in the modern state, either organize themselves as a political party, or enter into a close relationship with political parties."[30] There has not been a close affiliation of the antinuclear movement with the Democratic party, but many of the goals of the movement were "coopted" by the Democrats for their own political advantage. The Carter administration, however, was extremely ambiguous in terms of actual support for antinuclear goals.

Social movements are so much a part of the American political system that they have become institutionalized much in the same way that interest groups have. In one sense, social movements are a part of the normal functioning of the social system, revitalizing social structures and introducing (or resisting) innovative changes. Social movements are more often than not the bearers of significant social change, and this role determines their function in a modern society. When we consider the consequences of the antinuclear movement, we should be aware that movements have recognizable functions within a political system.

Research Difficulties

Social action theory helps one analyze social movements by providing a means of classifying groups that are part of the antinuclear network. Other insights into the movement derived from social action theory have to do with the *dilemmas of orientation* that activists may experience. Individuals in a social movement have an ambiguous status and often experience this conflict subjectively as a dilemma between the self and the collectivity. Activists have different statuses within and outside of the movement. Their status may have a broad or diffuse significance to them. Opposition to nuclear power could result in alienation from technological systems in general and perhaps even from the entire political system as the conflict with political authorities grows sharper. On the other hand, the significance attached to activists' status in the movement may be quite specific. For instance, if the main criticism of nuclear power plants is that radioactive wastes are produced, a satisfactory solution to this problem could soften their opposition to nuclear power. There is much variation in the intensity of participation over time in a social movement. Events can drastically change the public image of activists, while the government may choose to intervene by suppressing the movement.

Both social action theory and the resource mobilization perspective on social movements facilitate a better understanding of what occurs when groups seek change through collective action. However, it is almost impossible to distinguish collective episodes from a large number of events and even more difficult to assess modes of communication and psychological interaction among members of a movement.[31] Newspapers and social movement literature become primary sources for our knowledge of the sequence of important events, while their relative significance to the movement must be largely left to the analytical abilities of the observer.

The structure of events pertinent to the antinuclear movement can be found in the movement literature as well as in major newspapers such as the *New York Times* over a specified time period.[32] This longitudinal method is much more useful than a cross-sectional analysis of movement groups at a particular point of development. Do the groups change over time by getting larger, do they merge into coalitions, or do they gain publicity and then drop from the public arena? Answers to these questions can only be incomplete due to selective inattention on the part of the mass media, but if certain groups continually appear in newspaper items and have the resources to continue producing their own literature, they may be identified as important organizations in the movement.

A more difficult methodological problem is finding a way to show how social conditions are related to social movements at individual and collective levels. Much of the classical sociological literature revolves around questions of how social or economic deprivation and frustration are directly related to individual participation in movements. We must keep in mind that the social movement becomes a part of the conditions of life for participants, who subjectively experience the significant events in the history of the movement. The beliefs of participants become in part a new definition of their social conditions, and in some instances they may not be related to the original life situation at all.

The problem of the origin of the antinuclear movement is somewhat distinct from the problem of how antinuclear groups and organizations survived and developed as a movement. The resource mobilization school gives us excellent clues on how to analyze the organizational growth and decline in the movement.[33] Resources such as power, labor, publicity, and finances are all a generalized medium that the pronuclear and antinuclear groups use to struggle with the issue.[34]

The problem of how social conditions relate to individual participation in a movement is identical to the problem of analyzing the psychological motivations that propel individuals into collective action. Perhaps the resolution of this problem lies in the orientations, values, and belief, held by *groups* rather than essentially idiosyncratic individual motives. But social conditions should not be ignored. The general political and economic conditions during the life span of the movement—the energy crisis of 1973–1974 and the ensuing years of recession and political anxiety—are obviously sources of collective action by antinuclear groups.

Notes and References

1. Dorothy Nelkin, *Nuclear Power and Its Critics* (Ithaca, N.Y.: Cornell University Press, 1971).

2. Steven Ebbin and Raphael Kasper, *Citizens Groups and the Nuclear Power Controversy* (Cambridge: MIT Press, 1974). A more recent case study of the regulatory and hearing process has been made by Donald W. Stever, Jr., *Seabrook and the Nuclear Regulatory Commission* (Hanover, N.H.: University Press of New England, 1980).

3. Ronald Reagan, "The Time is Now . . . to Recapture Our Destiny," *Washington Post* (18 July 1980), p. 10.

4. An excellent introduction to this school of thought can be found in Mayer Zald and John D. McCarthy, eds. *The Dynamics of Social Movements* (Cambridge, Mass.: Winthrop Publishers, 1979).

5. Social action theory originates from the now classical work of Max Weber, *The Theory of Social and Economic Organization,* ed. Talcott Parsons (New York: Oxford University Press, 1947).

6. See Talcott Parsons, Edward A. Shils, and James Olds, "Categories of the Orientation and Organization of Action," in *Toward A General Theory of Action,* ed. Talcott Parsons and Edward A. Shils (Cambridge: Harvard University Press, 1951), pp. 30–79.

7. Rudolph Heberle, *Social Movements* (New York: Appelton, 1951).

8. Ibid., pp. 12–13.

9. Neil Smelser, *Theory of Collective Behavior* (New York: Free Press, 1962).

10. Bert Useem, "Solidarity Model, Breakdown Model, and the Boston Anti-Busing Movement," *American Sociological Review* 45 (June 1980): 357–69.

11. Heberle, *Social Movements,* p. 131.

12. Hans Gerth and C. Wright Mills, *Character and Social Structure* (New York: Harcourt, Brace & World, 1964).

13. Ibid., p. 440.

14. John Wilson, *Introduction to the Study of Social Movements* (New York: Basic Books, 1974), p. 118.

15. Heberle, *Social Movements,* p. 432.

16. Herbert Blumer, "Social Movements," in *New Outline of the Principles of Sociology*, ed. A. M. Lee (New York: Barnes & Noble, 1951), pp. 199–220.

17. Smelser, *Theory of Collective Behavior*, Chapter 1.

18. Wilson, *Introduction to the Study of Social Movements*, pp. 288–89.

19. Ibid., p. 286.

20. See Joseph Helfgot, "Professional Reform Organizations and the Symbolic Representation of the Poor," *American Sociological Review* 39 (August 1974): 475–91.

21. Hadley Cantril, *The Psychology of Social Movements* (New York: Wiley, 1941).

22. Hans Toch, *The Social Psychology of Social Movements* (New York: Bobbs-Merill, 1966).

23. Quoted in Toch, *Social Psychology*, p. 87.

24. Ibid., pp. 117–18.

25. John Wilson, *Introduction to the Study of Social Movements*, p. 338.

26. Herbert Blumer, "Social Movements," pp. 199–220.

27. Steven E. Barkan, "Strategic, Tactical and Organizational Dilemmas of the Protest Movement Against Nuclear Power," *Social Problems* 27 (October 1979): 19–37.

28. John Wilson, *Introduction to the Study of Social Movements*, p. 236.

29. A conceptualization of control movements and countermovements is present in Ralph H. Turner and Lewis M. Killian, *Collective Behavior* (Englewood-Cliffs, N.J.: Prentice-Hall, 1957).

30. Heberle, *Social Movements*, pp. 150–51.

31. Smelser, *Theory of Collective Behavior*.

32. This methodology has been employed by Charles Tilly in his studies of collective action in nineteenth–century Britain and France by reconstructing events of a prerevolutionary nature documented in historical archives. See *From Mobilization to Revolution* (Reading, Mass.: Addison-Wesley Publishing Co., 1978).

33. Mayer Zald and Roberta Ash, "The Transformation of Social Movement Organization," *Social Forces* 44 (1966): 327–41.

34. See part 4 of *Explorations in General Theory in Social Science*, ed. Jan Loubser, Ranier Baum, Andrew Effrat, and Victor Lidz (New York: Free Press, 1976), for an analysis of the concept of generalized media.

APPENDIX B
The Nuclear Fuel Cycle

Robert Dahl, a political scientist, notes the error in assuming that anyone who is not an engineer or physical scientist would be incompetent to research the esoteric subject of nuclear technology. Social scientists are capable of grasping the technical complexities of the physical sciences that pertain to their own research.[1]

One of the outstanding characteristics of the antinuclear movement is that activists have a high level of knowledge of an advanced technological system. One fundamental distinction *must* be kept in mind when analyzing nuclear power. This is the difference between a *fission* and a *fusion* reaction. Uranium is a fissionable material, for when its nucleus absorbs a neutron, it can split or fission into two smaller nuclei and release significant amounts of energy and two or three neutrons. All of the nuclear reactors that are opposed by movement groups operate on the fission principle. In a second process, hydrogen nuclei and deuterium atoms are fused together to produce energy. Fusion reactors remain at the research stage, but they are a potential unlimited energy source. Fusion is the process by which the sun produces energy. Almost by default, the antinuclear movement has precluded nuclear fusion as an alternative energy source. This may well be an unanticipated consequence of the antinuclear movement, in addition to a negative effect on the development of alternative reactors such as thermal converters, which utilize thorium rather than uranium, or high temperature gas–cooled reactors.

The issues and controversies perceived by antinuclear activists revolve around what is known as the nuclear fuel cycle, a generic term given to all the phases of production involved in utilizing nuclear energy as a com-

171

mercial power source. An understanding of the nuclear fuel cycle provides insight into the problem areas of nuclear power that concern antinuclear groups.

Uranium is the basis of fuel for nuclear power plants, but it can be used in its natural state only in a specific type of plant manufactured in Canada. Thus, the mining and milling of uranium ore is the first stage of the nuclear fuel cycle, but to be a fuel for most reactors, uranium oxide must undergo an expensive and complex industrial process of isotopic separation to "enrich" the element so that it may be used in the most common type of nuclear reactor. The third major stage is power plant operation, followed by fuel reprocessing and storage of radioactive wastes. There are many types of nuclear reactors, several alternative methods of uranium enrichment, and many different kinds of radioactive wastes.

The Economic Role of Nuclear Power

Industrialized societies cannot exist without electric power, which is also an important stimulus to the economic growth of underveloped countries. Since per capita income is *roughly* proportionate to per capita gross national product, the predicted exponential growth in energy consumption must take into account the role of nuclear power. However, some antinuclear groups, particularly the Environmentalists for Full Employment, have contested the assumption that a growth economy based on increased energy consumption is really necessary. Nevertheless, the technological foundation of industrial society rests on an abundant supply of energy.[2]

The Energy Policy Project of the Ford Foundation had predicted that by the year 2000 nuclear power would supply 25 percent of energy needs in the United States as natural gas and oil production leveled off. These researchers assumed that although production of coal and alternative forms of energy would increase, the proportionate growth of nuclear power would be even greater, reaching 60 percent of electric power generation. These predictions are unlikely now, but they indicate the relative importance of nuclear power to government and industry.[3]

An increase in the use of nuclear power does not necessarily mean that dependence on foreign oil would be greatly reduced, for oil consumption will still be substantial until at least the year 2000.[4] Electricity generation requires vast amounts of energy, and as the need for electricity increases to offset the use of depleting fossil fuels, more power plants will have to be constructed that will not utilize oil or natural gas. The costs of producing energy are also a major factor in the energy problems of the United States. According to the Energy Policy Project of the Ford Foundation, industrial and transportation sectors will continue to increase consumption of energy, while household and commercial use of energy will rise moderately because the United States has an advanced energy infrastructure.[5] This study, however, probably underestimates the effects of conservation policies.

In the United States, energy and energy-intensive industries account for at least 10 percent of all employees: 3 percent in the energy industries, and 7 percent in energy–intensive manufacturing. A study by the House Committee on Science and Astronautics shows where these employees are located.[6] These employment figures, summarized in Table 6, do not reflect the large number of transportation employees or government and scientific personnel involved in energy research and development.

Energy is also related to inflation. In the year ending January 1974, the wholesale price index rose by 20.8 percent in the United States, with two-thirds of that increase due to food and fuel prices. The mechanization of American agriculture is so intensive that the rise in the cost of food was energy related. Oil is important in the manufacture of fertilizer as well. Fuel costs rose by 74 percent, with the blast furnace and steel industries the most affected, followed by petroleum refining, paper milling, and plastics and synthetics.[7] This inflationary trend has continued into the present decade.

High costs are the rationale given by the nuclear industry for the creation of nuclear parks, such as those once proposed for Pennsylvania and the Delaware Valley. These would be complexes of as many as thirty to forty nuclear power plants and related facilities. Since nuclear power plants have enormous energy conversion losses, locating energy intensive industries such as aluminum smelting and fabrication nearby would allow excess heat to be used for productive purposes and increase the efficiency of nuclear power. The waste heat from just one nuclear power plant could be used in this way. The idea of nuclear parks is a version of the "nuplex" concept once advanced by Oak Ridge National Laboratory.[8] It is representative of the economic potential of nuclear power, but also a symbol of adverse consequences to society from the standpoint of the antinuclear movement.

TABLE 6

EMPLOYEES IN U.S. ENERGY INDUSTRIES

Industry Classification	Number of Employees (1971)	Percent of 1971 Total Employment
Total employment in U.S. energy industries	2,190,000	2.96
Coal mining	138,000	.19
Oil and natural gas	261,000	.35
Pipeline transportation	18,000	.02
Petroleum & coal products	191,000	.26
Electric & gas companies	464,000	.63
Combination companies	190,000	.26
Gasoline service stations	618,000	.84
Petroleum bulk stations	212,000	.28
Fuel and ice dealers	99,000	.13
Total employment in energy intensive manufacturing	4,828,000	7.31
Examples:		
Primary metals	1,178,000	1.60
Stone, clay, and glass	588,000	.80
Food products	1,582,000	2.10
Paper products	635,000	.90
Chemical products	845,000	1.10
TOTAL EMPLOYMENT IN ENERGY AND ENERGY INTENSIVE INDUSTRIES	7,603,000	10.27

Source: Committee on Science and Astronautics, *Energy Facts 1973*, (Washington D.C.: Government Printing Office, 1973), p. 144.

The Nuclear Industry

Nuclear power supplied almost 13 percent of the total electricity generated in the United States by the late 1970s. Currently there are over seventy nuclear power plants authorized to operate within the United States and approximately two hundred reactors operating worldwide in noncommunist countries. Approximately ninety reactors should come on line during the next few decades in the United States. Since 1975, the order of new nuclear power plants has remained at a virtual standstill, although many construction projects are near completion.

The greatest growth in nuclear power has been planned in New England, because transportation of low-sulphur western coal to eastern markets is expensive. Stack gas scrubbers, which reduce air pollution from coal-fired plants, are expensive. In order to meet stringent air quality standards in the Northeast, the cost of coal-fired stations increases by as much as 20 percent. However, the same standards do not exist in the Midwest, and winds carry emissions to the Northeast where they contribute to a serious acid rain problem.

Reliability and economic efficiency of nuclear reactors are important factors in the decision to build them. The environmental director of Chicago's Businessmen and Professional People in the Public Interest, David Comey, is critical of the reliability of nuclear power plants, asserting that they run at a lower capacity than coal-fired plants, and are often out of commission for safety checks or refueling. Comey calculates that if capacity falls below 55 percent, coal-fired plants will be cheaper to operate than nuclear power plants, and that by 1983 nuclear power will be 10 percent more expensive. Coal plants generally run at 60 percent of capacity.[9] Capacity figures for nuclear power plants are based on statistical means. For example, in May 1975 the mean capacity at which plants operated was 57 percent, with Yankee Rowe operating at 97.6 percent and Palisades reactor at 19.7 percent of capacity.[10]

Increasing capital costs lead to most cancellations and delays of nuclear power plants. Construction costs almost quadrupled from 1970 to 1975, although the figures were comparable for coal plants.[11] There is no clear economic advantage of nuclear over coal or vice versa. Some companies have divested themselves of nuclear plants. Consolidated Edison, for example, sold their Indian Point reactor to the state of New York. The recent slump in the nuclear industry has been due to financial obstacles rather than environmentalist considerations in nuclear power plant construction.

The nuclear industry was a government monopoly throughout most of its history. The House Select Committee on Small Business found common ownership of fuel sources to be a trend, particularly in oil company acquisitions of coal properties, uranium, and natural gas supplies. The Committee reported that the major oil corporations account for 84 percent of refining capacity, 72 percent of natural gas production, 30 percent of coal reserves, and 25 percent of uranium milling capacity.[12] The Justice Department contests very few of these mergers.

Exxon, Gulf, Sohio, Continental, and Phillips are among the petroleum companies with significant interests in the nuclear industry. Westinghouse and General Electric are the most important manufacturers of nuclear equipment, but the Thomas Register indicates nuclear reactor components are also manufactured by Atomics International, Rockwell, Kaiser Engineers, and over thirty smaller companies. There is no monolithic nuclear industry, for Westinghouse and General Electric play a minor role in relation to the utilities industry in nuclear power plant construction. Much of American industry would appear to have a direct or indirect interest in the nuclear industry.

The Nuclear Fuel Cycle

Mining and Uranium Reserves.   In the first stage of the nuclear fuel cycle, natural uranium is mined and then milled (crushed) to a concentrate containing about 85 percent uranium oxide. The mills extract uranium from its ore to obtain the "yellowcake."[13] Since uranium ore only contains about 1 percent of uranium, large amounts of wastes accumulate on a tailings pile. These radioactive wastes discharge radon-222 gas into the air, and the presence of thorium-230 makes the tailings radioactive for thousands of years. The Environmental Protection Agency estimates that individuals in the surrounding population receive radioactive exposure to the lungs from these radon releases,[14] and the Union of Concerned Scientists has conducted studies indicating that tailings piles are a hazard to he health of miners.[15] The mines themselves are even more hazardous.

Uranium reserves in the United States are concentrated in the Wyoming Basins, the Colorado Plateau, and the Gulf Plains, with the cheapest recoverable reserves in New Mexico, Wyoming, Texas, Utah, and Colorado. In addition, the United States consumes almost half of world uranium production. Canada, South Africa, Sweden, Spain, France, Gabon, Niger, and Australia all have large reserves.[16]

Projections of reserves depend on many factors, such as the location and depth of the ore, transportation facilities, cost of extraction technology, and percentage of uranium oxide in the ore. Uranium is mined in open pits and through strip mining, which presents an environmental problem. Stockpiles of uranium exist for nuclear weapons programs, and an embargo prohibiting uranium ore imports into the United States has been phased out. It is not known if large-scale exploration will uncover new reserves. The adequacy of reserves has also been controversial. Critics argue that an expansion of nuclear power on the scale proposed by the federal government cannot take place unless large new uranium reserves are discovered.

The issue over the adequacy of reserves is tied into the future of the liquid metal fast breeder reactor, which produces more fuel than it consumes. Proponents of nuclear power believe that with perfection of the fast breeder for commercial use, the problem of fuel supply will disappear. If the breeder reactor is successfully blocked by the antinuclear movement, then the uranium supply for present and future light water reactors may become an acute problem. A scientist critic, M. C. Day, succinctly states one position of antinuclear forces: if projections of uranium supply are based on an unproven technology, then a moratorium or slowdown in the construction of light water reactors is justified until uranium reserves are proven to be adequate.[17] Other critics, of course, reject nuclear power totally on other grounds.

With international use of nuclear power, uranium is becoming even more valuable as a resource. Some researchers have explored the possibility of a uranium exporters cartel, which would make the United States vulnerable to a uranium embargo in the future.[18] Since oil corporations have been expanding horizontally into uranium mining, the potential for monopolistic price fixing by a domestic cartel is more likely. These fears were substantiated in hearings before Congress that documented the existence of a conspiracy between Gulf and Tenneco to raise the price of uranium.

Uranium Conversion and Enrichment. After milling operations, uranium oxide is converted into uranium hexafluoride (UF_6), which can be maintained in a gaseous state. Conversion is followed by enrichment, which is the process of increasing the concentration of fissionable U-235 atoms above what occurs in natural uranium. This is the most complex step and involves diffusion of the gaseous UF_6 through porous barriers so that the lighter U-235 molecules are diluted from the heavier U-238 molecules. There must be continuous diffusion through thousands of barriers, and the UF_6 gas is pumped into the barriers by compressors driven by electric motors that consume vast amounts of electricity. Enrichment plants easily cover ninety acres of land, use about 400 million gallons of recirculating cooling water a day, and consume 1,300 megawatts of electric power.[19] The United States government owns all three gaseous diffusion plants, located at Oak Ridge, Tennessee; Paducah, Kentucky; and Portsmouth, Ohio. Conversion plants are located in Hematite, Missouri; Apollo, Pennsylvania; and Erwin, Tennessee.

Gas centrifugal processes are also available for the isotopic separation necessary for uranium enrichment, but are not as technologically developed as gaseous diffusion separation. Soviet and American scientists working independently discovered a third process involving focusing a laser beam precisely turned to the vibrational frequency characteristic of an isotope to free it from its chemical compound. If applied to the extraction of U-235 from uranium ore, the process would bypass the centrifuge and diffusion methods and make enriched uranium easily available.

The Atomic Industrial Forum, a trade asssociation of the nuclear industry, proposed in 1969 that uranium enrichment facilities be put into the hands of private industry. The proposal was supported by President Nixon and the Atomic Energy Commission but failed to gain support in Congress for fear that it would create a government "enrichment directorate." Legislation to transfer future enrichment facilities to private enterprise was also requested of Congress by President Ford but not pursued by the Carter administration.

The significance of these proposals are for nuclear exports. The federal government restricts the sale of enriched uranium, and with private control the industry would be more competitive with French and German firms on the world market. Large corporations such as Bechtel, Goodyear, Exxon, and General Electric formed consortia to enter the uranium enrichment field hoping to be stronger in international competition. The fear often expressed is that these corporations would have conflicts of interest from vertical and horizontal integration that would have an adverse impact on pricing and lessen the competitive power of solar energy technologies. Although the uranium enrichment market could reach billions of dollars a year, the United States monopoly is being eroded. The Soviet Union now exports enriched uranium, and France is leading an effort to develop a gaseous diffusion complex known as EURODIFF. West Germany, South Africa, and Brazil are also developing enrichment facilities.

The nuclear industry has been concerned with the profitability and availability of uranium for export rather than with the effectiveness of safeguarding nuclear materials in the expanding world market. The industry believes that the United States would profit from increased sales of enriched uranium and reactor exports in its balance of payments, offsetting losses suffered from policies set by OPEC.

Nuclear Power Plant Operation. Enriched uranium is converted chemically to metal or oxide and fabricated into fuel elements which are clad in alloy tubing. Fabrication facilities are located in Oklahoma (Kerr-McGee)[20] California (Gulf General Atomic), and in Connecticut and Virginia. The fabricated fuel elements are transported to a nuclear reactor, loaded, and irradiated for approximately three years.

In nuclear power plants, electric power generation operates on the same principle as in fossil fuel plants, except that steam is generated by nuclear fission rather than by the combustion of fossil fuels. Nuclear reactors are classified according to the type of fuel used, the moderator which controls the fission process, and the type of coolant. Not all plants use enriched uranium. Moderators may be ordinary or "light" water, carbon, or "heavy" water, which contains deuterium. Heavy water is the best moderator but is very expensive. Carbon is cheap but cannot serve as both a moderator and coolant. Because water can serve as both a moderator and coolant, light water reactors are the most common. Since light water cannot moderate well enough to sustain a chain reaction in natural uranium, it must be used with enriched uranium. Heavy water and carbon may be used with either natural or enriched uranium, and in more advanced reactors molten salt and gas are used as coolants.[21]

Individual reactor units have a capacity of up to 1,200 megawatts. The plants have a lower thermal efficiency than modern fossil fuel plants and, therefore, a higher conversion loss of energy. Open cooling systems discharge heat into lakes, rivers, canals, and evaporation ponds. To protect the environment, many nuclear power plants are constructed with closed cooling systems which transfer excess heat directly into the atmosphere through cooling towers, or recycle the cooling water back to the condenser.[22] Nevertheless, thermal pollution and the efficiency of plants are major concerns of antinuclear groups.

Fossil fuel plants produce sulfur oxides, carbon monoxide, nitrogen oxides, hydrocarbons, and dust. Nuclear power plants produce radioactive materials, which are largely contained within the reactor fuel elements. Normal radiation emitted from plant operation is minimal.

The fear symbolized by Three Mile Island at this stage in the nuclear fuel cycle is the possibility of a nuclear accident if the cooling system of the plant were to malfunction and contribute to a core meltdown, releasing large amounts of radioactive materials into the environment. One of the most important precautions in nuclear power plants is the construction of a containment enclosure around the reactor core to prevent the release of radioactive materials in the event of an accident.

Two perspectives on normal nuclear power plant operation are exemplified by Bernard Cohen, a nuclear physicist, and David Comey, an environmentalist. Cohen has argued that air pollution from a coal-fired plant kills more people every few days than a nuclear power plant would kill in thirty years if there are no nuclear accidents.[23] On the other hand, Comey claims that by building all nuclear power plants as scheduled, 5.7 million deaths would occur over the next 80,000 years. Since most would occur outside of the United States, the predicted deaths would be a "paradigm example of imperialism."[24]

Spent fuel from a nuclear reactor is removed and the highly radioactive material shipped in heavy lead casks to chemical reprocessing plants. Nuclear fuel reprocessing involves the recovery of uranium and plutonium produced during normal power plant operation. Plutonium is both one of the most toxic substances known to man and a primary weapons–grade material. It is a transuranium element that can also be recycled for use in the fast breeder nuclear reactor. All nuclear fuel reprocessing took place in government installations in Washington, Idaho, and Georgia until the first private corporation received a construction permit in 1963 for a plant in West Valley, New York. From 1966 to 1971, radioactive emissions from this plant were so high that major modifications were required in its design. It has since been closed permanently.

In a reprocessing plant, spent fuel assemblies are unloaded under water and cooled before being mechanically chopped into small pieces and dissolved by a Purex process. The dissolved fuel is run through extraction cycles to separate uranium and plutonium from waste fission products, while solid wastes are buried near the plant.

Krypton-85 is released to the environment during reprocessing, and 25 percent of the tritium is also emitted. Highly radioactive liquid wastes are reconcentrated and stored in underground tanks. Some 600,000 tons have accumulated thus far. A permanent waste disposal plan has not been approved, although ultimately the wastes may be deposited in salt beds or geologic caverns.

Among these wastes, strontium-90 concentrates in human bones, cesium in muscles, ruthenium and cobalt in the lining of the intestines, and tritium in the entire body. Most of these isotopes have a long physical half-life. Proposals for disposal of these wastes have included storing them in underground caverns excavated by nuclear weapons, placing them in solar orbit, and burying them under Antarctic ice. Savannah, Georgia, has been chosen as the site for interim above–ground storage, and Carlsbad, New Mexico, has been designated as a site for permanent disposal. Other sites have been suggested in poor rural states such as Maine and Mississippi. One hope has been that the chemistry of fuel reprocessing may improve in the future to allow separation of the long-lived transuranium wastes from actinide wastes in order that they may be burned in fast neutron reactors.[25]

Transuranium wastes are the products of the fission of U-235. After 800 years, fission product decay drops by a factor of several million and the wastes have a toxicity only fifty times greater than a similar volume of natural uranium. Only a minute percentage of uranium and plutonium remains in radioactive wastes after reprocessing. Plutonium is the most toxic transuranic element. Decay of Pu-239 takes 250,000 years. Plutonium is hazardous if only 10^{-6} grams are deposited in lungs or bone tissue, where it tends to concentrate. The radiological hazard of plutonium is 10,000 times that of natural uranium and its daughters. The yield of Pu-239 and Pu-240 from one metric ton of nuclear fuel is seventy grams after 500 years. With the projected 700 or more nuclear reactors worldwide by the year 2000, there would be 25,000 tons of accumulated wastes and 24 tons of Pu-239.

Since World War II, 90 million gallons of liquid wastes have been stored as slurries in underground steel tanks at Hanford Works in Washington and at Savannah River, South Carolina. Leakage from these tanks has been reported, and an Atomic Energy Commission document even speculated that a chain reaction might possibly occur from the spilled wastes. Disposal of wastes in solar obit brings the danger of reentry burnups, as occurred in April 1964, when a thermoelectric satellite containing 9000 grams of plutonium disintegrated in re-entry. Deposit of wastes in Antarctic ice poses the danger of the materials melting their way into underground channels leading into the sea, while deposits in caverns excavated by nuclear explosions risk the creation of geologic strains.[26]

Wastes are associated with each stage of activity in the nuclear fuel cycle. Solid wastes are commonly metallic and are stored in concrete silos on site for radioactive decay. Sea disposal has been used by some countries. Highly radioactive wastes contain the bulk of radioactive fission products, and these are accumulating on the site of nuclear power plants because reprocessing plants have not been operative in the United States. Since nuclear material is not dangerous until it is enriched, the critical transportation lines are between enrichment plants and power plants to reprocessing plants, and then back to power plants. Antinuclear activists believe that these transportation lines may be hazardous to the public as accidents may occur in the shipment of wastes.

The Fast Breeder Reactor. One future source of energy promoted by government policy and the nuclear industry is the fast breeder reactor. This reactor can "breed" nuclear fuel from natural uranium by converting it into plutonium. The plutonium can be used again in the breeder reactor or recycled as fuel in conventional light water reactors. The two main types of breeders are the liquid metal fast breeder reactor (LMFBR) and the high temperature gas–cooled reactor (HTCGR). Gas–cooled reactors are being developed by the Gulf Atomic Corporation at Fort St. Vrain in Colorado. Many scientists think this reactor is the safest alternative of all nuclear reactors, but is has not received significant federal funding. The government is funding the liquid metal fast breeder reactor concept.

The United States breeder program is considerably behind its European counterparts. France and Britain have breeders in operation, as does the Soviet Union. The only breeder ever to have gone into operation in the United States was the Fermi reactor near Detroit, Michigan. In 1966, there was a partial core meltdown of this reactor and it was shut down.

The Fermi reactor is still too radioactive to be disassembled, although a portion of it is used for joint experimental research by the United States and the Soviet Union.[27]

A breeder reactor is capable of undergoing a minor nuclear explosion, or hypothetical core disassembly accident (HCDA). Since the breeder also produces plutonium, the development of this reactor is greatly feared by antinuclear groups.

The liquid metal fast breeder reactor may cost over $10 billion in research alone, and would not make electricity that much cheaper, if at all. It has the advantage of providing electricity with an unlimited source of fuel. The high temperature gas–cooled reactor partially breeds U-233 from thorium-232 and does not produce plutonium, but it does produce the same waste fission products as light water reactors. This reactor would expand the quantity of nuclear fuel because the United States is self-sufficient in thorium reserves.

A test installation for the breeder reactor, the Fast Flux Test Facility in Richland, Washington, is near completion, and the first plant utilizing the breeder concept is under construction on the Clinch River in Tennessee. The United States government has already invested $2 billion in the project, equalling the total investment in the Manhattan Project to develop the atomic bomb.

If sodium coolant is blocked off to the core of a breeder, it may reach "autocatalytic criticality" in a few minutes: the fuel is compressed and collects on the walls of the reactor core, allowing a spontaneous and uncontrolled nuclear reaction to occur. Dispersion of plutonium in a nuclear accident would have severe consequences, for plutonium is a self-distributing aerosol that travels on small air currents. If 4.4 pounds of plutonium were released into the air, inhabitants 1,000 feet downwind would be certain to contract cancer, and forty miles downwind 1 percent of inhabitants would get cancer. If inhaled, 1/28,000th of an ounce of Pu-239 oxide would cause death within weeks by destroying lung tissue, and amounts 500 times smaller can cause cancer of the lung, lymph, liver, bone, and other organs.[28]

These fearsome possibilities have made government insurance liability limits controversial. Since private industry refused to underwrite the fledgling nuclear industry in the 1950s, government insurance was an important first step in commercializing nuclear energy. The Price-Anderson Act of 1957 provided for liability of $560 million for any one accident, regardless of the number of people or amount of property involved. Private insurance companies now make $60 million worth of insurance available to each plant, and the balance is provided by the federal government. But the estimate of property damage from a nuclear power plant accident ranges from $17 to $280 billion dollars. The government insurance program is actually being decreased and phased out under 1974 amendments to the Price-Anderson Act. New plans are under consideration, but this insurance does not cover all phases of the nuclear fuel cycle, only normal power plant operation.

Notes and References

1. Robert Dahl and Ralph S. Brown, *Domestic Control of Nuclear Energy* (USA: Social Science Research Council, 1951). The sources used in writing this appendix were numerous and varied. For a detailed account of the nuclear fuel cycle, the reader can consult the following: Albert V. Crewe and Joseph J. Katz, *Nuclear Research U.S.A.* (New York: Dover Publications, 1964); Bernard J. Cohen, *Nuclear Science and Society* (New York: Doubleday, 1974); United States Environmental Protection Agency, *Environmental Analysis of the Uranium Fuel Cycle* (Washington D.C.: U.S. Government Printing Office, 1973); Mason Willrich, *Global Politics of Nuclear Energy* (New York: Praeger, 1971); the Union of Concerned Scientists, *The Nuclear Fuel Cycle* (Cambridge, Mass: The Union of Concerned Scientists, 1974); American Nuclear Society, *Nuclear Power and the Environment* (Hinsdale, Ill,: The American Nuclear Society, 1975); Hans Bethe, "The Necessity of Fission Power," *Scientific American* 234, no. 1 (1976): 21–30; and the International Atomic Energy Agency, *Nuclear Power and the Environment* (Vienna: International Atomic Energy Agency, 1973). I would like to thank Dr. William McLean, Department of Physics, Rutgers University, for his comments on an earlier draft of this appendix.

2. The unilinear relationship between energy consumption and economic development is no longer being taken for granted, as much of the energy consumption in advanced societies is wasted—a problem that conservation policies hope to correct.

3. Energy Policy Project, *Exploring Energy Choices* (Cambridge, Mass: Ballinger Publishing Co., 1974).

4. Mason Willrich, *Energy and World Politics* (Riverside, N.J.: Free Press, 1975); Joseph A. Yager and Eleanor B. Steinberg, *Energy and U.S. Foreign Policy* (Cambridge, Mass.: Ballinger, 1974); and Peter R. Odell, *Oil and World Power* (Harmondsworth, England: Penguin Books, 1974) all make this point. See also Edward Friedland, Paul Seabury, and Aaron Wildavsky, "Oil and the Decline of Western Power," *Political Science Quarterly* 90, no. 3 (1975): 437–50.

5. Ford Foundation, *A Time to Choose* (Cambridge, Mass.: Ballinger, 1974).

6. U.S., Congress, House, Committee on Science and Astronautics, *Energy Facts 1973* (Washington D.C.: U.S. Government Printing Office, 1973).

7. *National Journal Reports,* Washington D.C.: Government Research Corporation, 1974), pp. 328–30.

8. See International Atomic Energy Agency, *Nuclear Energy Centres and Agro-Industrial Complexes,* Technical Reports Series no. 140 (Vienna: Interntional Atomic Energy Agency, 1972).

9. David Comey, "Chasing down the Facts," *Bulletin of the Atomic Scientists* 31 (February 1975): 42.

10. Federal Energy Administration, *Executive Summary, National Energy Outlook* (Washington D.C.: U.S. Government Printing Office, 1976), p. 46.

11. "Is Nuclear Too Costly?" *New York Times,* 5 October 1975, p. 1.

12. "Congressional Awareness of Energy Crisis: 1969–1972," *Congressional Quarterly,* (15 February 1973) p. 38.

13. Mason Willrich, *Global Politics of Nuclear Energy,* p. 16.

14. Environmental Protection Agency, *Environmental Analysis of the Uranium Fuel Cycle,* vol. 4, p. 73.

15. Union of Concerned Scientists, *The Nuclear Fuel Cycle,* pp. 92–115.

16. Environmental Protection Agency, *Environmental Analysis of the Uranium Fuel Cycle.*

17. M. C. Day, "Nuclear Energy: A Second Round of Questions," *Bulletin of the Atomic Scientists,* December 1975, pp. 52–59.

18. Mason Willrich and Philip Marston, "Prospects for a Uranium Cartel," *Orbis* 19 (1975): 166–84.

19. Mason Willrich, *Global Politics of Nuclear Energy,* p. 18.

20. This facility, the plant where Karen Silkwood worked, has been closed.

21. Mason Willrich, *Global Politics of Nuclear Energy,* pp. 14–16.

22. Environmental Protection Agency, *Environmental Analysis of the Uranium Fuel Cycle,* vol. 2, pp. 3–5.

23. Bernard J. Cohen, *Nuclear Science and Society,* p. 145.

24. David Comey, "The Perfect Trojan Horse," *Bulletin of the Atomic Scientists* (June 1976): 33–34.

25. American Nuclear Society, *Nuclear Power and the Environment.*

26. International Atomic Energy Agency, *Nuclear Power and the Environment.*

27. See John G. Fuller, *We Almost Lost Detroit* (New York: Readers Digest, 1975) for an account of this accident. A critical analysis of the fast breeder reactor has been written by Thomas B. Cochran, *The Liquid Metal Fast Breeder Reactor* (Baltimore: Johns Hopkins University Press, 1974). See also Department of Energy, *Final Environmental Statement for the Liquid Metal Fast Breeder Reactor Program* (Washington D.C.: U.S. Government Printing Office, ERDA-1535, 1975).

28. Daniel F. Ford and Henry W. Kendall, "The Nuclear Power Issue: An Overview," (Cambridge, Mass.: Union of Concerned Scientists, 1974).

APPENDIX C
The Sample of Antinuclear Groups

The initial sample of antinuclear groups was taken from a list entered into the *Congressional Record* 121, no. 75 (12 May 1975): 109, by Senator Mike Gravel (D-Alaska). Literature was collected from each group between March 1975 and November 1976 by mailing postcards requesting information about its activities and organization. I identified myself as a doctoral candidate in sociology at Rutgers University doing research on the antinuclear movement. Many of the addresses were obtained from a newsletter entitled *People & Energy,* published by the Center for Science in the Public Interest in Washington, D.C.

Only two groups did not respond to requests for information, while several organizations, such as the Clamshell Alliance and the Environmentalists for Full Employment, never appeared on the initial list. Forty groups were selected on the basis of the attention given to them by the mass media and my own evaluation of their significance to the movement for more intensive study. The literature sent to me was only one of many sources of my knowledge of their activities.

Three asterisks indicate that the group was selected for intensive study and two asterisks show that it was only of secondary importance. One asterisk merely indicates that the group was contacted for information (not all groups were contacted). The categories for the groups are my own creation.

Antinuclear Groups with a National or Regional Support Base
***Businessmen and Professional People in the Public Interest, Chicago
  *Common Cause

***National Intervenors
***New England Coalition on Nuclear Pollution, Inc.
***People for Proof
***Supporters of Silkwood
***Task Force Against Nuclear Pollution
***Western Bloc

Environmental/Ecology Groups
***Congresswatch
  *Environmental Action Foundation
  *Environmental Policy Center
 **Florida Audubon Society
***Friends of the Earth
   Hudson River Sloop Restoration, Inc.
***National Resources Defense Council
   Piedmont Organic Movement
***Sierra Club
  *Wilderness Society
   Zero Population Growth

Farmer Organizations Against Nuclear Power
   4-H Earthkeepers, Croton, N.Y.
   Jefferson County Farm Bureau, Wisconsin
   Kansas Farmers Union
   National Farmers Organization, Wood Falls, Wisconsin
  *Nebraska Low-Energy Agriculture Project
   Vermont Natural Food and Farming Association

Labor Unions Against Nuclear Power
   Amalgamated Meat Cutters and Butcher Workmen, Executive
      Board, Local 525, Asheville, N.C.
   American Association of Retired Persons, Chapter 727, Tuckerton,
      N.J.
  *Central Labor Union, Catawba, S.C.
   Communication Workers of America, Executive Board, Local 5503,
      Milwaukee, Wisconsin
   UAW Community Action Program Council, Lima, Ohio

Local Environmental/Antinuclear Groups

Alternative Energy Coalition, Turners Falls, Mass.
Americans for Safe Energy, Lafayette, Ind.
Anti-plutonium League, Urbana, Ill.
Biocides Recyling Group, Denver, Colo.
Carolinians for Safe Energy, N.C.
Citizens Action for Safe Energy, Okla.
Citizens Against Nuclear Dangers, Berwick, Pa.
Citizens Association for Safe Energy, Croton, N.Y.
Citizens Association for Sound Energy, Dallas, Texas
Citizens Committee for Protection of the Environment, Ossining, N.Y.
Citizens Energy Council, Allendale, N.J.
Citizens Energy Council of West New York
Citizens for a Safe Environment, Harrisburg, Pa.
Citizens for Environmental Action, Iowa City, Iowa
Citizens for Safe Power, San Antonio, Texas
Citizens for Tomorrow, Wis.
Citizens League for Education About Nuclear Energy, New Rochelle, N.Y.
Citizens to Preserve the Hudson Valley, Catskill, N.Y.
*Citizens United for Responsible Energy, Iowa
Coalition for a Safe Environment, Seattle
Coalition for the Environment, Fort Wayne, Ind.
Columbia County Survival Committee, Germantown, N.Y.
Committee for Nuclear Power Plant Postponement, Willington, Del.
Concerned Californians, San Pedro, Calif.
Concerned Citizens for Nuclear Safety, N.Y.
Concerned Citizens of Highland, N.Y.
Concerned Citizens of Tennessee
Connecticut Citizen Action Group
Delaware Valley Committee for Protection of the Environment
Delaware Valley Conservation Association, Stillwater, N.J.
Detroit Area Coalition for the Environment, Mich.
Dubuque Environmental Coordination Committee, Iowa
Dutchess County Environmental Association, N.Y.
Eau Claire Area Ecology Action, Eau Claire, Wis.

Ecology Alert, Bloomsburg, Pa.
Ecology Information Center, Sacramento, Calif.
Energy Conservation Organization, Hilyard, Oreg.
*Environmental Action of Colorado
**Environmental Coalition on Nuclear Power, Jenkinstown, Pa.
*Eurgene Future Power Committee, Oreg.
Hudson Valley Citizens Watch on Nuclear Safety, N.Y.
Illinois Citizens for a Nuclear Moratorium, Chicago
Kansas League Against Nuclear Dangers
Keys for Education for Environmental Protection, Summit, N.J.
Knob and Valley Audubon Society, Louisville, Ky.
*League Against Nuclear Dangers, Wis.
Mid-America Coalition for Energy Alternatives, Kansas City, Mo.
Minnesota Environmental Control Citizens Movement
North Anna Environmental Coalition, Charolottesville, Va.
*N.Y. State Safe Energy Coalition
Ohio Valley Citizens Concerned About Nuclear Pollution, Ohio
People Against the Atom, New York City
People for Energy and Environmental Responsibility, Lacomb,
    Oreg.
People's Action for Clean Energy, Conn.
People's Energy Project, Lawrence, Kans.
Prince Georges County Environmental Coalition, Md.
Protect the Peninsula's Future, Sequim, Wash.
Rhode Islanders for Safe Power
*Safe Power for Maine, Stockton Springs, Maine
Sassafras Audubon Society, Bloomington, Ind.
Save Solanco Environment, Quarryville, Pa.
Southeastern Confederation for Safe Energy, Asheville, N.C.
Southerners for Safe Power, Nashville, Tenn.
**Stop Nuclear Power, Margate, N.J.
Stop Nuclear Power Plants, New Orleans, La.
Vermonters Against Splitting Atoms
York Committee for a Safe Environment, Pa.
Wappinger Conservation Association, Wappinger Falls, N.Y.

Political/Quasi-governmental Organizations
California Democratic Council
Iowa Democratic Party

Natural Resources Council of Maine
New York City Environmental Protection Agency
New York County legislatures: Ulster, Greene, Columbia, Niagara,
    Dutchess
*N.Y. State Conservation Council
Oregon State Democratic Party
Washington Environmental Council, Seattle

Scientist Antinuclear Groups/Health Groups
  *Committee for Nuclear Responsibility
***Federation of American Scientists
  *National Health Federation
  Northern Michigan Medical Society
***Union of Concerned Scientists

Student Organizations
  Central Pennsylvania Committee on Nuclear Power, State College
  *ENACT, Ball State University, Indiana
**Public Interest Research Groups (PIRG): Iowa, Mass., N.J.
  Purdue Environmental Action
  *Student Government, University of Texas
  *Vanderbilt Energy Study Group, Tennessee

Women's Groups Against Nuclear Power
  American Association of University Women, Peekskill, N.Y.
  *Women's Club, Linwood, N.J.
  Church Women United of Tennessee
  HIPS—Housewivs Involved in Pollution Solutions, Ill.
  League of Women Voters, Riverhead/Southold, N.Y.
***National Organization of Women
  Stewardess Alumnae Association, Florida Chapter
  Women's Christian Temperance Union, Quarryville, Pa.
  Women for Peace, Chicago

Religious Groups Against Nuclear Power
  Council of Churches, Springfield, Mass.
  Dubuque Council of Churches, Iowa
***National Council of the Churches of Christ
  New Jersey Friends (Quaker) Council, Princeton, N.J.
  Religious Society of Friends, (Quakers), Harrisburg, Pa.

SELECTED BIBLIOGRAPHY

I have included below some of the more recent books that pertain to the controversy over nuclear power, as well as a few earlier works that would still be worth reading to help focus the issues. Most of these books were cited at some point in the text.

1. General: The Energy Crisis
Cohen, Bernard J. *Nuclear Science and Society*. New York: Doubleday, 1974. By far the most readable analysis of the technical characteristics of the nuclear fuel cycle.
Energy Policy Project of the Ford Foundation, *A Time to Choose: America's Energy Future*. Cambridge: Ballinger Publishing Co. 1974. Many of the current policy choices still revolve around commitments to growth scenarios outlined by the Energy Policy Project. It is useful to understand one of the approaches to resolving the energy crisis that had a definite impact on government energy policy.
Fischer, John C. *Energy Crises in Perspective* New York: John Wiley, 1974. A comparison of sources of electricity utilitizing the concept of economies of scale.
Ford Foundation/Mitre Corporation, *Nuclear Power: Issues and Choices*. Cambridge: Ballinger Publishing Co., 1977. An overview of some of the basic issues related to nuclear energy.
Friedland, Edward; Seabury, Paul; and Wildavsky, Aaron. "Oil and the Decline of Western Power," *Political Science Quarterly* 90, no. 3 (1975): 437–50. An excellent summary of what OPEC means to the Western nations.
Odell, Peter. *Oil and World Power*. Harmondsworth, England: Penguin Books, 1974. Although dozens of books exist on the oil crisis, this one has the distinction of explaining the structure of the oil industry in a low-key and nonalarmist manner.

Schuur, Sam H., ed. *Energy in America's Future: The Choices Before Us.* Baltimore: The Johns Hopkins University Press, 1979. This volume was prepared for Resources in the Future, Inc., and is highly recommended, although it is decidedly pronuclear. The chapters on health, environmental, and catastrophic effects of energy technologies warn us that dependence on coal could be even more disastrous than dependence on nuclear energy.

Stobaugh, Robert, and Yergin, Daniel, eds., *Energy Future.* New York: Ballantine Books, 1979. This is the result of a project on energy at the Harvard Business School and leans toward conservation and solar energy as the mix most likely to resolve the energy crisis.

Willrich, Mason. *Energy and World Politics.* New York: Free Press, 1975. Willrich is a professor of law at the University of Virginia and perhaps the foremost expert on the energy crisis and its implications. This book is not frequently cited but is still one of the better ones in the area.

2. Nuclear Technology and Social Change

Cochran, Thomas B. *The Liquid Metal Fast Breeder Reactor.* Baltimore: The Johns Hopkins University Press, 1974. Although cutbacks of the Clinch River breeder project have softened this issue, it still divides the United States and its Western European allies developing breeders. Cochran's book is a good comprehensive analysis of the fast breeder.

Fuller, John G. *We Almost Lost Detroit.* New York: Reader's Digest, 1975. In the wake of Three Mile Island, this book seems better than when it first appeared. It documents the crisis when there was a partial core meltdown of an experimental breeder reactor near Detroit in 1966.

Nau, Henry P. *National Politics and International Technology: Nuclear Reactor Development in Western Europe.* Baltimore: Johns Hopkins University Press, 1974. This is a very scholarly account of the development of nuclear power in Western Europe and the growth of organizations such as EURATOM.

Skolnikoff, Eugene. *The International Imperatives of Technology.* Berkeley: University of California Press, 1972. This monograph is highly recommended for those wishing to understand the role of technology in social change.

3. Foreign Policy and Energy

Rodgers, Barbara, and Cervenka, Zdenek. *The Nuclear Axis: Secret Collaboration Between West Germany and South Africa.* New York: Times Books, 1978. An account of one of the many intrigues that surround nuclear power as the technology diffuses from one nation to another.

Szyklowicz, Joseph S., and O'Neill, Bard. *The Energy Crisis and U.S. Foreign Policy*. New York: Praeger, 1975. Although published in the mid-1970s, this book is still helpful in understanding the immense foreign policy ramifications of the energy crisis.

Yager, Joseph A., and Steinberg, Eleanor B., *Energy and U. S. Foreign Policy*. Cambridge: Ballinger, 1974. This book gives a panoramic view of the impact of energy on major nations and the lesser developed countries, as well as the basics on international safeguards.

4. Nuclear Energy and National Security

Gilpin, Robert, and Wright, Christopher, eds., *Scientists and National Policy Making*. Princeton: Princeton University Press, 1962. A classic sketch of some of the issues involved when scientists and politicians both lay claim to decision-making power.

Rogin, Michael, *The Intellectuals and McCarthy*. Cambridge: The MIT Press, 1967. This book does not deal directly with atomic energy but is useful reading for those who wish to understand the political environment of the late 1950s, which affected our nuclear policy for many years afterward.

Schneir, Walter, and Schneir, Miriam. *Invitation to an Inquest: Reopening the Rosenberg Atom Spy Case*. Baltimore: Penguin Books, 1973. This is good reading for those who are concerned about the rise of a garrison state to protect nuclear materials.

Schurmann, Franz. *The Logic of World Power*. New York: Pantheon Books, 1974. An historical study of the rise of the national security state.

Shils, Edward. *The Torment of Secrecy*. New York: Free Press, 1956. One of the most erudite sociologists reflects on the meaning of the McCarthy era.

Willrich, Mason, and Taylor, Theodore B., *Nuclear Theft: Risks and Safeguards*. Cambridge: Ballinger, 1974. Required reading for all interested in possible dangers posed to society through the theft of nuclear materials.

5. Energy and the Environment

Caldwell, Lynton K., Hayes, Lynton R., and MacWhirter, Isabel M., *Citizens and the Environment*. Bloomington: Indiana University Press, 1976. This is a primer on citizen action, with case studies involving a wide range of environmental issues, including those of energy. One case involves an early struggle over nuclear energy in Oregon by the Eugene Future Power Committee.

Liroff, Richard. *A National Policy for the Environment: NEPA and its Aftermath*. Bloomington: Indiana University Press, 1976. The Burger court changed the basic meaning of NEPA in cases involving nuclear power. This book indicates how the act was originally intended to operate.

Norwood, Christopher, *At Highest Risk: Environmental Hazards to Young and Unborn Children.* New York: McGraw-Hill, 1980. A book that students don't put down until the entire narrative has been read. The chapters on radiation and other environmental toxins can be extrapolated to hazards presented by energy technologies.

Odell, Rice. *Environmental Awakening: The New Revolution to Protect the Earth.* Cambridge: Ballinger Publishing Co. 1980. Odell has provacative chapters on energy resources, problems, and analysis. In addition, the book is concerned with other current issues such as chemicals and public health.

Ramsay, William. *Unpaid Costs of Electrical Energy: Environmental Impacts from Coal and Nuclear Power.* Baltimore: Johns Hopkins University Press, 1978. The title indicates the importance of this book, which was a main source utilized by the project on energy directed by Sam Schurr for Resources in the Future, Inc.

Schnaiberg, Alan. *The Environment: From Surplus to Scarcity.* New York: Oxford University Press, 1980. A theoretical treatise on environmental issues from a neo-Marxist perspective. Schnaiberg should be read by all environmental professionals.

6. Significant Case Studies of the Nuclear Controversy

Ebbin, Steven, and Kasper, Raphael. *Citizen Groups and the Nuclear Power Controversy.* Cambridge: MIT Press, 1974. A case study of citizen intervention in Atomic Energy Commission hearings for the licensing of Vermont Yankee and Michigan's Midland nuclear power plant before the antinuclear movement captured national attention.

Nelkin, Dorothy. *Nuclear Power and Its Critics: The Cayuga Lake Controversy.* Ithaca, N. Y.: Cornell University Press, 1971. Perhaps the first documentation of conflict over nuclear power written by someone very proficient in the analysis of modern issues concerning advanced technology.

Parkin, Francis. *Middle Class Radicalism: The Social Bases of the British Campaign for Nuclear Disarmanent.* Manchester, England: The University of Manchester Press, 1968. The CND has remerged in the 1980s, and Parkin's book explores reasons for the rejection of nuclear weapons by the English.

Stever, Donald W., Jr., *Seabrook and the Nuclear Regulatory Commission.* Hanover, New Hampshire: University Press of New England, 1980. The most detailed study of the regulatory process available, written by an official in the U.S. Department of Justice. The book is objective, often critical of the Nuclear Regulatory Commission, and an interesting insight into the Seabrook controversy.

7. Pronuclear Literature

Bethe, Hans. "The Necessity of Fission Power," *Scientific American* 234, no. 1 (1976): 21–30. A Nobel laureate physicist cogently argues why we must remain commited to nuclear power.

Garvey, Gerald. *Nuclear Power and Social Planning: The City of the Second Sun.* Lexington, Mass.: Lexington Books, 1977. An argument on why conservation alone will not solve energy problems.

Hoyle, Fred. *Energy or Extinction? The Case for Nuclear Energy.* Salem, N. H. : Heinemann Educational Books, 1977. Considered by the Atomic Industrial Forum to be one of the best and most concise explanations of energy and nuclear power.

Lilienthal, David E. *Atomic Energy: A New Start.* New York: Harper & Row, 1980. Although extremely critical of the nuclear energy program, Lilienthal opts for research into new reactor concepts.

Teller, Edward. *Energy From Heaven and Earth.* San Francisco: W. W. Freeman, 1979. A chapter on "Reactor Safety and the Anti-Nuclear Movement" is incisive in parts but biased in others; e.g., "even in California the nuts are a minority (p. 197)," in reference to groups seeking passage of the 1976 California Nuclear Safeguards Initiative.

8. Antinuclear Literature

Berger, John J. *Nuclear Power: The Unviable Option.* New York: Ramparts Press, 1977. Begins with an interesting fictional account of a nuclear disaster in "Santa Bonita, California," and has well-researched analyses of problems with nuclear power.

Commoner, Barry. *The Politics of Energy.* New York: Alfred A. Knopf, 1979. This book outlines the political program of the Citizens Party, of which Commoner was the presidential nominee in 1980. Advocates abandonment of nuclear power and transition to a solar powered economy.

Faulkner, Peter, ed. *The Silent Bomb: A Guide to the Nuclear Energy Controversy.* New York: Random House, 1977. An edited anthology of antinuclear articles written by prominent activists.

Gofman, John, and Tampblin, Arthur. *Poisoned Power.* Emmamus, Pa.: Rodale Press, 1971. Valuable because it is written by scientists who had their work suppressed by the Atomic Energy Commission.

Lewis, Richard S. *The Nuclear Power Rebellion.* New York: Viking Press, 1972. One of the more interesting accounts of the early phase of antinuclear activities.

Lovins, Amory, *Soft Energy Paths.* Cambridge: Ballinger Publishing Co., 1979. Along with several other books and important articles in *Foreign Affairs,* the British environmentalist has emerged as one of the most important critics of nuclear power.

Metzger, Peter. *The Atomic Establishment.* New York: Simon & Schuster, 1972. More criticisms levied at the now defunct Atomic Energy Commission.
Nader, Ralph, and Abbotts, John. *The Menace of Atomic Energy.* New York: Grossman, 1977. Written by one of the prime movers of the antinuclear movement.

INDEX